HISTORY OF ELEMENTARY EDUCATION

ENCYCLOPAEDIA OF ELEMENTARY EDUCATION SERIES

HISTORY OF ELEMENTARY EDUCATION

Edited by

M. Husain

ANMOL PUBLICATIONS PVT. LTD.

NEW DELHI - 110 002 (INDIA)

ANMOL PUBLICATIONS PVT. LTD.
4374/4B, Ansari Road, Daryaganj
New Delhi - 110 002
Ph.: 23261597, 23278000
Visit us at: www.anmolpublications.com

History of Elementary Education

First Edition, 2004

ISBN 81-261-1528-9

PRINTED IN INDIA

Published by J.L. Kumar for Anmol Publications Pvt. Ltd., New Delhi - 110 002 and Printed at Mehra Offset Press, Delhi.

Contents

Preface

'Elementary education' is much debated universal issue, which is given emphasis as a fundamental right of each and every human being. All the nation-states the world over have made statutory provisions to ensure that none could be deprived of elementary education. Many world organisations are playing vital role in advancing the status of elementary education. Despite all these measures a large number of children in different parts of the world are still deprived of basic education.

This work in three volumes intends to focus on some vital issues pertaining to the theme. Attempts are made to gather the well researched material, based on the empirical findings of different scholars of repute from various settings.

As the information is drawn from various authoritative sources, no claim is of originality. We are deeply beholden to all those whose works and views are cited or substantially borrowed herein for making the work comprehensive and more useful. Besides these, we are grateful to one and all who have rendered the assistance while executing the plan of the work. Finally Mr. J.L. Kumar, Managing Director, Anmol Publications Pvt. Ltd. deserve all appreciation for undertaking the publication of this venture.

—**Editor**

1
Elementary Education in Historical Perspective

The Tradition of Elementary Education

The history of elementary education, more than any other branch of education, is an epitome of the social and political history of each nation. In it are reflected the place of the Church and of religion, the gradual suppression of the influence of the Church by the State, the change in social organization and the status of social classes, the gradual emergence of nationalism and of nationalist indoctrination, the rise of the working classes and an appreciation of the importance of economic life and organization, and the gradual development of an appreciation of the worth of the individual as a human being, and therefore of the meaning of democracy. From another point of view, the development of the elementary school represents all the changes which have taken place, not only in social values, but in the attitude to knowledge and literacy, in the kind of knowledge that is of most worth, in the meaning of intelligence and the methods of its development, in the relation of mental and physical activities, in the learning process, and, in general, in the concept of what makes a whole individual.

Elementary education in the nineteenth century was everywhere, except in the United States, regarded as an instrument for training the children of the masses, the lower classes, to be content with the position in which it had pleased the Lord to place them. Through instruction in the elements of literacy, the three R's combined with religious instruction, it was expected that society would find a protection against immorality, superstition, and crime. As the spirit of nationalism developed, another aim, training in loyalty and patriotism, was added. The purposes of the elementary school were determined by a deep-rooted faith in knowledge as power and knowledge as virtue; literacy was regarded as the best panacea for all social ills. Hence the wide acceptance of Guizot's slogan, "Open a school and close a jail." Through the acquisition of knowledge, the individual was to acquire, not merely the skills and techniques which would adjust him to his environment, but a training in character. As circulated by Herbart, the theory of education was that knowledge provides the basis of ideas and ideas make the man. The type and amount of knowledge considered desirable to secure these ends were selected by the adult generation without any attempt to take into account the stages of immaturity or maturity of the educand, the pupil to be educated, a principle which has survived to the present in the French statement that the pupil in the elementary school should learn those things of which no individual should be ignorant. To the objection that a programme or curriculum based on this principle was too difficult, the answer was that the very difficulties themselves were valuable, since they called for effort, hard work, and perseverance, which are moral virtues and so provide a training for character, and, in addition, they train the mind. Whether from the moral or the psychological point of view, the fundamental basis upon which education rested was discipline.

Gradually the curriculum of the elementary school was expanded under the influence of Auguste Comte to and the positivists, of Herbart, and of Herbart Spencer; to this expansion the emergence of the working classes, the rapid growth of industry in factories, the development of adult education, the rise of the press and the supply of cheaper books, and the increase in the means and methods of communication also contributed. But the emphasis continued to be upon knowledge, and the expansion of the elementary school curriculum meant additions and accretions to the information which was to be imparted. The increasing difficulties of this situation were met by the development of methods which would simplify and facilitate the acquisition or the learning process. The good pupil was the one whose mind was well filled with the knowledge, facts, and information supplied by the teacher or obtained from books, as tested by annual examinations. The result of such an education, which was to provide a store of knowledge as a preparation for life, was an emphasis on intellectualism, bookishness, memorization, repetition, and discipline. In the development of a perfect technique for successfully carrying out the principles of such an education, the German system attracted widespread attention.

The defects of this education were that it ignored the nature and needs of the individual, accepted a static concept of the culture to be transmitted to the new generation, and was unrelated to the changing demands of society. Under such a system the successful teacher was he who faithfully carried out the prescriptions of a detailed course of study and produced good results which could be measured by examinations. In such a system there was no room for the teacher who sought to develop the individual as an all-round personality. The distinction between the two methods was to be found in every country in the distinction between elementary and secondary education: the function of the former was to impart a certain amount of information; the function of the latter to train students and scholars in methods of acquiring information. The work of the former was completed, except where it was continued in part-time education more directly related to vocational purposes, when the pupils were released from compulsory school attendance; the work of the latter was looked upon as a foundation for further study and the cultivation of new interests. The distinction between the two was not merely one of class, but of quality, a distinction expressed in Germany by the different connotation of the words *Akademiker* and *Nicht-Akademiker*; or in the connotation of the French *esprit primaire*, the elementary school mind, as distinguished from the mind trained by secondary or higher education.

Social Status of the Elementary School

The opening of the twentieth century witnessed the beginning of a changing attitude to elementary education. The United States had already given an example of an educational system in which the elementary school constituted the lower part of a continuous system, although in general character it did not differ from the elementary school elsewhere. The changes in Europe are moving in the direction of the American system—the recognition of the elementary school as the school which provides a common educational foundation for all, to be followed at the next stage by differentiated types of secondary education. This movement, which is in its infancy, is accompanied by a movement to change the terminology and to avoid the connotations which have grown up around the term "elementary" education. The first stage is to be called "primary," to be followed by "secondary" education. Russia and Italy have adopted the ladder system, an organization in which the primary school is the common foundation for all; Germany requires all pupils during the first four years of compulsory education to attend the common foundation schools (*Grandschule*); France, since 1925, requires the same curriculum and course of study to be followed in all primary schools, whether public or private; in England the movement to reorganize the whole system on the foundation of a primary school is well on its way in the principle stated by Mr. Stanley Baldwin that

> One of the strongest bonds of union between men is a common education. England has been the poorer that in her national system of schooling she has not in the past fostered this fellowship of the mind. The classification

of our schools has been on the lines of social rather than educational distinctions...The great new fabric is already taking shape; the outworn "elementary" structure is at last being superseded[1].

The Elementary School and the Progress of Educational Theory

As democratic institutions develop, the elementary school as an institution for the education of the masses is changing to an institution for the common education of all. But the development of a higher and more comprehensive appreciation of the significance of democracy implies more than a change in the social status of the elementary school as an organization; because it connotes a change in the attitude to the individual as an independent, responsible personality and recognizes his worth as a human being, it implies also a change in the character of the internal organization and work of the elementary school. This change, which has accompanied the broader conception of democracy, has been supported by changes in educational theory and in the sciences upon which it is based. The metaphysical, structural psychology, on which the faculty psychology of the nineteenth century was based, has yielded to physiological and genetic psychology, directed to the scientific study of the individual as a whole. A new educational philosophy has undermined the importance attached to knowledge *qua* knowledge and stressed the principle that its worth and value can only be measured by its reality, meaningfulness, and use to the learner. On the side of the learning process, the result of a combination of the new psychology and the new philosophy has been to direct attention to the importance of active participation by the learner in place of the passive memorization and learning which had characterized the traditional school. The individual, in other words, learns through his own experience—through sensory, perceptual, motor, and emotional activities, he must be a free and active participant in his own education, and the function of the school is to provide an environment which will introduce the learner to a variety of many-sided experiences, growing out of and related to his interests, needs, and capacities. Not knowledge for its own sake, but knowledge related to life, methods of thinking and criticism, the acquisition of the tools and technique of acquiring experience, interpreting it, and using it as an instrument of control should be the aim of education. The definition of the content of school work in terms of experience means the inclusion of activities which in the traditional scheme, if they were given any consideration at all, were regarded as subordinate to intellectual training—music, fine arts, drama, physical and manual activities.

The Individual and Society

As a immediate reaction against traditional practices and methods, the new psychology and philosophy were seized upon by extremists as a justification for abolishing all controls in the school—external discipline, curriculum fixed in advance, extrinsic standards and tests. The advocates of freedom, guided by respect for the child's individuality, were willing to follow the child whithersoever he might lead. Experiments, conducted on the principle that the only true freedom is that which originates in the true self of the individual, free from the control of material or quasi-material forces and laws, have been valuable because they illustrated the pitfalls of the extremist position and drew attention to the fact that the individual represents only one datum in the educative process.

The individual is born with certain tendencies, abilities, and potentialities; the function of education is to provide the environment and the experiences by which the individual will grow into a responsible member of society, responsible not merely for his own self-realization, but also for the realization of the best in the society to which he belongs. The school is not merely a vacuum for the spontaneous self-expression of the individual; it is itself a social organization which mediates between the individual and society and provides opportunities for sharing in activities which society regards as valuable. It may be objected that the traditional school performed this function, but the objection is not valid, because the activities of the traditional school were selected without any consideration for the individual's interests or capacities and he was adjusted to them through discipline and authority. The only activities which can be of values in developing the individual as a socially responsible personality are those which represent the major aspects of culture of the society in which he lives, but they must be meaningful and of significance to the learner according to the stage of his development; only in this sense can he become an active agent in acquiring mastery of his environment. This means further that the teachers must be, not a dictator of lessons to be learned, but a guide and organizer of the activities in which the pupil is to engage and through which he realizes himself.

Even when the claims of activities which are meaningful to the individual and of value to society as representing a part of its culture are accepted, there are those who fear that a definite programme in the mind of the teacher—or a curriculum fixed in advance—would militate against the self-expression and creative originality of the pupil. The advocates of self-expression and creative originality are content with anything which they regard as the direct result of the pupil's own experience, forgetting that such immature experience needs guidance, that expression requires training in rules and techniques, and that for the immature their reaction to any experience is creative. The emphasis of this group is always on the process rather than on the acquisition or the result. For this position, as in the radical interpretations of freedom, the reason is to be found in a swing of the pendulum away from the traditional practices of formalism, mechanical learning without comprehension, dictation, and indoctrination. The compromise will be found in a proper adjustment between activities or curriculum closely related to the developing interests of the pupils and expanding in range and richness with their own development and active methods of instruction and learning to merge into the accepted values of society, or, to put it in another way, in a reconciliation between freedom and responsibility. The so-called child-centred school is meaningless unless it implies that the child is but the starting-point of a process which is guided by the teacher.

Early Education

The forces which have led to a change in the function and organization of the elementary school, because they have directed attention to a consideration of the child, have equally stressed the importance of the early years. The development of the individual is determined, not only by his nature, but also by his nurture or environment. Compulsory education generally begins at about the age of six; some countries have provided schools for children before this age, but the infant schools of the nineteenth century, whether in England, France, or Italy, were regarded as preparatory to the elementary schools and introduced formal subjects in a rudimentary form; the kindergarten, which pointed in another direction and laid stress on games and activities, whether Froebelian or neo-Froebelian, were mainly private institutions for children of the well-to-do, and the Montessori method of auto-education came still later. Influenced by the kindergarten and Montessori methods, by the new psychology, and by the recognition of the importance of health and good physical habits, the infant schools were gradually transformed and more attention was given to play, games, and activities of children in a healthy environment. Still more recently, as a result partly of the contribution of psychoanalysis and its insistence on the dangers of early miseducation, and partly of a movement from considerations of social welfare to provide for the children of the working classes an environment comparable with that enjoyed by children of the well-to-do, the nursery schools have been established and are exerting an influence on the character of the educative care given to very young children. Similar attention is being given to the stage which precedes nursery and infact schools; care is being given in institutions (*creches,*

Krippen, children's homes, day nurseries) to children as soon as they can be left by their parents. All these movements represent a realization that education is a lifelong process, and all the influences, physical and spiritual, that affect the individual determine the character of his development.

Curriculum and Courses of Study

As long as the function of the elementary school was restricted to imparting a fixed amount of knowledge, the three R's to which enrichment subjects were later added, and as long as it was believed that the same content would serve all educative purpose—training of character, development of skills and techniques, and mental training—the problem of who should prepare the curriculum and courses of study was relatively unimportant. Because teachers were inadequately trained, or because they were trained merely to carry into practice what was prescribe, or because the State definitely intended to use the schools for purposes of nationalistic indoctrination, curriculum and courses of study have in the main been prepared and prescribed by a central authority. Even in the United States, where central control was negligible, they were prepared in each area by the administrative efforts, and in England, where the central authority was in the main an agency for the inspection of schools and for distributing grants, the work of the elementary schools was dominated by the annual examinations conducted by the inspector.

The movement for greater freedom for the child has been accompanied by its correlative, greater freedom for the teacher. If the child and his interests are to be the starting-point, and if education is the process of understanding and mastering one's environment, then the work of the school must be related to both, and a curriculum or course of study uniform for a large area becomes ananomaly. Hence the tendency is at present to abandon the prescribed curriculum and course of study, and to issue suggestions which serve as a basis for adapting the work of the school to the locality in which it is situated. Hence, also, a movement for the better preparation of teachers on a higher standard. France and the United States alone have retained prescribed courses of study, but in the former country permission is given to the teachers to make adaptations to local needs, and in the latter there is a tendency to enlist the participation of teachers in the preparation of courses of study to be adopted, however, in all the schools of a system. In England, the German states, the Soviet Republics, and Italy, the practice of issuing suggestions instead of prescribed regulations has been adopted.

Freedom to adapt the curriculum and course of study to the needs and interests of pupils and to the local environment furnishes only the starting-point from which the work of the school is to reach out until the pupils are introduced to the larger environment of the society, the nation, and the world in which they live. Such culture is obviously coloured by the history and traditions of the country in which it has been developed. With the development of the nationalistic spirit in the nineteenth century, it was further coloured by an attempt to utilize it for nationalistic indoctrination out of narrow loyalties. The development of patriotism is important and cannot be denied a place in education, but unless it involves at the same time a series of loyalties to the home and the social institutions of which the pupil is a member, and with them a sense of service and a realization that culture and civilization have been a collective achievement in which one's own nation has borne a share along with others, such training will result in a nationalistic spirit which looks upon other nations with suspicion and hatred. The narrow type of patriotic education has not disappeared, but much has been achieved already in so far as it is possible today to talk in the schools of international understanding and of a common humanity based on common knowledge and devoted to common ends.

Methods of Instruction

Education, accordingly, must have a definite end or purpose: to base it solely on the growth of the individual and his interests is to court anarchy; to impose on the individual content whose significance he does not understand but which he learns, in the superficial sense of memorizing, is to court failure. The tendency today is to bring the two together—the individual with his interests and capacities, and the culture which he is to make his own. The method which mediates between the two is the activity of the learner motivated by recognition of meanings. The school is accordingly being changed from a passive, learning school (*Lernschule*), which cultivated verbalism and the use of books, into an active school (*Arbeitsschule; école active*) in which the pupil is an active participant in the learning process, no longer limited to the acquisition of knowledge and information from books or from the teacher, but engaging in a variety of activities which train him in the use of hand and eye, give him opportunities for the exercise of his mind and body, and do not neglect the development of his emotions through aesthetic experiences.

Such are the general tendencies in the progress of elementary education. The conflict between the old school and the new school has not yet been settled; but as the following sections will show, the new tendencies are dominant in every country, with the exception of France, with her strong convictions that the function of the school is to transmit those things of which no individual should be ignorant and with a proud faith in her own cultural traditions, all the other countries which are discussed in the following sections illustrate the new tendencies. There are differences, to be sure, which result from national traditions, national characteristics, and national value, and from the conceptions of the State and society in relation to the individual. Russia uses her school system as an instrument of indoctrination in socialistic principles; in Italy education is dominated by Fascist ideals; Germany and England, but England less consciously than Germany, stress the importance of the cultural heritage; the United States because there has not yet been developed any deep or profound conviction or faith in a national culture, emphasizes the individual more and is restlessly searching for the best means and methods appropriate for the promotion of his growth and development.

The Present a Stage of Transition

Elementary education is thus in a stage of transition full of uncertainties and groping for new expression. The preparation for teachers in this process of reconstruction has not yet been adequately adapted to the new situation, except perhaps in Germany and in a few English training colleges. This much has been achieved, that the nineteenth-century tradition is no longer accepted as adequate to present conditions. Science has accumulated a vast store of knowledge about the nature of the individual, even though complete agreement has not yet been (and perhaps never will be) reached on the subject. Much thought is being given to the nature of the content of the elementary school curriculum and to the process of instruction. The standardized methods and formulas of the nineteenth century have given way to countless experiments which will bear fruit in the future. How much of these results, and whether the genuinely valuable aspects of an education can be submitted to objective measurement, is another question which only the future will answer. Upon this, however, the tendencies which will be described in the following sections are agreed, that the purpose of elementary education is to lay the foundations for, or to initiate the development of, an independent individual, as a member of society, trained to think and feel, and conscious of his responsibilities, with a mastery through appreciative understanding over himself and his environment. The individual with his original nature is the starting-point, society and all that it means with its culture and civilization, and the world of nature and of man, furnish the environment from which the educative experiences, or curriculum content, are derived. That the school can go beyond this and be used as an instrument for the reorganization and reconstruction of society not even a Russian educator, like Pinkevitch, accepts, ready though he is to believe in the theory that education can change human nature.

We are not supporters of the thesis that an existing society can be changed through the school. To make the school the embryo of a future socialistic order is impossible for the simple reason that the school cannot be independent of its environment. Moreover, the school should be most intimately related to the contemporary life; it should study, observe, and participate in an organized way in that life. The school will of course reflect the existing situation; and the children because of their imitativeness and suggestibility, are naturally influenced by their surroundings.

To adopt the French phrase, "the school is the school," an institution created by society to perpetuate itself; but the school must be responsive to contemporary life it is to save itself from the danger of becoming artificial and meaningless, formal and mechanical. The weakness of elementary education in the nineteenth century lay in the fact that it was directed solely to transmission of the acquired heritage and the perpetuation of existing social and political orders. Today the world finds itself in a stage of change and transition, still uncertain of the future, confronted with economic, national and international problems which it has never before in its history been called upon to solve, and standing at the beginning of an era in which every aspect of life is being affected by the advances of science whose progress is apparently unlimited. In the light of these conditions, education assumes a new function; the school becomes an instrument of reconstruction, not in the sense that it creates a new social order, but that it so equips the individual that he understands the world around him, has some appreciation of the civilization and culture which have made it what it is today, and with an interest, because of a sense of social responsibility, in contributing to its progress. This is the function of education in general, in which the elementary school is only one stage, but an important stage because its task is today to lay the foundations of a process which should continue through life. The elementary school can only interpret the life of the society which it serves, express the highest aspirations and ideals which society sets before itself; as an institution for creating a new social order, it would be meaningless, even if it were tolerated.

1. ENGLAND

History

Elementary education in England does not lend itself to easy classification by any convenient pedagogical formula. It cannot be described as conservative or progressive, but has in it the elements of both. It has none and yet has all of the characteristic features of other systems. It is not, like the French system, inspired by a deep-rooted passion for national culture, although its curriculum is founded on a belief in the value of the best that has been said and thought. Unlike the German system, it does not bear the stamp of any dominant philosophy or theory of education, but is ready to tolerate any experiment in curriculum or method which a teacher can justify. It is not dominated, like Russian or Italian education, by any particular political or economic or social ideology, and yet is able to cultivate loyalty to ideals of government and democracy. Finally, while it is not governed, like the American, by efficiency as an aim and encourages variety and freedom, with all its vagueness it is administratively efficient. While England, like France, can point to a distinguished list of educational statesmen—Bentham, John Stuart Mill, Lord Brougham, Sir James Kay-Shuttleworth, Lord Shaftesbury, W. E. Forster, Sir Michael Sadler, and H.A.L. Fisher—with a few outstanding exceptions (J.J. Findlay and Sir Percy Nunn) she has on the whole not made any important contribution to the philosophy of education; the progress of education has not been influenced by great theories, although some influence has been exercised, but as a rule indirectly, by Pestalozzi, Froebel, Herbart, Kerschensteiner, and John Dewey. Since the abolition of the "payment-by-results" system in the nineties, elementary, like secondary education, has relied upon the personality of the teacher more than on nationally accepted theories or governmental rules and regulations.

The English system of elementary education had its origin in the philanthropic and religious movements at the beginning of the nineteenth century and was provided until 1870 by voluntary organizations. To some of these the State began in 1833 to give financial assistance, which soon led to the establishment of a National Education Department (1839) and the introduction of a system of inspection on the principle of "no grants without inspection." It was not until 1870 that public authorities, school boards, were permitted by the Education Act of that year to establish elementary schools out of local rates, where the supply was inadequate. There was thus created a dual system of elementary schools, some established and maintained by voluntary organizations, mainly denominational, others provided by publicly elected school boards, which were not permitted to give denominational religious instruction. Although the schools under the dual system were intended for children of the lower orders, the well-to-do providing for the education of their children at home or in private schools, fees were charged in all schools, with exemption for the poor, until they were abolished in 1891. Compulsory attendance at school was not introduced until 1876, the Act of 1870 having empowered local authorities to pass by-laws requiring children to attend school between the age of five and twelve; the Act of 1876 made education compulsory up to the age of ten and based the employment of children from ten to fourteen on the attainment of certain scholastic standards; in 1900 local authorities were permitted to pass by-laws requiring full-time attendance up to the age of fourteen; in 1914 there were still 70,000 children of school age who were engaged in half-time employment.

The aim of the elementary schools was to impart the essentials of an education, the three R's mainly and religious instruction. The work of the schools was regulated first by inspection, and after the publication by Mr. Robert Lowe, vice-president of the Committee of Council on Education, of the Revised Code in 1862, by annual examinations of all the pupils conducted by the government inspectors. The government grants were based on the results of the examinations. For thirty years, until the practice was abolished in 1895, and for some years following the abolition, the chief features of elementary education were moulded by the payment-by-results system with its emphasis on drill and discipline, repetition and memorization. While the effects were in the main harmful to the progress of education, the system did not fail at the same time to stress the importance of the ideals of accuracy and thoroughness. Nor was the curriculum of the schools restricted altogether within the limits of a few subjects; some subjects were obligatory in all schools, others were optional for pupils above the first class (Standard I), and others, known a "specifics," were optional for pupils in the last three years of the course (Standards IV to VI); a Seventh Standard and even a so-called ex-Seventh standard were added after 1961.

The larger industrial centres, in which elementary education was administered by enlightened school boards, were unwilling, in the absence of an adequate supply of secondary education, to restrict the opportunities of abler boys and girls, and not only added the extra standards, but also organized higher grade or higher elementary schools which gave a form of lower secondary education. The refusal of a government auditor to sanction expenditure by the London school board on subjects which were not strictly elementary (the Cockerton Case), combined with the universal recognition, following the *Report* of the Bryce Commission, of the need of a system of public secondary education, precipitated a situation which made a revision of the education law inevitable. The elementary school of the nineteenth century had outlived its usefulness. The voluntary organizations were no longer able to secure adequate funds to maintain their schools, and more and better education in a genuinely national system was demanded. The Board of

Education was created in 1899 by a combination of a number of national departments concerned with various aspects of education, and in 1902 the administrative organization was changed and the provision of secondary education out of public funds, local and state, was made possible[2]. A new spirit had already been injected into elementary education before this by the abolition of the payment-by-results system and the substitution of inspection for examinations.

PRESENT SYSTEM

Provision of Schools

By the Act of 1902 the dual system of elementary schools was continued, but placed under one authority—the county, county borough, municipal borough, or urban district councils. In areas which are unorganized for educational purposes—that is, rural areas—elementary education is under the control of the county authority. Each of the authorities mentioned is responsible for the maintenance of both the denominational and the strictly public schools. The difference between the denominational, voluntary, or, more usually, "non-provided" schools and the "provided" schools is that the buildings of the former are the property of a body of trustees and rented to the education authority at a charge sufficient to cover the cost of reasonable "wear and tear"; the trustees retain certain rights in the appointment of the teachers with respect to their ability to give religious instruction of their denomination. The "provided" schools are built and maintained wholly by the education authority. Both types of schools now constitute parts of the public system of elementary education.

Religious Instruction

Religious instruction is given in all schools, but in the provided schools it is controlled by the Cowper-Temple Clause (Clause 28 of the Education Act, 1870), which requires that "no religious catechism or formulary which is distinctive of any particular denomination shall be taught in the school."

This has meant in practice the inclusion of the reading of the Bible without comment, and the teaching of the Apostles' Creed, the Lord's Prayer, and the Ten Commandments. A number of local education authorities—the West Riding of Yorkshire, Cambridgeshire, Lancashire, Leicestershire, Oxfordshire, Hampshire, Middlesex, and others—have issued syllabuses for religious instruction which have been prepared by the cooperation of teachers, the clergy of the Anglican Church, and ministers of the Free Churches, and adopted not only in their own but in other areas. All children are expected to receive religious instruction, usually given by the class teacher, unless their parents claim exemption under the conscience clause of the Education Act. The first period of the day, usually half an hour, from 9 A.M. to 9.30 A.M., is set aside for religious instruction, a period which is often curtailed by taking of attendance and marking of registers.

In non-provided schools the religious instruction is definitely denominational and is given by the teachers, who may be selected for appointment because of their religious affiliation. New non-provided schools may be established, but if a local education authority refuses its recognition, which means the assumption of a certain share in the cost of maintenance, the final decision rests with the Board of Education. Religious instruction is not supervised by the Board's inspector; in non-provided schools it may be inspected by the managers or trustees of the school or as they may arrange, usually by a minister of the denomination concerned.

The increasing cost of education, the inability of most of the dominations to replaced their school buildings, which in many cases are old and outworn, the development of interdenominational syllabuses, and the recent movement to reorganize the system of schools, have focussed attention on the defects of the dual system and the need of some reform. The *Church Assembly Report of the Commission on Religious Education*, known as the Archbishops' Commission, recommends that local education authorities be empowered by Parliament to make such arrangements as they may think fit for religious instruction for all children of their area, in accordance with the religion of their parents, notwithstanding the prohibition of the Cowper-Temple clause.

The Commission also recommended state building grants for the purpose of adapting the buildings of non-provided schools to the needs of the proposed senior schools[3].

The first recommendation would mean the organization of elementary schools as interdenominational schools (the German *Simultanschulen*); the second would relieve the denominational organizations of one of the chief causes of their present difficulties—inability to find money for new buildings. No action has yet been taken to give effect to these recommendations, but two authorities, Bradford and West Riding, have entered into a Covenant "for twenty-one years or more" to take over non-provided schools on condition that the religious instruction follow the regular syllabuses of the authorities and that the denominations concerned provide for denominational religious instruction at their own expense on two days a week at such times and places as they may elect.

The time has passed when the reform of elementary education and the religious question were synonymous, as they were in 1902 and 1906. All the denominations, except the Roman Catholic, because of financial pressure and the education authorities in the interests of economy and a common public system, are ready to compromise on the subject of religious instruction and the dual system.

Private Schools

Beside the public elementary schools, there is a large number of private schools, which are required to be efficient, but which at present are not subject to inspection except under the indirect requirement of the law that children of compulsory school age must be efficiently educated.

Compulsory Attendance

The Education Act, 1921, places upon parents the obligation of causing their children of not less than five nor more than fourteen years of age to attend school, unless under efficient instruction in some other manner, for reasons of health, or because a public elementary school is not available within two miles of the residence of a child under eleven, or three miles if over that age, and suitable means of conveyance are not provided by the local education authority beyond these limits. The law thus requires compulsory education, and may be met by attendance at any school, public or private, or by instruction at home, provided that the education is efficient. Since 1918 no child may leave school except at the end of the term in which the fourteenth year is reached. Local authorities were also empowered by the Act passed in that year to pass by-laws extending compulsory attendance to fifteen or even sixteen with the approval of the Board of Education; the number of authorities which have availed themselves of this power is negligible.

Compulsory attendance regulations are administered by the local education authorities through their school attendance committees and school attendance officers. The latter are responsible for the preparation of the school census and investigations of absences. With the improvement of education and the introduction since 1907 of a system of school medical inspection, the large majority of absences are no longer due to truancy and neglect, but to illness. It has even been suggested that the functions of school attendance officers should be taken over by school nurses. In any case, the position of the school attendance officers has become more like that of the welfare workers. Cases of repeated absence without cause are caught first before the school attendance committees or their sub-committees, and only in the last resort to the magistrates'—usually juvenile-courts. Habitual truants may be committed to special schools—reformatory and day industrial schools.

The percentage of average attendance for the whole of England and Wales in 1930-31 was 89 per cent. This high percentage is attained not only through the efficiency of the administration of attendance and the growing popularity of the schools, but by the fact that a part of the government grant is calculated on the basis of attendance, the interest of the teachers who have emphasized the importance of regularity and punctuality, and competitions between schools, classes, and pupils. It is not improbable that a higher percentage of attendance might be attained were it not for the rigorous regulations of the school medical service.

The Organisation of Schools

The elementary school is rapidly becoming the common school of the whole population, a position which it had secured, not through pressure of official regulations, but because of its progressive improvements in buildings, teachers, and curriculum. There is, however, a complete absence of uniformity in the organization of the schools. Because of its separate origin in the nineteenth century, the infant school, intended for children between the ages of five and seven, has everywhere continued to be organized as a separate department with its own principal and staff, and even in small schools it is usual to have a separate teacher for the infants. Under the pressure of economic conditions, many working mothers are compelled to send children to school before the age of five, but no child is admitted under the age of three. For these children there have been organized, although for reasons of accommodation the upper limit is sometimes exceeded, babies' classes, which are gradually being transformed, under the influence of the nursery school movement, into nursery classes.

Beyond the infant school all uniformity of organization ceases even in the organization of schools under the same authority. In some schools boys and girls from seven to fourteen may be in separate departments; in others they may be in junior mixed departments from seven to eleven and continue the last three years in senior mixed departments; elsewhere they may be in junior mixed departments and then separated for the last three years into departments for senior boys or senior girls. The *Handbook of Suggestions for the Consideration of Teachers and Others Concerned in the Work of Public Elementary Schools,* issued by the Board of Education[4]; is based upon four stages of school life: (1) the "nursery" stage for children under the age of compulsory attendance (three to five); (2) the "infants" stage from the age of five to about eight; (3) the "junior" stage up to the age of eleven plus; and (4) the "senior" stage including the last three years of schooling. At the close of the "junior" stage, the better pupils are usually selected by examination for transfer to a central or a secondary school.

The movement for the provision of some form of post-primary or secondary education for all pupils is based in general on the organization adopted by the Board. The *Report on the Education of the Adolescent* (1926), followed by the Board's pamphlet, *The New Prospect in Education* (1928), recommended a definite break at or about the age of eleven; education up to that age was to be given in the primary school, including the infants' and junior departments; beyond that age and up to the age of fifteen, which was proposed as the upper limit of compulsory attendance, pupils were to attend a variety of schools according to their ability and bent—the modern school, selective and non-selective, or the secondary school. The failure to enact the School Attendance Bill, which would have given effect to these recommendations, left the local authorities with the reorganization of the school system in their own way. Many have already begun to organize senior schools as separate units for pupils between eleven and fourteen: the difficulties are not so great in the larger areas, but in the rural areas they are intensified by the existence of the dual system and the refusal of trustees to send their older pupils to the senior schools without some guarantee as to their religious instruction and to face a reduction in the size of their own schools.

The Consultative Committee, in its *Report on the Primary School,* (London, 1931), repeats the recommendation made in its *Report on the Education of the Adolescent,* that pupils should be transferred to some form of secondary school at the age of eleven plus. It proceeded to recommend that the education of children up to eleven be given in two stages, one extending to the age of seven plus and the other from seven plus to eleven plus. The recommendations of the Consultative Committee will undoubtedly constitute the basis on which the elementary school system of the future will be organized throughout the country, as it has already begun to be reorganized in a few areas. The present organization is indicated in the following figures which give the number of departments for 1931:

> there were 426 departments for senior boys, 421 for senior girls, 505 senior mixed, 2797 for boys, 2928 for girls, 12,815 mixed, 348 for junior boys, 416 for junior girls, 3285 junior mixed, and 6422 for infants—a total of 30,363.

Articulation

One of the difficulties involved in the present organization of schools by departments is to secure an unbroken articulation between them. In the absence of specific requirements prescribed by a central authority, each department is autonomous and articulation depends upon voluntary consultation and cooperation between the head teachers concerned. The problem of articulation is particularly difficult at a time when theories and practices, especially in the education of young children, are changing; the work of infants' departments are tending to become freer and the transition between this and the next stage is at times too abrupt. The *Report on the Primary School,* while recommending the retention of the infants' department as a separate unit, emphasizes the importance of articulation with the junior school, which constitutes the next stage.

Size of Class

There are no rigorous or standardized regulations on the size of classes. For some time the Board of Education has encouraged the adoption of forty-five children in a class as the maximum. Owing to the economic situation and the fluctuations in enralments since the War, this maximum has frequently been exceeded. *The Primary School Report* recommends that "A class in a primary school should not contain more than forty pupils, and, where there are a considerable proportion of retarded children, it should be much smaller."

Nursery Schools

The necessity, which became urgent during the War, of providing for the care of infants and young children whose mothers were absent from home and at work during the day, helped to focus attention on their needs. The actual situation, combined with the emphasis of the school medical service on the importance of a sound foundation of good health and with the rapidly developing study of the growth of children, helped to arouse public interest in a type of school, the nursery school, which had been first established by Rachel and Margaret McMillian in one of the slum districts of London in 1908. The Education Act, 1918, permitted local education authorities to establish and maintain *creches* or day nurseries in which infants might be received from one month old and kept until they are three years old or more, and nursery schools for children between the age of two and five years, out of local rates, half the cost being borne by grants from the Board of Education. The value of the nursery school, which aims to provide for young children living under social conditions detrimental to their health and good training an environment similar to that enjoyed by children in good homes, has been universally recognized. The financial conditions of the last decade have, however, prevented any extensive establishment of such schools. The general principles of the nursery school have been adopted in the reorganization, in infants' schools, of babies' classes for children between the ages of three to five, into nursery classes. From the point of view of the health of the pre-school child, nursery classes and nursery schools continue the work begun in Maternity and Child Welfare centres which have been established under the Maternity and Child Welfare Act of 1919: beyond this stage the care of the child's health is supervised under the system of school medical inspection, established in 1907.

Administration of Elementary Schools

The responsibility for the administration of elementary schools or departments of such schools rests upon the head teacher, head master, or head mistress. There are no uniform regulations governing the appointments to this position; each authority has its own system. Generally the position is filled by promotion from the ranks of teachers within a system, sometimes by inviting application through advertisements; some authorities have an eligible list of candidates prepared on the recommendations of the local inspectors. The tendency at present is to appoint only certificated teachers who have had a number of years of successful experience; in very small schools, owing to unsatisfactory conditions of salary and living, uncertificated teachers are still appointed to headship.

Head teachers are expected to devote a number of periods a week to class instruction, but their chief functions are to guide and supervise their staff; to promote the unity of school work by frequent consultations, discussions, and conferences; to prepare the curriculum, time-schedule, and course of study with the advice and assistance of their teachers; to conduct periodical examinations, and to assume a large share of the responsibility for the classification and promotion of pupils. They are expected to supervise the work of their teachers and in particular to give as much assistance as possible to young teachers; and, finally, they are responsible for the general routine work of administration, the keeping of records, and the preparation of reports.

Aim of Elementary Education

The aim of elementary education varies somewhat in the different stages. The purpose of the nursery schools and classes is to provide an environment which will promote the health and happiness of the children and at the same time cultivate their early interests through play and games, movement and exercise, from and colour, song and story. This aim is continued into the infants' classes, where the activities expand in range and become the basis of what are later organized as subjects.

The aim of elementary education has been defined as follows in the Annual *Code* issued by the Board of Education from 1904 to 1926:

> The purpose of the public elementary school is to form and strengthen the character and to develop the intelligence of the children entrusted to it, and to make the best use of the school years available in assisting both girls and boys, according to their different needs, to fit themselves, practically as well as intellectually, for the work of life[5].

To this statement may be added the more recent definitions of the aim of the primary school:

> Its primary aim must be to aid children, while they are children, to be healthy, and, so far as is possible, happy children, vigorous in body and lively in mind, in order that later, as with widening experience they grow towards maturity, the knowledge which life demands may more easily be mastered and the necessary accomplishments more readily acquired[6].

Referring to the curriculum of the primary school, the Consultative Committee in its *Report* declared:

> Its aim should be to develop in a child the fundamental human powers and to awaken him to the fundamental interests of civilized life so far as those powers and interests lie within the compass of childhood, to

> encourage him to attain gradually to that control and orderly management of his energies, impulses and emotions, which is the essence of moral and intellectual discipline, to help him to discover the idea of duty and to ensue it, and to open out his imagination and his sympathies in such a way that he may be prepared to understand and to follow in later years the highest examples of excellence in life and conduct[7].

As in all English definitions of education, character-formation comes first; it implies the development of certain habits of conduct and behaviour, intellectual, emotional, and moral, and the cultivation of certain ideals. Beyond and contributory to this common aim, the elementary school has the task of development of health and vigour of body, of cultivating intellectual habits, of arousing alertness and a taste for further study and work, and of laying the foundations and giving the tools for self-education. As compared with the aim of the elementary school in the nineteenth century, with its emphasis on thorough mastery of a few subjects, the aim today is to impart the elements of liberal education, or, in the words of Sir Michael Sadler, to give "new things to love and admire."[8] Through individual as through cooperative activities the pupils are to be trained to discipline themselves and to become sensitive to the meaning of duty for themselves and to society. All those qualities which are implied by freedom and independence must be developed, but they must be tempered by an appreciation of the similar rights of others.

In the elaboration of these aims a distinct change is noted. The English school has always emphasized character-formation, but the methods in the past have been in the main extra-curricular; increasingly the contribution which may be made by a suitable organization of the curriculum and content of instruction has begun to be recognised. This represents a movement toward the recognition of the education of the whole man; whatever contributes to the education of the individual cannot be divided into separate and distinct departments which are unrelated to each other. A similar change has taken place in the concept of discipline; discipline, it is recognized, cannot be discarded, but the external discipline of tradition, suppression of the individual by authority, must be replaced by free self-discipline accepted because it is necessary to the existence of any social organization. Corporal punishment has not been abolished, but it is administered with less frequency and reserved for serious offences.

Curriculum and Courses of Study

The work of the nursery school is determined by its aim—provision for the healthy and active growth of young children, and to some extent by the nature of its buildings and equipment. Some nursery schools, following a principle insisted upon by Margaret McMillian, consist of gardens and buildings attached, and most of the work is carried on in the open air; others, including also nursery classes, have buildings with gardens or playgrounds attached, and the major part of the activities are carried on indoors. The nursery schools take care of children for the whole day, from 8 A.M. to 5 P.M.; the nursery classes for the shorter school day. In both provision in made for feeding the children; the parents as far as possible, contribute what they can. So far as one can speak of a curriculum at the nursery stage, it is directed to the cultivation of good habits through bathing and washing, dressing and undressing, cooperative activities in the preparation for meals and other activities. Much of the time is devoted to play and games, training of the senses through colour, size and number; formal subjects, as such, have no place, but a foundation is laid for them through the care and observation of animals and plants, singing, group games, story-telling, art work, and the development of good habits of speech. In some cases the work of nursery schools and classes has been influenced by the spirit, but not by the details, of the Montessori method. Although attention is given to the individual child, the nursery schools have not been established as centres for psychological research, as have

Model Programme of Nursery Classes

A.M.	
9:00-9:50	Arrival and registration. Hymn. Prayer. Visit offices. Put on handy bags. Handy drill. Breathing exercises.
9:50-10:00	Rhythmic exercises or games.
10:00-10:15	Charts and picture talks.
10:15-10:50	Preparation for lunch. Wash hands. Set table. Have lunch. Tidy up.
10:50-11:05	Free play.
11:05-11:35	Short rest. Sense Training on Monday, Wednesday, and Friday; singing on Tuesday and Thursday.
11:35-11:50	Nursery rhymes and drawing on Monday and Friday; aloplast on Tuesday; paper tearing or folding or cutting on Wednesday, finger plays or beads on Thursday.
11:50-12:00	Learning to put on coats, etc. Grace and dismissal.
P.M.	
1:30-2:30	Arrival and registration. Inspection of class. Handy drill. Visit offices and prepare for rest. Quiet occupations for those who do not sleep.
2:30-2:40	Wake up and put on shoes or clogs.
2:40-2:55	Free play.
2:55-3:30	Story followed by dramatization on Monday; free drawing on Tuesday; Brick building on Wednesday; toys on Thursday, rocking horse and singing rhymes on Friday.
3:30-3:45	Dressing. Prayer. Dismissal.

many similar institutions in the United States. Because of the age of the children, the nursery schools and classes have attracted the interest of parents and in that way have become centres that influence the home environment to which the children return from school.

In infant and elementary schools neither the Board of Education nor the local education authorities prescribe either the list of subjects to be taught—the courses of study, or the time-schedules. The legal definition of elementary education is that it is "that education which constitutes the whole or the principal part of the work of an elementary school." The Board of Education until 1926 issued an Annual *Code* in which the subjects of an elementary school curriculum were indicated without any requirement that all subjects should be taught in all schools, but the practice has been discontinued. The only guidance furnished by the Board is the *Handbook of Suggestions for the Consideration of Teachers and Others Concerned in the Work of Public Elementary Schools,* first issued in 1905 and revised periodically until 1927. The *Handbook* is prepared by the inspectors of the Board on the basis of their observations in the field and with the cooperation of teachers. The *Handbook* is thus a compilation which is eminently practical and a guide which represents what can actually be achieved. The *Suggestions* are not governed by any particular theory or philosophy, but illustrate the variety of practices which result from the freedom enjoyed by the teachers. The only subject in which the Board, influenced by the medical inspection branch, requires its syllabus to be followed is physical training, but even in this case a local authority may use its own syllabus provided that it can secure the approval of the inspectors.

The Board definitely refrains from prescribing the curriculum or its details because, according to the *Suggestions*:

> It is not possible to lay down any rule as to the exact number of the subjects which should be taken in an individual school. The choice, indeed, cannot be in practice absolutely free. It is in part determined by public opinion as expressing the needs of the community in which the scholars live. [Language, reading and writing, arithmetic and measurement, hygiene, physical and moral training cannot be omitted.] But in selecting other subjects the decision is not always so easy...The curriculum must vary to some extent with the qualifications of the teaching staff...Variations in the curriculum will often correspond to the special needs and circumstances of the scholars[9].

This does not mean that the English elementary school is curriculum-centred or that the interests of the children are ignored.

> He [the teacher] certainly must become, if he is not one already, a close and sympathetic students of the nature of his pupils. He must be able to range himself mentally alongside them and ready to modify his teaching to meet their needs. Briefly, his task is to make the most of the mental qualities which already exist in them and are seeking opportunities for exercise, their motives, interests, and instincts; their sense of wonder and romance; their natural curiosity, constructiveness, competitiveness, and so forth. His starting point must be no rigid syllabus or subject, but the children as they really are; he must work always with the grain of their minds, try never to cut across it[10].

But if the children are the starting-point, the ends are determined by the purposes for which the school exists and the civilization and culture which they are to share. Freedom must be combined with its correlative, responsibility.

An almost unlimited degree of freedom for children is sometimes advocated nowadays. It has been proposed that they should choose their own subjects, make their own rules and time-tables, work or not as they feel inclined. Nothing of this kind is suggested here, except perhaps in the case of individual pupils who are nearing the end of their school life. There is a due mean between a system which counteracts the natural aspirations of the children and one which in the name of freedom refuses them the aid and guidance they require. Children cannot be treated from the outset as if they were possessed of mature judgment, experience, and self-knowledge. But they can be treated as natural beings, and the teacher should see to it that the purpose of the work they are required to do does not remain a mystery, either to them or to himself. Its ultimate purpose may not be fully within their comprehension, or may be too remote to appeal to them directly. The teacher should then endeavour to invest it with an immediate purpose which should, if possible, take the intrinsic form of putting it to some practical use, rather than an extrinsic form, such as the gaining of marks[11].

The success of education at any stage depends upon the personality of the teachers, free and responsible, understanding children, but also appreciating the purpose of education guided not by plans and methods prescribed by others and exacted by rigorous supervision, but by their own insight and experience. In view of the tendency in the United States toward curriculum-making by experts, the periodic vogue of methods, the control through administrative devices, supervision, standardized tests, and so on, students of education cannot too often be reminded of the importance of the teacher in the educational process. On this point it is pertinent to quote two statements from the *Report on the Primary School.*

The National Association of Inspectors of Schools and Educational Organizers argue that the greatest single factor in education was, or should be, the personality of the teacher, since schools were neither made nor marred by curricula.

Different methods will be used not only in different subjects, but also in teaching the same subject in different circumstances of school organization, numbers, situation, and equipment, and different teachers will face similar problems in different ways. In a vital sense, method is the teacher's style, the outward expression of his educational faith and experience. If his instruction is to be a living influence upon his pupils, his methods must in the end be an individual expression of his modes of thought, feeling, and outlook, and not merely the application of general rules, however sound.

Freedom for the teacher who understands his pupils is the first essential. The curriculum will represent an "introduction to the major interests of society as derived from man's civilization and culture, or certain elements of experience, because they are part of the common life of mankind."

Here is the touchstone, Sir Percy Nunn has declared, by which the claims of a subject for a place in the time-table can be infallibly tested. Does it represent one of the great movements of the human spirit, one of the major forms into which the creative impulses of man have been shaped and disciplined? If it does, then its admission cannot be contested. If it does not, it must be set aside; it may usefully be included in some special courses of technical education, but it is not qualified to be an element in the education of the people[12].

In no part of English education has a greater transformation taken place than in the infants' schools. From classrooms equipped with galleries in which large classes were huddled together under a disciplinary regime as strict as in the upper schools and a curriculum which in the main was formal and preparatory, the infants' schools have become centres of free movement and activities proper to the interests of the children in attendance. No longer is the emphasis placed upon the acquisition of the three R's and adjustment to the demands of the next Standard, but upon a variety of activities and experiences out of which the need for the rudiments of the so-called subjects emerge. Play and games, speech-training with clear articulation and freedom in expression, story-telling and conversation, painting, drawing, music, dancing, nature study, and manual activities provide a range of experiences on which are based the introduction to reading, writing, and arithmetic with an emphasis on concreteness and reality and within the scope of the pupils' comprehension. The common-sense principle is followed that a normal child, as a result of the environment in which he has been brought up, even before he enters school has an interest in the so-called formal subjects, despite modern theories to the contrary. The change in the character of the infants' school has been effected in party by the greater freedom introduced into the school atmosphere in general in the last generation, in part by the progressive methods of the kindergarten and by Montessori methods, and to some extent by the nursery school. In turn, the methods of the infants' school are affecting the work of the early years of the elementary school and the transition from the one to the other is not as abrupt as it once was.

Time-Schedule of an Infants School

		Class 1 (min.)	*Class 2 (min.)*	*Class 3 (min.)*
Registration and religious instruction—A.M.		150	150	150
Registration, grace and personal hygiene —P.M.		75	75	75
Prayer, songs and dismissal		25	25	25
Free play—A. M. and P. M.		150	150	150
Free movement between periods (3)		75	75	75
Number		125	125	125
English	Reading and doing	190	200	200
	Composition, grammar, and dictation	150	100	75
	Script writing, poetry, and words of songs	65	75	95
Nature. Conversation. Stories. Picture. Chats. History and geography		140	115	165
Physical exercises	Games and dancing, exercises personal hygiene	150	150	150
Music and band		60	50	50
Handwork	Knitting and needlework Drawing Expression work Plasticine Toymaking Individual occupations	220	235	190
Total number of minutes		1,575	1,575	1,575

The normal subjects of an elementary school are religious instruction, English language and literature, writing, arithmetic, drawing and modeling, nature study, geography, history, singing and music, hygiene and physical training, manual work, and domestic subjects (needlework, cooking, laundry work, and household management). Moral instruction is rarely taught as a separate subject. The *Education Act*, 1918, contained a provision, now incorporated in the *Education Act*, 1921, Section 20, requiring local authorities to include practical instruction suitable to the ages, abilities, and requirements of the children, and to provide courses in advanced instruction for the older pupils. The curriculum, courses of study, and time-schedules are prepared in each school, sometimes by the head teacher, most usually by the head teacher and his staff. Wherever possible a teacher who has specialized in some subject of the curriculum prepares the syllabus in that subject for the whole school. The responsibility, however, rests upon the head teacher; the courses of study or syllabuses and the time-schedules must be approved by the government inspectors, who do not withhold approval if the head teacher can justify his position.

Time Schedule of a Junior Mixed Elementary School

Subjects	*IIA*	*II*	*IIIA*	*III*	*IVA, VA*	*IV, V*
Religious instruction	175	175	175	175	175	175
Arithmetic	230	230	230	230	230	230
Physical training*	75	75	75	75	75	75
Geography	110	110	110	110	110	110
English †	195	195	195	195	230	230
Recreation	100	100	100	100	100	100
Drawing	150	150	150	150	150	150
Needlework ‡	120	120	120	120	120	120
History	70	70	60	60	60	60
Handwork	60	60	60	60	60	60
Poetry	70	70	60	60	60	60
Music	70	70	60	60	60	60
Dancing and rhythmic exercise	50	50	50	50	50	50
Optional	70	70	110	100	110	110
Observational Lessons ...	80	80	80	80	80	80
Reading	145	145	140	135	100	100
Total	1,650	1,650	1,650	1,650	1,650	1,650

* Boys attend baths for swimming on Friday afternoons.

† English includes grammar, composition, and exercises auxilary to composition.

‡ Needlework is correlated with arithmetic, drawing, nature study, geography, history.

In the preparation of courses of study, head teachers and teachers are guided by tradition, by their professional knowledge, by the *Suggestions* and *Memoranda* of the Board of Education, by special reports, such as that on *The Teaching of English,* and in some areas by suggestions issued by the local education authority. Another source of influence is to be found in the increasing number of short summer courses on the subjects of the curriculum, organized either by the Board of Education and given by its inspectors or other specialists, or by education authorities, such as those of Kent and West Riding of Yorkshire, and courses and conferences for teachers provided during the school year by some education authorities. Such a system permits adaptation to the local environment encourages freedom, and elicits responsibility. It is characteristic of the system that the courses of study are rarely printed, sometimes typewritten, usually written by hand, evidence at least that they are not intended to be permanent and are subject to modification as the occasion requires.

The Consultative Committee in its *Report on the Primary School* recommends that in the early years the curriculum be integrated on the basis of the common experience underlying all subjects (the German *Gesamtunterricht*) and correlated with the natural movement of children's minds. Such integrated instruction, whether in the form of projects or through close correlation of subjects, must, as the child grows older, give place to subjects "which have their own self-sufficient motives," and in which regular and systematic work is desirable. Similarly, while room should be provided for individual study, this must be alternated with group instruction. On the question of methods, the English attitude is pragmatic—those methods are best which produce the best results. The statement on the subject in the *Report on the Primary School* is as follows:

> Since the immediate aim of teaching is that the pupil shall become an active learner, any method which is claimed, on reasonable grounds, to conduce to that end is worthy of unbiased study.

The well-tried methods of corporate teaching have an indispensable place in the school economy, and should not be discarded wholesale in obedience to insufficient tested theories.

Nevertheless, there are occasions and purposes for which they are clearly not so suitable as methods which, while not depriving pupils of the stimulus, inspiration, and guidance of the teacher, yet leave him reasonable scope to ensue his own special interests, to learn in his own way, and to acquire the priceless habit of independent purposeful work.

While these considerations are of general validity, they apply specially to small rural schools, where from the nature of the use, class-organization and class-teaching must have a particularly limited value.

Finally, while we deprecate experiments ill-considered or carried out under conditions clearly unfavourable to success, we hope that as teachers come to grips with the special problems of the primary school, ways and means will be found of giving effect to what is sound in the suggestions of those who criticise the present predominance of the class-method. In particular, we hope that where individual methods are employed with unmistakable success in an infant school, the teachers in the lower classes of the primary school will consider carefully the propriety Qof so adjusting their own methods that there is no serious break in continuity as the child passes from the one to the other[13].

Curriculum Organization and Standards

The general character of the infants' school curriculum has already been indicated. The fact that compulsory education begins one year earlier in England than in any other country and the acceptance of the principle that young children do manifest an interest in what are usually called formal subjects, render it possible to set up a standard whereby pupils at the age of eight of nine may, in addition to the variety of other activities in which they engage, be expected to be able to read an easy book, tell or write a simple narrative and have a command of the first notions of arithmetic and measurement. From this stage on, the work becomes more systematic with less emphasis on mere freedom and pleasure than on exactness. The standard to be attained by pupils at about the age of eleven is that.

The scholars should be able to express themselves with fair ease and correctness on matters which fall within their experience or which they have read about in books. They should have learned accurately all the simple process in arithmetic and made at least the first steps in mensuration. In landwork and drawing, they should now be showing more technical skill and be aiming at more difficult subjects and a closer finish. The outlines of history and geography will be forming in their minds, though no attempt should have been made to teach them details, or generalizations, which they cannot properly assimilate[14].

The weakest part of the work of the English elementary school has in the past been that of the senior stage (pupils from eleven to fourteen). This has been due to a number of causes; under the selective system the best pupils were generally transferred to an intermediate or secondary school at about the age of eleven; much time was wasted on repetition of work already done; the smaller number of pupils made an adequate system of classification difficult; in the last year, until the Education Act, 1918, required pupils to remain in school until the end of the term in which they reached their fourteenth birthday, the classes were constantly reduced as pupils dropped out. The Education Act, 1918, attempted to attack the difficulties by imposing upon local authorities the duty of providing advanced instruction and a variety of practical work for pupils in the senior stage. The *Suggestions* recommended in the advanced instruction laid more emphasis on self-education through extensive reading, local, social, and European history, practical work in science and geography, and in mathematics the introduction of algebraical symbols and graphical methods. For practical work, the opportunities for a variety of manual activities for boys and for housecraft or domestic science were increased, in the larger schools by the provision of workshops and model apartments, for pupils in the smaller schools by the organization of central workshops or domestic science centres used in common by pupils from a number of schools.

It is possible here to give only the main features of the English course of study as defined in the Board's *Handbook of Suggestions*. The subject which is regarded as the most important, because it is a means of expression and understanding and underlies the work in all other subjects, is English. Every teacher should, in fact, be a teacher of English. The aim of the school should be to encourage good and correct English and its simple, direct, and unaffected written and oral expression. While aiming to correct bad English, the use of dialects should not be altogether discouraged, because they "have a history and associations which entitle them to respect." English should be regarded as a unified subject which offers opportunities for a variety of exercises through speech, reading, and writing. Beginning with conversation which should develop naturally out of concrete situations (the home, play, pictures, stories, and dramatization), the pupil is introduced to reading and oral and written expression. The subjects for composition and spelling lists should be within the range of the pupils' ability and experience. The purpose of reading, prose and poetry, should be to cultivate pleasure and appreciation; after the preliminary foundations through the use of readers, pupils should as early as possible be introduced to the masterpieces of literature appropriate to their stage of development. The range of reading suggested for the senior stage includes Scott, Dickens, Shakespeare, Kingsley, *Robinson Crusoe, Masterman Ready, Tom Brown's School-days* and books of travel, adventure, and biography. Attention is given both to reading aloud and to silent reading, and special emphasis is placed upon good speech, accurate voice-production and careful articulation[15]. Freedom and breadth have taken the place of the narrow, formal drill in fundamentals; practice is regarded as necessary in spelling, some grammar is essential, and rules and techniques are desirable in writing compositions, but the practical needs have replaced the formal and deductive methods.

Although the teaching of arithmetic has undergone considerable change, the subjects is still regarded as one of the most important in the elementary curriculum and absorbs about one fifth of the weekly time allotment. Meaningless drill has been replaced by ability to apply number to everyday life, and the practical and useful are kept constantly in mind. Simple geometry and mensuration through handwork and drawing are associated with arithmetic. Graphic methods and algebraical symbols are taught to older pupils where circumstances are favourable.

In the teaching of history and geography, there is an absence of any attempt to use these subjects for purposes of nationalistic indoctrination. The purpose of history instruction is to develop a sense of continuity and of cause and effect. The teaching of history varies with the capacity and interests of the teacher.

It is of more value to give the pupil some idea of the right spirit in which he may approach the study of history in later life than to burden his memory with details which can have little or no significance for him. If the subject is made so attractive that the pupil is constantly asking himself "What comes next" and if when his schooldays are over he continues to read and study history, the teacher has achieved his purpose[16].

In the lower classes an appeal should be made to the imagination through simple and attractive narratives, legend, and the story of the British and foreign heroes, and, if taught at all, as a subject, history at this stage should be limited to the older period of British history which is the least complex and the most picturesque. The older pupils should acquire a connected view of the main outlines of British history and of the changes which have led to the social and industrial life of the present. Controversial aspects of economic and political development should be omitted, since "There is scope enough for all children's powers in those aspects of history which are not of this character, and the discussion of topics on which they are unable to exercise their judgment is useless."[17] In addition to its value as a cultural subject, history may also be made an instrument of moral training in lessons of heroism, unselfishness, loyalty to an ideal, and "how the patriot has helped his country." Finally, the history of Great Britain and of the British Commonwealth of Nations should be taught as a part of world history leading to a discussion of international cooperation, the League of Nations, and the ideals for which it stands[18].

Geography, which may be closely associated but not necessarily integrated with history, is a subject which provides opportunities for observation of and reasoning upon scientific facts within the child's experience. Through it the teacher should awaken an interest in the environment, lives and habits of people, illustrate the interdependence of the world, and develop a knowledge of the principles of geography and power to apply them. As a subject, geography is a link between the humanistic and scientific subjects and is accordingly a study of man and his world.

Elementary science developed out of the nineteenth-century object lessons. Starting with the observation of common things, the subject aims to deepen the pupils' interest in the world around them and in the simple phenomena of nature, to train them in habits of scientific observation and thinking with an avoidance at this stage of technical terms. The selection of the topics to be treated depends upon the interest of the teacher and his ability to use the opportunities provided by the environment of the school. Like geography, elementary science can be correlated with other subjects.

The school journey has long been advocated as a valuable aid to instruction. First promoted by the School Journeys Association, the school journey has been adopted widely and in many areas special facilities are provided for reducing the cost of travel. In history, geography, science, and art, the school journey provides endless opportunities, not only for making the work of the classroom concrete and real, but in developing an appreciation and knowledge of the local resources and in their historical and geographical significance as well as through museums and art collections. More than this, it can cultivate an appreciation of the pleasures of open-air life and the opportunities available for educational and recreational activities. The recent establishment of Youth Hostels is a valuable contribution to this aspect of school life.

Finally, an important part of the work of any English school is the attention given to physical training for the promotion of health and for the development of character. All schools are required to have a playground, which is in most cases unsatisfactory; in addition, the regulations of the Board of Education permit teachers to take their pupils to open spaces an playing-fields, often set aside in municipal parks, or made available by the National Playing Fields Association. Physical training, which includes also formal classwork in hygiene, is on the formal side dominated by the Swedish system and on the informal side provides for a great variety of games, dances, and sports; for swimming, pupils are taken to public swimming baths. The emphasis in physical training is on honest, cheerful, and strenuous play and the cultivation, not of perfection of skill, but of an appreciation of the rules and spirit of the games[19]. In many areas special organizers, half the cost of whose salaries is borne by the Board's grants, have been appointed to coordinate physical training, to offer courses for teachers, to supervise and in general to promote the progressive development of this branch of the work of the elementary school.

Textbooks

The Board of Education does not publish a list of textbooks for the use of schools, nor are they in the elementary schools used as extensively as in the United States, partly because of the cost, partly because the "recitation" method has never been widespread, and partly because there is gradually developing a tendency to use a wider range of books and sources than are provided by the textbook. Suggestive lists are drawn up by a number of local education authorities (*e.g.*, London, Kent, West Riding of Yorkshire), and central stores are available where teachers may examine books; the selection is made, however, by the head teachers and their staffs for each school. Free textbooks are provided to the pupils, but remain the property of the schools and in most cases are kept in the schools. For a long time schools have cooperated with public libraries in securing books for general reading; more recently many schools have begun to create their own libraries; here and there teachers organize class libraries consisting of books lent for a period by the pupils themselves. The limitation on expenditures imposed by economic conditions rather than by administrative regulations restricts any extended purchase of textbooks and libraries. In any case, however, as is true in the making of courses of study, head teachers and their staffs enjoy freedom of choice, with such guidance as may be afforded, in the selection of the books used in their schools[20].

Control of Elementary Education

Throughout the discussion of English elementary education, the outstanding characteristic has been freedom. The work of the elementary school is not controlled by prescribed time-schedules, curriculum, or courses of study. Each school is a unit and the responsibility for its progress rests upon the head teacher and his staff. There is thus an absence of standardization and of uniformity; reliance is placed upon the insight and personality of the teachers and opportunities for reasoned experimentation are provided. Public elementary education is marked by variety of practice ranging from the traditional and formal to a radical free school[21].

There are, however, certain controls which, though indirect, are none the less effective. There is as everywhere an undefined public demand, which, whether sound or not, expects the schools to achieve certain results. From professional preparation, even though all teachers have not had it, certain norms are derived which guide the work of the school. The *Suggestions* and other publications of the Board, lectures, courses, and conferences organized by the Board, local authorities, or professional associations set up a definite standard of aims and ideals. The system of inspection by inspectors of the Board and of some local authorities, although not as rigorous as supervision in the United States, tend to spread common standards, which are suggestive, if not prescriptive. External examinations for pupils in elementary schools are discouraged. There has, however, developed out of the necessity of a system which does not provide free secondary education for all the practice of holding an examination for pupils at about the age of eleven on the basis of which the selection of the abler boys and girls to be transferred to secondary or central schools is made. In some areas all pupils at this age are required to take the examination; in others, only those who are recommended by their teachers are presented; in all cases, the examination tends to be indicative of the standard of attainment expected by pupils at the age of eleven; leaving out of account the danger of cramming, the examination becomes normative. On the whole, however, the pressure of this examination is not felt, and as will be seen later, the examination is administered and organized in such a way that direct cramming or preparation is discouraged.

Movement for Reorganization of the Education System

The arrangements suggested for the improvement of the work in the senior stage of elementary education neglected the pupils over eleven who were retarded and remained in the lower Standards, likely to leave without any preparation for the life before them. This situation, combined with the movement to provide for all pupils above the age of eleven the advantage of some form of secondary education, has led to proposals for a reorganization of the whole system of education into four well-defined stages; the pre-school or nursery school for children up to the age of five; the infants' stage, up to seven; the primary stage, up to eleven; and the secondary stage, divided into two stages —one up to fourteen or fifteen, the other up to eighteen. The first three stages will offer a common foundation for all; the last stages will provide a variety of schools and courses.

The transition would have been facilitated if the School Attendance Bill, which passed the House of Commons, but was rejected by the House of Lords in 1931, had been enacted. The bill sought to give effect to the recommendations of the Consultative Committee on the Education of the Adolescent, which urged a break at eleven plus, the extension of compulsory education to fifteen, and the provision in the last four years of some form of secondary education. The pamphlet of the Board of Education on the *New Prospect in Education,*[22] issued in 1928, encouraged local education authorities to proceed with the reorganization, to establish senior schools, and to transfer to these all pupils at age of eleven, irrespective of scholastic attainments. Since the senior school constitutes a new stage above the primary, and since classified as a part of the provision of secondary education, it is more convenient to consider it, together with other types of schools already in existence, as a part of the system of intermediate education. This classification is perhaps not altogether happy, but it distinguishes the schools within it from primary and from secondary schools and places them in a category side by side with the French *écoles primaires supérieures* and the German *Mittelschulen*. The movement for reorganization, it will be noted, is similar to that which has been taking place in the United States in the development of what is known as the six-three-three plan (six years of primary education, followed by three years of junior high school and three years of senior high school), with the important distinction, however, that the junior high school is definitely intermediate between the primary school and the senior high school, while intermediate education, except for the minority, is not articulated with a continuing higher stage in the European system.

Central Schools

The origin of the central schools has already been given. They are schools intended for boys and girls who can remain in school for four years beyond the age of eleven, and have proved their ability in a selective examination, but are not considered sufficiently able to profit from a secondary education. The distinction between those who do and those who do not proceed to a secondary school is somewhat arbitrary; the general assumption is that the secondary school is intended for the academically minded and the central school for the practical minded. The difference in the curricula of the two types of school is also based on this distinction.

The central school offers a course of four years (occasionally five). It differs from the elementary school in that classes are smaller, the equipment somewhat superior, and the teachers selected and paid a bonus in addition to the elementary teachers' scale of salaries; as compared with the secondary schools, the classes are somewhat larger, the teachers are not always university graduates, although they are trained, the salaries are lower, and the work becomes more practical in the last two years. One very important consideration in the establishment of the central schools is that they are cheaper. A few years ago it was estimated that the cost per place in an elementary school was £26, in a central school £38, and in a secondary school £66, while the average cost per pupil was £1110s. in an elementary school, £18 in a central school, and £34 in a secondary school.

The aims of the central schools, as announced at the opening of such a school at Morely in 1928, are as follows:

1. To widen the outlook of the pupils so that they may become intelligent citizens.

2. To give them the basis of a sound literary and scientific training so that they may learn to reason correctly and draw legitimate conclusions.
3. To train them to use their hands so that, if need be, they can afterwards follow skilled occupations, and make intelligent and profitable use of their leisure time.
4. To develop the aesthetic taste through the medium of art (drawing, painting, and music).
5. To teach them the elements of a foreign languages (French) to open their minds to the difficulty of nations speaking different languages under-standing one another, and to assist somewhat in the "rapprochement" of the nations of the world, which is so much to be desired.
6. To give them physical training and games to develop their bodies, to train them in swift judgment, accurate movement and cooperation, and to inculcate the ideals of fairness and good-will together with self-reliance, restraint and courage[23].

The London central schools, which have served as a model for others, have provided for all pupils in the first two years, including English, mathematics (algebra and geometry), science, history, geography, art, music, handwork, and domestic science and needlework; French is included especially for pupils who plan to continue in the commercial course of the last two years. The work of the second half of the course becomes more definitely practical; without being definitely vocational, the courses are given a bias—commercial, industrial, or domestic. In the course with a commercial bias, bookkeeping, economics, commercial correspondence, shorthand, and typewriting, are added; in the industrial course more time is given to manual work of various kinds; in the domestic course for girls domestic science, household management, and the needlecrafts are given special attention. In some central schools the general course is continued in the last two years.

Time-Schedule of a Mixed Selective Central School in a Rural Area

Subjects	*IV A (min.)*	*IV B (min.)*	*III A (min.)*	*III B (min.)*	*II A (min.)*	*II B (min.)*	*I A (min.)*	*I B (min.)*
1	*2*	*3*	*4*	*5*	*6*	*7*	*8*	*9*
English	210	210	210	210	245	245	245	245
History	105	105	70	70	70	70	70	70
Geography	105	70	105	70	105	105	105	105
French	175	..	175	..	175	175	175	175
Mathematics	175	245	210 / 175 *	245	210	245 / 210 †	210	210
Needlework (girls)	70	140	70	140	70	70	70	70
Mechanical drawing (boys)	..	70	..	140	70	70	70	70
Mechanical drawing (girls)	..	..	..	..	..	..	35	35
Surveying	..	70	..	..	..	..	..	..
Science (boys)	70	210	140 / 70 *	210	140	140	140	140
Science (girls)	..	140	..	140	140	140	105	105
Art (boys)	70	70	70	70	70	70	70	70

Contd. . .

1	2	3	4	5	6	7	8	9
Art (girls)	70	140	70	140	70	70	70	70
Handicraft	140	210	140	210	140	140	140	140
Housecraft	140	210	140	210	140	140	140	140
Commercial	175	..	175	..	..	..	..	..
Music	35	35	70	70	70	70	70	70
Physical training	35	35	35	35	35	35	35	35
Games	70	70	70	70	70	70	70	70
Gardening	..	..	140*	..	..	140†	..	..
Private study	70	..	70	..	..	..	..	..

* These are boys who will not be completing a full Form III course and who may be taking up Farm Service. Instead of French and part of the commercial course they take gardening and extra periods in mathematics, devoted to rural problems; they study bookkeeping and have extra science.

† These are boys who are judged unable to profit by a study of French; they, therefore, take up school gardening and extra mathematics.

A comparison of the time allotted to the different subjects of the corriculum in secondary and central schools how very slight is the distinction between the two types.

Because the first four years of the secondary course culminates in an examination whose certificate carries some weight in securing employment, a number of central schools in London and elsewhere have tended to prepare their pupils for this examination and have not only sacrificed the interests of many pupils for the sake of the few, but have departed from the original purpose of the central schools to provide a differentiated type of education. It is now proposed, since certificates play an important part in the vocational career of the adolescent to establish a distinct system of examination for central schools. An experiment along these lines has been tried in Manchester.

The chief source of the difficulty has, of course, not been attacked, nor can the problem be solved until it is recognized in England (as well as in France and Germany where the problem is similar) that all education beyond the break at about eleven should be classified as secondary, but that within this category there is room for differentiated types of schools for pupils of different abilities and capacities. Such a system would demand alertness on the part of the authorities and of teachers to see that pupils are adequately classified and that opportunities for transfer from one type of school to another are always open. England has already reached the realization that educational organization cannot be based, without encountering considerable difficulties, on social considerations. The opportunity for a reorganization on educational grounds and the abilities of pupils will be provided when all children will be assured of an education for four years beyond the age of eleven. The problem was well stated by the Director of Education for Kent, Mr. E. Salter Davies, before the Consultative Committee on the Education of the Adolescent:

It can be laid down as a postulate that the organization of the education of children in the bulk up to fifteen or sixteen years of age cannot be carried out effectively so long as the practice prevails of thinking in terms of more or less parallel educational systems instead of concentrating on the problem of the education of adolescent as a whole[24].

The United States, in solving the problem, has adopted the common school for all, providing differentiated courses within each school[25]. England and other European countries, have an opportunity of creating a democratic system of education in which schools will be organized on a functional basis, and in which the right pupil will find his way into the right school with the right curriculum adapted to his needs and capacities.

Conclusion

Elementary education in English has made remarkable progress since the beginning of the century, a progress in which the guiding hand of the Board of Education may be seen, but which has in no small manner been due to intelligent and sympathetic direction of administrators who have been called forth by the opportunity and by principals and teachers who have wisely used the freedom which is granted to them. That there are backward districts, no one would deny. Those, however, who would judge the progress of education by the amount of money spent or by the material fabric of the schools (buildings, equipment, and supplies) will fail to catch the spirit underlying the educative process. The absence of standardization of uniformity in methods and courses of study, and of a dominating philosophy of education is apt to mislead the superficial observer. Particularly is this likely to be true in the case of the observer armed with a list of detailed objectives, based on a mechanistic psychology and on the principles derived from the canons of industrial efficiency, and convinced that certain results can only be obtained by specific methods adapted to their attainment. Nowhere is this better illustrated than in the teaching of reading and the fundamentals of language; an examination of the *Suggestions* on this point would reveal methods which have long been discarded by the scientific students of education and yet the results of the two systems would be discouraging to the advocates of a "science" of education. There would here be found some arguments for the theory that those methods are best which work best.

Not only has progress been made in methods of instruction, but the courses of study have undergone a process of revision and reconstruction; the formal and disciplinary elements have been discarded and greater emphasis is being placed upon those elements which have meaning and significance to the pupil. Here again the reform has not been carried out under the eagis of any philosophy or theory, but largely by trial and error guided by a more sympathetic understanding of the child. The change which has taken place in the internal organization of the elementary school reflects also the change in the public attitude toward it. The elementary school has gradually become the common school for all. With this concept as the starting point, the whole system is beginning to be reorganized on the principle that national welfare and progress depend upon sound education and the provision of equality of educational opportunity to each according to his ability. This is the stage which has been reached; the reorganization is not complete, and, as usual in all matters of social progress in England, the problem of reorganization is being solved by trial and error. When the desirable form has been achieved, legislative action will follow to consolidate the gains which have been made and to provide for the advance to the next stage. If convincing proof is desired of the achievements of the English elementary school, it will not be found in results of examinations or by objective tests and measurements, but in a concrete visual comparison such as is afforded by the photographs of children in elementary schools in the same districts of London thirty years ago and today[26]. More remarkable perhaps than the progress itself is the fact that the major portion of it has taken place in the period of economic strain following the War. Whatever the results may be on the intellectual side, there has been an improvement in manners and in physique; there may be, although it has not been proved, less accuracy and thoroughness, but they are balanced by greater alertness and adaptability. In other respects England, like all other countries, is confronted by problems which always accrue in a period of social transition, unrest, and uncertainty, when society is released from its old moorings and values and has not yet found new objects of allegiance.

2. FRANCE

General Character of French Education

In an era of educational reforms, when virtually all her neighbours are reorganizing their educational systems and practices, France stands out for her staunch loyalty to theories elaborated in a period of intellectual revolt and put into practice when the Third Republic was established. France has produced a long list of distinguished educational statesmen—Jules Ferry, Paul Bert, Octave Gréard, Felix Pécaut, Ferdinand Buisson, and Louis Liard—who laid the foundations of her educational system; through Gabriel Compayré she contributed to the study of the history of education, and through Alfred Binet and Dr. T. Simon she gave to the world an instrument of educational research which has been more fully elaborated and applied in other educational systems than her own; the French concept of culture has exercised a dominating influence over a large part of Europe, Asia Minor, and South America. In the field of educational theory, however, it would be difficult to discover any French educator whose work is known outside of his country[27]. The French system of education is peculiarly national and rooted in the soil of French ideals, French philosophy, and French culture.

The explanation of this situation is not to be found in the rigid centralization of educational administration, centralization is to be explained rather by the French emphasis on logical organization, by profound faith in and reverence for French culture, which must become the heritage of all her citizens, and by the desire to preserve French national solidarity through imparting the common heritage in the schools. There is another important factor which can be cited as an explanation of the character of French education in general and elementary education in particular; France has not developed a child psychology which in other countries has been so effective in changing the character of the elementary school. The child is still regarded as a miniature adult, and instruction still emphasizes the cult of reason and logic rather than activity and behaviour at the child's level. By development and growth of the child, French pedagogy still understands increased mastery of subject-matter through the development of reason, and subject matter is built up, not on the interests of the child, but as an introduction to French culture. The place of reason in French life has been excellently illustrated by Cloudesley Brereton in his discussion of "Moral Instruction in France." Referring to the varied uses of the word *raison* in the French language he writes:

> They intrude, in fact, into the moral domain and even into the sphere of action...Note for instance the moral *nuances* in the uses of *avoir raison* (to be in the right), *donner raison à quelqu'un* (own that some one is in the right), *dire avec raison* (rightly, justly, equitably), *entendre raison* (to comply with something just), *comme de raison* (as is just), *pour valoir ce que de raison* (in equity), *entrer en raison avec quelq'un* (to remonstrate, reason together,—as to *rights* and *wrongs), lui demander raison de quelque chose* (ask him to justify himself), *rendre raison de quelque chose* (to justify), *point de raison* (justification).
>
> Note again the *nuance* of action implied in the phrases *avoir raison de ses raison* (to get the better of his vices), *demander raison qu tyran* (challenge, attack), *faire raison* (render justice), *conter ses raisons* (business). But the full strength of the word raison is best seen or felt in such phrases as *raison suffitride* (sovereign reason), *raison d'être or raison d'état*[28].

Where the English language emphasizes conduct or behaviour, the French stress reason.

The character of elementary education is thus derived from the emphasis on French culture and on the development of reason. The work of the school must provide for the progress of the pupil in both directions. Through a curriculum based on French culture, he will be introduced to the great spirit of humanism and a body of knowledge and information common to all French citizens; through the cult of reason he will develop the highest and most important human quality. To culture he will be introduced gradually as he passes through the various stages of his psychological development; at first the emphasis will be on the concrete and training of the senses; the next stage will give him the foundation of knowledge and information; at the third stage the emphasis will be more on the abstract and on training in deductive reasoning.

The course of the child's education is mapped out in advance and the map is gradually filled in as he grows more mature; hence the curriculum is organized on the concentric method, and expands by reviews and repetition through the three stages of the pupil's development. Facts first, then ideas, but facts and ideas derived from the body of knowledge which society has come to regard as the proper heritage of its members. The principles of method are based, not on the activity of the child based on his interests as they react to his environment, but on the theory that the child must learn first before he can express himself or create. Activities, problems, projects, which are in the foreground of the new educational philosophy, have not replaced the French emphasis on receptivity, assimilation, and then creation. The pupil must understand, in the best sense of the word, all that is taught him, but what is taught him is determined by the kind of individual that society desires to reproduce as man and as citizen, for "the civilization which education must transmit is something different from the nature of the individual and cannot be attained by following nature," that is, the interests and urges of the child. The intellectual sympathy with the child which "is carried to extremes, even to the point of wishing to derive the methods of education solely from a consideration of children's characteristics," makes little appeal to the majority of French educators. He agrees with the new philosophy of education that the aim of education is the development of the personality of the child, but he starts, not with the premise of the autonomy of the child, but with the conviction that the family, society, and the State are the trustees of the child's right to an education, and differs from the progressives in his interpretation of personality.

French philosophers, as is well known, distinguish between individuality and personality. The individual is such by virtue of the fact that he is different from others. He is a person to the extent that he represents the conscience of truths valid for all and the will to undertake duties common to all. The individual ought to become a person, that is, in a sense he should de-individualize himself, and this is the work of education and of personal effort[29].

From the point of view of the new education this attitude to the curriculum to be imparted in the school would be described as "extrinsic," as "fixed in advance," as "impositions." The same attitude governs the views on discipline. Beginning in the family, the French notion of discipline is based on authority, at first of persons, then of moral law. The school as a miniature society must be governed by a body of rules, a code which is gradually converted into a moral law, whose atmosphere dominates the spirit of the school. On the theory of self-discipline, the French educator is skeptical.

> Experiments along these lines [says M. Pécaut] have been made here and there, but too infrequently to justify any generalized conclusions; in fact, where they succeed, it is difficult to discern what is the result of pupil effort and what is due to the authority, concealed but ever present, of the teacher[30].

Elementary education, then, represents the will of the State, of the adult members of society, their culture and their traditions, and their aspirations. Because the French State has determined, since the establishment of the Third Republic, for reasons which have their origin in history and not because of antagonism to religion, to separate Church and State, the French school is a lay, secular school. The State, desiring to maintain impartiality in matters of religion, decided to establish its school on principles acceptable to all. But in remaining lay and neutral in religion, the State has not surrendered its right and responsibility to impart instruction in moral ideas acceptable to all and a common spiritual bond to all. The State has not, however, refused to recognize the right of parents to provide for the religious instruction of their children in their own way. For this purpose all schools are closed on Thursday, and parents may follow the dictates of their own consciences in arranging or refusing to arrange for the religious instruction of their children through the spiritual teachers of the denominations to which they belong. Such religious instruction may not be given in a building used as a public or private school, nor by a public school teacher, nor during regular school hours; the only exception which is permitted is that pupils may be excused during school hours to attend religious exercises during the week preceding their first communion.

The ideal of the lay schools, it must be remembered, is not an innovation of the Third Republic. It was inherent in the educational thought of the Revolution; and the ideal of the lay teacher as the priest of intelligence and the leader of progress was expressed by Victor Hugo, *A propos d' Horace (Les Contemplations, 1831)*:

> Chaque village aura, dans un temple rustique
> Dans la lumière, au lieu du magister antique,
> Trop noir pour que jamais le jour y pénétrat,
> L'institutear lucide et grave, magistrat
> Du progrès, médecin de l'ignorance et prêtre
> De l'idée: et dans l'ombre on verra disparaître
> L'éternel écolier et l'éternel pédant.

THE ELEMENTARY SCHOOL SYSTEM

The elementary school system in France includes all those schools and institutions which belong to the branch of elementary as distinguished from higher education. There are accordingly included not only the elementary school proper (*l'école primaire*), but the maternal or infant school which precedes it (*l'école maternelle et la classe enfantine*), and the higher elementary school (*l'école primaire supérieure*), and the institutions for the preparation of teachers for these schools (*l'école normale primaire et l'école normale primaire supérieure*).

L'école Maternelle

The maternal or infant school is an institution for children below the age of compulsory attendance, which grew out of the *salle d'asile,* a charitable institution, based on the ideas of Oberlin and Père Girard, and established by regulations issued in 1837 "to provide maternal care and the early stage of education suitable to the ages of the pupils." The Law of June 16,1881, recognized the *salle d'asile* as a part of the system of free public education. Under the present title of *école maternelle et la classe enfantine,* this institution was incorporated into the system in the Law of October 30, 1886, the charter of elementary education, the organization and work of the school were defined by a decree and *arrêté* (regulation) issued on January 18, 1887, which have continued to constitute the basis of the maternal school up to the present. The provision of a maternal school is not, like that of an elementary school, compulsory, but it may be established at the option of the municipalities, but, once established, it must be maintained for a period of ten years by agreement between the commune and the State and State aid is given for its support. This regulation applies only to municipalities with a population of 2000, of whom 1200 are concentrated in a town or village; municipalities of smaller size may also establish such schools, but wholly at their own expense.

The maternal school is "an institution for the stage in education in which children of both sexes, between the ages of two and six, receive in common the care required for their physical, moral, and intellectual development." In municipalities with less than 2000 population, a *class enfantine* may be annexed to the elementary school, under the charge of the principal, and performs the same function as the maternal school which is an independent institution under its own principal (*directrice*). The construction and equipment of the material school are defined in detail by the regulations issued in 1927: waiting-rooms must be provided for parents, rooms must be set aside for classroom activities, rest and recreation; a court and playground must be available; the school must be equipped with a kitchen, a medicine cupboard, cloakrooms, washbowls, sanitary arrangements, and cots; the school furniture must consist of movable chairs and tables; for instructional and recreational activities each school must have a supply of toys, sand-trays, wagons, and carts, jumping-ropes, hoops, pails, balls, beads, paper for cutting, weaving, and folding, raffia, wool and cotton, scissors, and clay, cubes, bricks, rings, sticks, pictures, slates and crayons, and a tuning-fork. The regulations express a pious wish, on the whole, since the movement to reform the *école maternelle*, which began nearly thirty years ago, has not yet met with success, due in part to the scholastic tradition of the past and the demand of parents that their children be taught as early as possible to read, write, and cipher, in part to the inadequate differentiation in the preparation of the teachers, and in part to the fact that many of the schools are inspected by elementary school inspectors rather than by experts, a weakness which has been greatly reduced in recent years.

Children are admitted to the *école maternelle* at the age of two and remain until the age of six. No child may be admitted without a medical certificate; absences are carefully checked to prevent the spread of disease; and a medical officer is expected to visit once a month. The teachers must hold a *brevet supérieur*, with special qualifications in the theory of education in the maternal school, puericulture, hygiene, and the sciences applied to these subjects. Principals must have the same qualifications and five years of experience in a maternal school. In addition, there is appointed an unqualified assistant (*femme de service*) to look after the cleanliness and physical needs of the children. Increasingly the inspection of maternal schools is being entrusted to inspectresses with special qualifications; candidates for appointment must be twenty-five years of age and hold the *brevet supérieur* and the *certificat d'aptitude pédagogique* or some recognized equivalents, must have had five years of teaching experience in an elementary or secondary school, and must pass a special examination. The examination consists in the written part of two essays, one on some subject in the theory of education in the maternal school, and the other on the hygiene of the maternal school. The oral examination includes the discussion of some problems on the education and hygiene of the maternal school and questions on the law and administration of such school. In addition, a report of an inspection of a maternal school must be presented.

The size of a maternal school is limited to 150 pupils; where the number exceeds 50, an assistant principal is appointed. The size of each class is limited to 25, pupils being divided into two groups according to age and intelligence—usually those below and those above the age of five being grouped together. The curriculum consists of (1) physical exercises: breathing exercises, games, and movements accompanied by songs; (2) sensory exercises, manual work, and drawing; (3) exercises in observing things and familiar objects; (4) exercises for the development of moral habits; (5) exercises in language and recitation, and (6) introductory exercises in reading, writing, and arithmetic for the older pupils. In a circular issued by the Ministry of Public Instruction on November 10, 1931, the following distribution of time is suggested:

Recreation and personal care	5 periods
Rhythmic exercises	2 "
Sense-training and observation	2 "
Modeling and drawing	2 "
Manual work	2 "
Singing and music	2 "
Recitation and story-telling	2 "
Arithmetic	2 "
Language, speech, and oral exercises	10 "
Total	29

During the last few years a tendency in a new direction has been noticeable, with less concern for formal school work and instruction and more emphasis on play and free activities. This may be the result of the spread of the Montessori theory; it may be a return to the original method suggested by earlier regulations which stated that the best method is that which gives the name to the school—"the closest imitation of the educational procedure of an intelligent and devoted mother—a method essentially natural, personal, and always, open to new suggestions always ready to expand and to reform." Freedom, health and happiness, the promotion of spontaneous and joyful activity, training in observation and thinking and physical and moral development are the characteristics of the new tendency. Despite this, much still remains to be done to bring the French maternal school up to the level of the pre-schools elsewhere, and not the least important of the innovations, assuming that brighter buildings could be secured, would be the abandonment of the depressing, if useful and economical, black smock.

Elementary Education

Public elementary education has its origin in the *Loi Guizot* of 1838, which required every commune to establish an elementary school, but failed to impose compulsory attendance. The reactionary *Loi Falloux* (1850) practically placed the control of education in the hands of the ecclesiastical authorities and lowered the qualifications which the *Loi Guizot* had required of teachers; the slow progress of elementary education was indicated in 1865 by the fact that 26 per cent of the men and 44 per cent of the women were unable to sign the marriage certificates. Victor Duruy, recognizing the importance of education at a time when universal suffrage had been granted, proposed to make elementary education free and compulsory; the *Loi Duruy,* which was passed in 1867, failed to secure those two essentials of public education, but did succeed in requiring communes to tax themselves for the maintenance of schools, curtailed the influence of the Church, regulated the qualifications of teachers, introduced the school funds (*caisses d'écoles*) to aid poor pupils, and added geography and history to the curriculum.

The defeat of France by the German schoolmaster in 1870 at once drove home to the leading statesmen the recognition that the problem of elementary education must be one of the first tasks to be considered in the reconstruction which followed the establishment of the Third Republic. Jules Simon announced that he would introduce a bill to make school attendance compulsory, but the National Assembly showed no interest in it. Ten years later the programme of the reformers began to be realized: elementary education was made free by the law of June 16, 1881; by the law of March 28, 1882, school attendance was made compulsory for all children between the ages of six and thirteen and the lay secular course of study was introduced; finally, the whose system was codified by the Organic Law of October 30, 1886, defined by the decree and *arrêté* of January 18, 1887.

Compulsory Attendance

Elementary education is compulsory for all children between the ages of six and thirteen; they may attend public or private schools or be educated at home; in the last case pupils must be submitted, after the third school year, to an annual examination conducted by a committee consisting of an elementary school inspector or his deputy, a cantonal delegate, and another person holding a recognized certificate. In localities where a maternal school or infant class is not available children may be admitted at the age of five.

A school census is drawn up each year by the mayor, assisted by the school committee, and a notice is sent to parents who have children of school age. All children must be registered in a school fifteen days before the beginning of the scholastic year, or a statement must be submitted by their parents of the provision made for their education otherwise. Parents and guardians are responsible for the school attendance of their children or wards; in cases of inexcusable absence, the school committee (*commission scolaire*) may post the names of parents or guardians on the public notice-board of the town hall for a period of fifteen days or a month. For further repetitions, a penalty of a fine from eleven to fifteen francs, or imprisonment for five days or more, may be imposed.

The administration of compulsory attendance is perhaps the weakest feature of French education. School committees may exempt pupils above the age of eleven, if living and working for their parents or guardians, from attendance for three months in a year, provided the approval of the elementary school inspector is obtained for exemptions of more than fifteen days; with the approval of the departmental council, a school committee may exempt pupils for one or two periods a day to engage in farm work for employers other than their parents. Pupils who pass the examination, which they may take at the age of twelve, and obtain the *certificat d'études primaires*, are exempted from further attendance at school. Repeated efforts have been made to require attendance for the full period during which schools are in session, but the poor success of such efforts prevent further attempts to extend compulsory education up to fourteen. France did not sign the Geneva Convention of 1921. Teachers and inspectors are urged to use their influence to improve regularity of attendance. One result of the poor administration of compulsory attendance, which is explained by the lack of an adequate supply of labour in the agricultural areas, the unwillingness of school committees to use the authority with which they are endowed, and to some extent the failure, until recently, to adapt the school curriculum to rural conditions, has been a perceptible increase of illiteracy. France had succeeded before the War in reducing the percentage of illiteracy to 3 per cent; in 1924, of 235,325 conscripts called to the colours, 13,838; or 6.2 per cent, were unable to read or write[31]. The figure continued to increase and in 1928 had reached nearly 9 per cent[32].

The Elementary School

The elementary education of all French children is today the same, whether given in public elementary school, or in private schools, at home, or in the preparatory classes of secondary schools. The majority of children, however, attend public elementary schools, which must be provided in every commune. Separate schools are maintained for boys and girls in communes with more than five hundred inhabitants, unless special permission is obtained to establish a mixed school. The teachers (*instituteurs* and *institutrices*) must have recognized qualifications (the *brevet élémentaire*) granted on an examination in the work of a higher elementary school, the *brevet supérieur*, obtained by examination at the end of the normal school course, and the *certificat d'aptitude pédagogique,* conferred as the result of an examination after at least two years of service[33]. Boys must be taught by men, girls and mixed classes of boys and girls by women; in exceptional cases women, provided that they are related to the principal, may teach in boys, schools.

All elementary education is under the supervision of inspectors—general, specially assigned to this field academy inspectors, and elementary school inspectors[34]. A large number of the public elementary schools are single-teacher schools. In schools with two or more classes, a principal (*directeur* or *directrice*) is appointed; for this position no special examinations or qualifications are required except that candidates must be at least twenty-one years of age. Principals who do not have charge of a definite class, as they do in small schools, are required to give four hours of instruction each week in once of the essential subjects of the curriculum; from this duty they can only be exempted in schools with an enrolment of three hundred pupils. On the principal devolves the responsibility for the sound organization of instruction, of helping and supervising the teachers, especially the young teachers in his school, of providing for satisfactory articulation between the different classes, and of maintaining with his teachers constant relations between the school and the home, the locality, civic life, and educational institutions. Although not required by law or regulations, the practice of organizing a teachers' council (*conseil des maîtres*) has grown up since 1908, which through conferences and meetings maintains the unity of work in the school, promotes the interest of the teachers and their professional growth. Meeting at the beginning and end of each school year, and at least once a term, the council drafts regulations for the internal organization of the school, assigns pupils and teachers to their classes, and determines on promotions from the maternal school or infant class outside of the regular period. Disciplinary measures and rewards to pupils are meted out by the council. It is, however, the opportunity for discussing educational problems—the time-schedule, adaptation of the course of study, consideration of methods of instruction, provision and maintenance of the school library—which gives such councils their importance. Administrative action recommended by the teachers' councils are subject to the approval of the local elementary school inspector.

The Aim of Elementary Education

The aim of elementary education which determines the character of the curriculum was summarized in a statement by Octave Gréard, who organized the system of elementary education in Paris and later, as vice-rector of the University of Paris and chairman of many commissions, exercised a strong influence on the development of education in France. This statement, which was formulated by Gréard in 1887, and is still accepted as valid in the *Instruction* issued in 1923, is as follows:

The object of elementary education is not to burden the different subjects that are treated with everything that can be learned, but to learn well in each of the branches that of which we cannot be permitted to be ignorant.

The aim of elementary education is accordingly to preserve and transmit the treasures of acquired truth, to enlighten the consciences, to strengthen the judgement, and in general to develop the pupils physically, morally, and intellectually. Elementary education should be both utilitarian and educational, for:

We have no intention of abandoning either one of the two aims which have been assigned to elementary education. We do not overlook the fact that most of our pupils from the time they leave us, will have to work for a living; and we desire to supply them with a fund of practical knowledge which tomorrow will serve them in their vocation. But we do not forget, furthermore, that we should be forming in them the man and the citizen that they are to become tomorrow. Concern with urgent realities will not cause us to neglect the cult of the ideal[35].

The elementary school pupil is expected to leave school with a fund of practical knowledge and some appreciation of the meaning of civilization. French philosophy of education, as interpreted by the Ministry of Public Instruction, thus emphasizes social control and adult needs rather than the direct and immediate needs and interests of the pupils.

Curriculum and Course of Study

It follows from this aim and from the character of the French administrative system that the curriculum and course of study of the elementary schools are prescribed and defined by law, and by decrees and regulations issued by the Ministry of Public Instruction. In the preparation of the courses of study the inspectors and the Higher Council of Public Instruction cooperate, but responsibility and authority for its enforcement are vested in the Ministry. The basic foundation of the curriculum and the course of study was laid by the Decree of January 18, 1887, and the regulation of the same date. It is significant of the French conviction on the subject that no extensive revision was made until a new course of study was issued on February 23, 1923, followed by *Instruction* published on June 20 of that year. The revision was undertaken, as is explained in the *Instruction,* not because the historical curriculum and course of study were unsound, but because they had not been put into practice in the spirit which had been intended.

"What demand does the reform meet? Has the system drafted by the authors of our school laws revealed itself as defective?" are questions asked in the new *Instruction*. The answer is:

> By no means. Each time that one reads over the statement in the *Instructions* of 1887, one is filled with admiration. It is thus not without apprehension that we have decided to apply to this structure the modifications that time has rendered necessary. We have taken care, of course, not to affect the outstanding features, and however important certain innovations may appear, the general tone remains the same. In reforming the institution, we intend to remain faithful to the principles of the founders.
>
> But experience has proved that, in order to obtain a better application of these principles, there was need of a definite statement on the proper use of the time allowed, of simplifying and graduating the programmes, of vitalizing the methods, and coordinating the subjects. To define, to simplify, to graduate, to vitalize, and to coordinate, such has been our aim[36].

Teachers had failed to understand the regulations, had not followed the organization of the course of studies strictly, had tended to crowd it into a shorter period than was intended through fear lest pupils might leave school without completing it, and had overburdened the pupils. The new *Instruction* aimed to clarify the organization, to simplify the programme, and, as a result of the simplification, to leave greater freedom to the teacher in retaining or adding or even omitting certain topics, and in adapting the work to the needs of his pupil and the conditions of local life.

The course of study is organized, not by years or classes, but by course: for children from the age of six to seven (*cours pré paratoire*), one year; for children between the ages of seven and nine (*cours élémentaire*), two years; for children between the ages of nine and eleven (*cours moyen)*, two years; for children between the ages of eleven to thirteen (*cours superieur*), two years. In each course beyond the preparatory the second year was in the old course of study largely a repetition and review of the first; while something of the concentric method of organization is retained, it has lost its rigidity in the new *Instruction*, for

With pupils ranging from six to thirteen years of age, it would be dangerous to give up all repetition and review. There are lessons to which it is necessary to return in the various courses, so that the pupil may complete, according as he is more capable of understanding and reasoning, the notions previously taught. But if it is desired that the child should study with pleasure and profit, the monotony of repetition and distaste for what as already been studied should be avoided... Give, then, to your pupil the impression that he is progressing, that he is discovering a new realm. Instead of the concentric, take in preference the progressive method[37].

The prescribed subjects of instruction in the elementary school curriculum are as follows: moral and civic instruction, reading and writing, French, arithmetic and the metric system, history and geography (especially of France), object lessons and elementary science, drawing, singing, manual work for boys (applied chiefly to agriculture), and needlework for girls, physical and military training. The language of instruction must be French except in Alsace-Lorraine where bilingualism has been sanctioned since 1926. The time-distribution of the subjects are as follows:

Official Time-Schedule

	Prep. Sec	*Elem. Course*		*Middle Course*		*Higher Course*		*Total*	
	Hrs.	*B. Hrs.*	*G. Hrs.*	*B. Hrs.*	*G. Hrs.*	*B. Hrs.*	*G. Hrs.*	*Boys Hrs.*	*Girls*
Moral and civic instruction	1¼	1¼	1¼	1¼	1¼	1½	1½	5¼	5¼
Reading	10	7	6½	3	3	2½	2½	22½	22
Writing	5	2½	2½	1½	1½	¾	¾	9¾	9¾
French	2½	5	5	7½	7	7½	7	22½	21½
History and geography		2½	2½	3	3	3	3	8½	8½
Arithmetic and geometry	2½	3½	3½	4½	4½	5	5	15½	15½
Physical and natural science ...	1¼	1½	1½	2½	2	2½	2½	7¾	7¼
Drawing	1	1	1	1	1	1	1	4	4
Manual work	1½	1	1½	1	2	1½	2	5	7
Music (inc. singing)	1¼	1	1	1	1	1	1	4¼	4¼
Physical training	1¾	2	2	2	2	2	2	7¾	7¾
Recreation	2	1¾	1¾	1¾	1¾	1¾	1¾	7¼	7¼
Total hours	30	30	30	30	30	30	30	120	120

Within this distribution each school may make up its own time-schedule subject to the approval of the elementary school inspector.

It is clear from the discussion on the preceding pages that the work of the French elementary school continues to be based on the dualism between subject-matter and pupil, which the new education seeks to eliminate. The French theory is that there is a body of facts, information, knowledge, of which no person can be permitted to be ignorant:

> We do not ask that each child be left to do just as he likes, according to his fancy; the school is no more a playroom than it is a prison; the school is the school—a gathering of children who work whole-heartedly for their common education, under the guidance of the teacher.

The function of the teacher is to act as an intermediary between the subject-matter to be learned and the pupil by appealing to his interest and inspiring him with enthusiasm for his work. The pupil should be guided to take pleasure in his work, "Conscious of working towards the realization of a beautiful ideal."

The only method that is suitable to teaching elementary grades is that which provides for an interchange between the teacher and the pupils, which maintains between them, so to speak, a continuous exchange of ideas, varied, flexible, and cleverly graded.

The methods of instruction follow in the main three steps—exposition by the teacher, discussion through questions and answers, and summaries in the form of an idea, a formula, a *cliché,* a short statement to be entered into the pupils' exercise books and memorized. These steps are illustrated with particular clarity in the textbooks on moral instruction; the teacher makes a general statement, develops it by questions and answers, and leads up to a summary sentence which synthesizes the point reached and which is then entered into the exercise books as the resolutions to be adopted by the pupils; this is followed by reading of selections to illustrate the discussion, and then by an exercise to be done by the pupils. The resolutions reached in a lesson on good health intended for pupils between the ages of nine and thirteen were as follows:

(1) Good health is incomparable wealth for all.

(2) Good health is not real and complete unless it applies both to the body and to all those faculties that are called the soul.

(3) He who only takes care of his body is like the workman who stops with the care of the body.

(4) Good health of the soul regulates that of the body.

(5) Only those are well who have a sound body and a sound soul.

Nothing could better illustrate the French emphasis on the abstract idea than a lesson of this kind.

The regulations set up a standard curriculum, but do not exclude freedom or variety which comes from the teacher's cultural background and skill in instruction. There appears to be an increasing tendency to permit adaptation to local conditions, a tendency which is due to the influence of foreign practice, the advocacy of new methods by *Les Compagnons,* and the realization that the failure of the rural schools is the result of failure to adapt the programmes to the rural environment. Recent circular have encouraged the normal schools to devote some attention to the preparartion of teachers for single-te acher schools, and elementary schools to stress the local environment and to give attention to the occupations of young children. What is demanded of all schools is that what is done should be done thoroughly. Knowledge and information continue to be emphasized, but so are attention, activity, observation, and judgment, as the desirable ends of education. The *Instruction* urges "more air, more ease, more freedom, more joy, and finally, more work." None the less, it would be a mistake to confuse these recommendations with those of the new education. France offers in her educational system an example of a country which has definite convictions as to what shall be taught; starting with a prescribed, standard curriculum, she recognizes the value of good expository teaching which, while it seeks to impart a definite round of subjects to be learned, does not fail to pay due regard to the child.

Of the subjects of the curriculum those which are considered as the most important besides the fundamentals are moral instruction and French. The training of character should take precedence over that of intelligence and overlaps both physical and intellectual training. The three forms of training really constitute one whole, for through intellectual training judgment is developed and the cultivation of the judgment is the best way of training the will, to which physical education also contributes. The process of moral instruction follows the three stages of the child's development—from the concrete through a mixture of concrete and abstract to ideas; hence it emphasizes habit-formation and opportunities for moral judgment in school conduct and culminates in a body of moral ideas. With moral instruction is combined civic training in the duties of the individual as man and as citizen, and the study of government despite the emphasis in the *Instruction* on the practical aspects of moral training. The course of study (the upper course with pupils from eleven to thirteen discusses conscience and character, self-education, and the various aspects of solidarity) and the textbooks on moral instruction bring out clearly the influence of Desecrates in French education and the emphasis on reason and the reasoned life.

The teaching of the French language derives its importance, not only because it is looked upon as an instrument for maintaining and disseminating a beautiful language and a beautiful literature, but because it is a valuable means for strengthening national unity. To overcome the *patois* of the village and the dialect of the province, particular attention is paid to recitation and elocution, to grammar and vocabulary exercises, until in the last stage the command of language and ideas is tested by exercises in composition and the pupil is introduced to simple canons of taste and appreciation through reading of French literature.

Through history and geography, the pupils is introduced to a knowledge of France and her relations in the past and in the present with the rest of the world. Both subjects have another function to perform than that of conveying information; both can be employed to develop and cultivate patriotic feeling; the rights of science and the rights of truth are not opposed. Hence "French patriotism has nothing to fear from truth...The place of France in the world is sufficiently great and her role sufficiently noble to justify a sincere kind of instruction, scrupulously truthful." And yet the French elementary school teachers through their largest professional organizations threatened in 1926 to refuse to use the current history textbooks unless all expressions of hatred were removed, and in addition, undertook the preparation of a textbook which, in the opinion of the organization, would be more accurately representative of the truth[38].

Some idea of the organization of the curriculum on the concentric method and of the emphasis on repetition and review may be obtained from the following analysis of the monthly and weekly course of study in geography and history contained in a handbook which was prepared for teachers by two normal school principals and which elaborates in detail the course of study prescribed by the Ministry[39]:

Geography

Elementary Course

First Year	*Second Year*
Local	Review (2 months)
Plans	Asia, Africa, Europe (1 month)
Terminology	France (6 months)
Asia	Reveiw (1 month)
Australia	
Africa	
America	
Europe	
Great Countries	
Review (1 month)	

Middle Course

France	Review (3 months)
Physical	France (7 months)
Industrial	France—Colonial Possessions
Review (1 month)	

Upper Course

France (8 months)	Europe
Industrial	Relief, Physical
Colonial Possessions	British Isles
Europe	All countries
Asia	Asia
Africa	France and her Colonies (5 months)
America	Germany
Review (1 month)	
France	

History

Elementary Course

First Year	*Second Year*
France to 1453	Review (3 months)
Review (1 month)	France to 1610
	Inventions and discoveries
	Art, Renaissance, Religion
	Review (1 month)

Middle Course

Review (1 month)	Review (2 months)
France to 1815	France 1815-1918
	Review

Upper Course

Review to 1919	Ancient History
Review of the Review (1 month)	Egypt, Greece, Jews, Romans, Christianity, Germans
	Review of France (7 months)
	Relations to England and Prussia
	Review (1 month)

It is unnecessary to discuss the other subjects of the curriculum in detail. They may be characterized, like the rest of the course of study, as somewhat formal, factual, and informational, but leaning somewhat to the practical implications. Increased attention is being given to local and regional studies, and excursions are being introduced to secure and supplement the materials of instruction. Such excursions (*excursions* or *promenades*), if made during regular class hours, must receive the authorization of the local inspector; if made on Thursdays or Sundays, such approval is not required, the State assuming responsibility for accidents which are not the result of serious negligence on the part of the teachers.

There is thus a tendency toward the new or progressive in education, but only within the limits of the prescribed curriculum. Educational experimentation of a radical character is not encouraged, except in extra-curricular activities, such as self-government and organization of pupils' cooperatives. In the literature of progressive education there is to be noted only one instance of a free experiment in the field of elementary education, that conducted by M.R. Cousinet, a government inspector, who was given an opportunity in his district to try out courses of study and methods of instruction, following the models of the new education developed outside of France.

Administrative Controls

Although the regulations speak of freedom for the teachers, the administrative controls have not been changed. The method of teacher preparation is still of the apprenticeship type and teachers grow up in the elementary branch of the educational system. In their school work they are supervised by inspectors whose approval is needed for every act not already prescribed and whose duty it is to see that prescribed regulations are carried out. In their instruction they are limited by the regulations which define the curriculum, course of study, and methods of instruction, and in addition, have available a number of manuals which work out the government regulations in detail and weekly professional journals which devote a part of each number to lesson plans and answers to examination questions. Every pupil is required to have an exercise book in which the first task in each subject is written at the beginning of each month (*cahier de devoirs mensuels*); at the teacher's option another exercise book may be provided in which a pupil enters the work of each day (*cahier de abudement*); both serve as records for inspectors and parents of the work done by the teacher, the progress of the pupils, and the care with which corrections and revisions are made; the *cahiers de devoirs mensuels* are retained by the school and not given to the pupils until they leave. Another important link with tradition in education is the close interest of parents in the work of their children, which, based on a strong faith in the tradition, manifests itself in a demand for the same kind of work as they did in their own school days. Two other methods of control are textbooks and examinations.

Textbooks

The selection of textbooks to be used in elementary schools passes through the hands of a number of committees. Each year fully appointed teachers in each canton meet under the chairmanship of a primary inspector and prepare a report recommending the addition and elimination of textbooks. This report is submitted to the academy inspector, who in turn transmits it to a departmental committee, over which he presides, consisting of the normal school faculties, of the teacher members of the departmental council, and cantonal delegates selected by this council. The list drawn up by the committee is submitted for approval to the rector of the academy and adopted, if he approves. In case of disapproval it is referred to the Minister of Public Instruction who has the final decision with the advice of the permanent section of the Higher Council of Public Instruction. No book, pamphlet, or manuscript may be introduced into a school except with the sanction of the academy inspector. Books for prize distribution may be selected by the teachers themselves or by the municipal authorities with the sanction of the primary inspector. The Higher Council may, however, prohibit certain books even here.

Under Article 7 of the Decree of January 29, 1890, the books that pupils are required to have are definitely prescribed. Thus, in the lower course a pupil must have a reader; in the middle course a reader, an elementary grammar with exercises, an elementary arithmetic, a small atlas, and a history of France; and in the upper course a reader, a grammar with exercises, an arithmetic, a history of France or a history covering the prescribed course, an atlas, and a textbook on morals and civics. A pupil refusing to use one of the books included in the list of the department may be excluded from school.

Examinations

Pupils are promoted each year on the basis of their records and the recommendations of their teachers to the principal or the *conseil des maîtres*. At the end of the course the State conducts an examination for the certificate of primary studies (*certificat d'études primaires*), which serves to test both pupils and schools. Pupils may present themselves if they are twelve years of age in the year of the examination. The examination is conducted by a commission consisting of a primary inspector, a representative of a normal school, higher elementary school or of an elementary school with a *cours complémentaire*, and two teachers not engaged in a school of the canton in which the examination is held. Each examination is held in the capital of a canton. Provision is made to include women on the commission for examining girls.

The examination is oral and written. The latter, the topics for which are selected by an academy inspector, includes an essay in a simple subject (50 minutes); dictation and questions on the sense and language (40 minutes); two reasoning problems in practical arithmetic and the metric system (50 minutes); an essay or questions on history and geography or everyday science applied to agriculture, industry, commerce, fishery (according to the locality), infant care hygiene (40 minutes), and a simple drawing exercise and handwork (50 minutes). The oral examination, lasting from twenty to twentyfive minutes and open to the public, includes a test in reading and questions on the sense and language of the text, recitation of a poem selected arithmetic, and a very simple physical exercise. The questions for the written examination are prepared by the academy inspector from the syllabus issued by the Ministry; the oral questions are based on the same syllabus, which covers in the main the work of the middle course with some selections from that of the upper course.

A definite system of marking is prescribed on a scale of 10, as follows; 1-2, bad; 3-4, middling; 5, passable; 6, sufficiently good; 7-8, good; 9-10, very good. The examining commission reports the result to the academy inspector who grants the certificate to successful candidates and transmits his report to the rector of the academy through whom it reaches the Ministry. Thus, in the last analysis, it is the Ministry that is the controlling authority in all matters affecting the school. The authorities have endeavoured in the last year to discourage preparation and cramming for the examination and to develop types of tests which would call for conservation and reflection, but without much success in either direction. The authorities do not appear as yet to have achieved their ideal.

The examination which crowns the work of the schools should not, because of poor selection of tests, result in setting a premium on bookish and abstract methods. In banishing them from the *certificat d'études primaires,* the Higher Council has tried again to affirm its confidence in those intuitive and active methods which should more and more be given a place of honour in the elementary school.

The examination has been subjected to criticism and has been fraught with certain dangers which the new *Instruction* and regulations seek to avoid. On the whole, however, its retention is strongly desired by parents, since it serves to establish standards and helps to link the public to the schools in a country in which certificates and diplomas play perhaps too great a part. The statistics do not indicated the number of pupils eligible to take the examination, but in 1931, of 98,583 boys who presented themselves, 82,490 passed the written examination and 82,372 the oral; of 90,116 girls, 75,878 passed the written examination and 75,805 the oral; about 84 per cent of those who took the examination obtained the certificate.

3. GERMANY

Education and the Revolution

The Revolution in Germany did more than substitute one form of government for another; it deprived the country of those objects of allegiance, to the cult of which the schools had been devoted. For elementary education a new aim had to be formulated to replace the traditional training of "Godfearing, loyal, and self-supporting subjects." The Federal Constitution redefined the aim in broad, general terms; Artical 148 provided that

> In all schools effort shall be made to develop moral education, public-mindedness, and personal and vocational efficiency in the spirit of the German national character and of international conclusion... Civic training and activity instruction shall be part of the curricula of the schools.

Religious instruction was retained as part of the regular school curriculum, but the rights of conscience, both the teachers and of pupils, were protected, and the establishment of secular schools or schools representing the spiritual outlook (*Weltanschauung*) of parents was permitted. A federal law to regulate the status of religious instruction was provided in the Constitution, but, as was pointed out in an earlier chapter, the Federal Government, despite several attempts has not succeeded in securing the enactment of a law (*Reichschulgesetz*) to regulate the organization of schools from this point of view. Finally, the Constitution provided for the abolition of the old methods of preparing teachers for elementary schools and by requiring the completion, of a full secondary school course before such preparation, substituted for an apprenticeship type of training a system organized on the university level.

In a country as intellectually restless as Germany, it would have been surprising if any delay in reforming education should have had to wait for the formulation of new theories and philosophies of education. Although the principles upon which the schools were founded and the practices within the schools were rigidly regulated by central authorities, there was no similar check on freedom of thought and of expression, providing that the existing political regime was not attacked. There was, accordingly, no lack of educational theories, psychologies of education, and new methods of instruction and curriculum-making, once the opportunity for considering them as practical issues was afforded. Teachers' organizations through their study circles, psychologists in their experimental laboratories, philosophers, and a small band of practitioners who had undertaken educational experiments in private schools had built up a body of literature which was at once critical of existing practices and pointed the way in new directions, to which the Youth Movement (*Jugendbewegung*) had sought to give expression.

The teachers' organizations maintained active study circles which not only provided opportunities for teachers in practice to extend the limited education which they had received in the normal schools, but which served as centres for the elaboration of materials of instruction in their own localities (*Heimatkunde*, especially history, geography, and nature study). In the latter connection, teachers had already begun to take their classes on excursions of discovery and exploration which tempered the bookishness of classroom instruction by contacts with the concrete (*Schulwanderungen*). Shortly before the War, the Prussian authorities had sanctioned a few experiments in environmental studies (*Heimatkunde*) in the elementary schools[40]. In Leipzig the teachers' association had organized an important laboratory for experimental psychology, inspired by the new tendencies in this field inaugurated by Wilhelm Wundt, Ernst Meumann, and Wilhelm Stern, who broke away from the traditional metaphysical and abstract discussions of psychology. Criticism of experimental, mechanistic, and voluntaristic psychology, led in time to the development of new schools of psychology with which the names of *Gestalt* and *Struktur* are associated, based on the objection that experimental psychology cannot explain all mental functions and emphasizing larger units or wholes rather than discrete nervous processes.

On the practical side, a number of private schools had been established as centres for educational experimentation. Free from all restrictions except the official requirement that their teachers must be as well qualified as teachers in public schools, and the pressure of parents that their children be enabled to pass the official examinations, these schools were in fact protests against many of the characteristic features of the public schools. To free education from the pressure of modern industrialization, they were established in the country and found there opportunities for healthy living, abundant physical activities, and a return to nature. In place of the competitive spirit, they sought to develop a sense of social responsibility and broad human sympathy. To offset the rigid intellectualism developed in the public schools, they emphasized the free play of emotional life through the cultivation of the fine arts, music, and manual skills and the provision of opportunities for self-expression and for self-government. In contrast to the public schools, some of these experimental schools were coeducational. Influenced largely by Ceci Reddie's experiment at Abbotsholme, England, Hermann Lietz developed in his *Landerziehungsheime* (country home schools) at *Ilsenburg* (1898), *Haubinda* (1901), and *Bieberstein* (1904) which soon became models for many other schools organized on the same principles. Other centres of reforms influence were the *Hauslehrerschule* established at Berlin-Lichterfelde (1906) by Berthold Otto, the *Freie Schulgemeinde Wickersdorf* (1906) of Gustave Wyneken, and the *Odenwaldschule* of Paul Geheeb.

Those progressive schools represented a general spirit of unrest which pervaded the country from the close of the nineteenth century and which was most widely represented by the Youth Movement, described by Friedrich Wilhelm Foerster, himself a radical critic of the official educational philosophy, as "a moral rejuvenescence of the German people, the return of the German soul to its best traditions." The Yough Movement was more than a rebellion of youth against the restrictions and conventions imposed on them by the adult generation and by the school authorities. It was inspired by clear and definite constructive ideas; it emphasized a return to nature and simplicity, free from the incubus of the conventions and artificialities of industrialized urban life; it laid stress upon freedom for youth to determine its own life in accordance with its own ideals rather than the standards imposed by others; it preached the gospel of social responsibility and brotherhood; and it sought to spread an appreciation of the real foundation of German culture—its music, art, drama, folkways, and folk customs—instead of the conventional culture of the schoolroom.

From various angles educational theory concentrated its attack upon the same weaknesses and defects as did the leaders of the progressive schools and of the Youth Movement. The schools were too mechanical and formal; they placed a premium on the mastery of knowledge and information without giving any training in its acquisition; the work was bookish, artificial, and unrelated to the life and interests of the pupils; false standards had been set up which resulted in pressure from the home or the pupils and from the authorities on the teacher; freedom and self-expression were unknown and the process of instruction had developed into a sterile method of questions by the teacher and answers by the pupils, who were themselves never allowed to question; aesthetic and creative activities were ignored, although formal training in drawing and singing were included in the curriculum. In a word, the elementary schools were dominated by the spirit of intellectualism derived from secondary and higher education, but limited, prescribed, and defined by the official regulations. Such a system afforded no opportunities for the development of free personalities, but moulded all according to a standard pattern, which, when supplemented by vocational and military training perpetuated the existing caste system.

Educational theorists were agreed in their criticisms of the existing system; and in their emphasis on the cult of personality they differed only in the solutions which they were prepared to offer. While all were ready to take the individual, his interests and needs, as the starting-point, some wished to leave the process of education wholly to the development of these interests and needs, others set up specific ends which they derived either from the claims of the State and of society or from a theory of cultural values. Common to all, but differing somewhat in the interpretation of its meaning was the advocacy of activity (*Arbeit*) on the part of the learner in the educative process rather than of the mere passive absorption of knowledge. Once the pressure of official control was removed, as it has been in the new German education, the school became the battle-ground of the educational theories which were associated with the names of Friedrich Paulsen, long an opponent of bureaucratic control in education, Wilhelm Dilthey, Eduard Spranger, Theodor Litt, Georg Kerschensteiner, Hugo Gaudig, and Paul Oestreich, each of whom stressed the importance of the educand as an individual personality to be developed, but differed in the ends to be attained. The radicals, under the leadership of Pail Oestreich, emphasized freedom above all else, *vom Kinde aus*; Gaudig and Kerschensteiner were the leading advocates of the activity principle (*Arbeitsprinzip*), but differed in their interpretations of it; Spranger and Litt stress the importance of a theory of cultural values and of cultural unity which educands are to make their own.

The influence of Spranger and Litt has dominated in the main the development of a theory of secondary education, but has not been without its effect on elementary education. Because of their more immediate applicability in school practice, the influence of Gaudig and Kerschensteiner, who had already put their theories into practice—the first in girls secondary school in Leipzig, the second as Superintendent of Schools in Munich—has been greater than that of the philosophers. Gaudig, starting with the potentialities of the child, advocated an emphasis on free spiritual development, or self-activity under the guidance of the teachers and of the schools as cooperative communities (*Arbeitsgemeinschaften*), but he limited the activities in the main to the methods of acquiring information rather than to the organization of new materials of instruction; the school is to be an *Arbeitsschule* rather than a *Lernschule*, but the techniques of learning rather than the content are to be changed. Kerschensteiner, perhaps because his work brought him more directly into contact with elementary and post-elementary school pupils, showed greater breadth in his interpretation of the activity principle through which each individual was to be trained to become a responsible, cooperating citizen for ennobling society and the State. Recognizing the importance of vocations in developing the worth of the individual as a person and a citizen, he emphasized the place of manual work, of drawing, of civic instruction, and gradually extended the application of the activity methods in these subjects to others. But in contrast to the encyclopedic character of the official courses of study, Kerschensteiner advocated less content, but more thoroughness, less bookishness and greater reality, less knowledge and more experiencing. Starting with manual activities, he gradually extended the principle of activity to intellectual (*geistige Arbeit*) and physical (*körperliche Arbeit*) sides of the school curriculum. From the concentration on civic training as the end of education, Kerschensteiner gradually accepted Spranger's philosophy, that a fully developed personality implies mastery and appreciation of cultural possessions—language, literature, fine arts and music, techniques and skills, science and religion, social customs and law—which serve two ends in providing the content for the development of personality, but only if the individual is an active agent in making them his own. Manysided character, developed emotionally as well as intellectually, can be cultivated only by a process through which the individual enters into the possession of values which are social. His early emphasis on civic instruction Kerschensteiner reconciled with his later point of view by defining the State, not as a preexisting entity, but as a cultural institution which exists for the free development of human personality.

The task which confronted the reformers of German education was defined, first, by the change in the form of government from a monarchy, which demanded the training of loyal subjects, to a republic which, by implication at least, rests upon the independent judgment of citizens. Secondly, the traditional division of the people into classes, each with its own form of education, had to be replaced by a system which for a period of years would train the future citizens in the same schools and which throughout their educational careers would seek to cultivate the same objects of loyalty as a basis of national solidarity. Third, there had to be substituted for bureaucratic control a certain measure of freedom to the localities and to the teachers. Finally, education in all its branches had to be imbued with the spirit of the new orientation, the emphasis on the individual as a growing personality as contrasted with the traditional aim of indoctrination and moulding of standardized patterns. Except for an extreme group which saw in the Revolution an opportunity for anarchy or an absolute concept of freedom, there was general agreement that the aim of elementary education must be to develop responsible, independent citizens, but citizens loyal to republican ideals and striving to appreciate and enrich the cultural foundations upon which the new Republic rests. For the State is more than a political instrument; it is a form of social organization which exists for the promotion of moral and cultural ends. Education must accordingly be conducted, in the words of the Constitution, "in the spirit of national character and of international reconciliation."

The data of the educational process are thus the individual and his environment. The process of education is the gradual acquisition by the pupil of mastery over and understanding of this environment in accordance with his developing potentialities. The content of the curriculum is not derived solely from books, but from experience in an enlarging environment. Education must be rooted in the soil of the people (*Bodenständigkeit*); and as the pupils grow, the process is one of expansion from their immediate environment (*Heimat*) to an understanding and appreciation of the meaning of life (*Loben*). The materials of instruction or curriculum must be derived from those aspects of life with which the pupils at each stage of development are familiar (*Heimatkunde*, knowledge of the environment), and which furnish the real and concrete relations between school and life outside. The function of the teacher is to create opportunities for the gradual expansion of the pupil's horizon, in part through vicarious experiences—that is, through books, in part through excursions. Through language and literature there is developed an appreciation of the best expressions of the ideals of the nation; through history a knowledge of the processes by which civilization and its institutions have developed; through geography an understanding of the relations of man to nature and of the interrelations of different parts of the world, through a study of nature an idea of elementary science and of the service of science to man. For the pupils the process must not be merely the acquisition of factual information, but a creative discovery. Beyond this, the school must develop the emotional side of the pupils' lives through the arts, music, manual, and physical activities. As the pupils grow older, they begin to realize that their own national culture has been and is influenced by the culture of other peoples and nations; *Heimatkunde*, knowledge and understanding of the national environment, is the common point of reference for elementary as for secondary schools, with the difference that the latter can take its pupils further afield in discussing foreign influences which have helped to mould German culture and civilization.

The process of education must be the active participation of the pupils, which will result in their intellectual, moral, and emotional development and growth. As contrasted with the traditional emphasis on precept and example, the method of activity (*Arbeitsprinzip*) implies on the part of the pupils ability to recognize and formulate problems to select the means and methods of their solution through independent planning, and to verify and criticize the results. Recognition of a problem, observation, and collection of data furnish the opportunities for a variety of forms of expression—oral, written, graphic, dramatic, musical, and manual. The necessity for observation, comparison, application, and verification in order to carry a task through to its desired end is in itself the basis of moral training, since it calls for perservance, self-control, and truth. But the school is not a collection of isolated individuals bound to a each other by common subjection to the authority of the teachers; it is a social organization, a section of life, a cooperative working community (*Arbeitsgemeinschaft*), which seeks through the promotion of group planning and group activities to develop the ideals of self-sacrifice, cooperation, and a sense of social duty and responsibility. The individual is free, but he learns that his freedom is restricted by the values created by his environment and by the right of his fellows to equal freedom.

The reform movement aims to cultivate the totality, the whose being of the individual. Experience is one and undivided; its logical separation into discrete compartments called subjects has no place in the minds of young children and even for older children; it is only tradition that has determined that the time of the school shall be distributed into a variety of periods assigned to disconnected activities to be studied. From this approach there was derived the demand for integrated programmes of instruction (*Gesamtunterricht*), which implies the abolition of time-tables and the splitting of the total activity of the pupils into separate subjects. It emphasizes the unity of experience in young children, the enrichment of that experience through the environment, and the gradual emergence of the need for techniques and the three R's. The traditional school, because it was artificially organized round subjects, set up a distinction between school and home, and school and the background which the child of the age of six has already accumulated. Through integrated instruction the home and background of the child are incorporated into the school as experience to be further developed. The principle of *Gesamtunterricht* has in general been adopted as the basis of instruction for the first two years of school life; drill in the fundamentals still continues to be regarded as an important educational foundation by all but the most radical theorists, but the fundamentals must be drawn out of the matrix of the child's experience rather than be imposed upon him. In other directions integrated instruction, an expansion and reinterpretation of the earlier concept of correlation, is followed; the excursions in particular lend themselves to such treatment, or it may be found in combinations of various forms of expression round one subject.

These in general are the trends of the new German theories of education—respect for personality (*vom Kinde aus*), the derivation of materials of instruction from the expanding environment (*Heimatkunde*), training of a common loyalty to German ideals and culture (*Bildung zum Deutschtum*), excursions as a method of enrichment (*Wandern*), integrated instruction (*Gesamtunterricht*), and activity methods (*Arbeitsunterricht*). It would be a fallacy, however, to conclude that all these features will be found in all German schools, but what is true is that all forms of education from the absolutely free to the conservative can be discovered, even in the schools of one city. Human nature being what it is, this is to be expected. The majority of teachers in the German schools were trained under the old methods; some with long years of experience were satisfied with the old system; others, who were applying the prescribed methods and courses of study under protest and against their convictions, readily broke away in new directions as soon as opportunities for liberalism were created. For some the Revolution meant the abolition of all supervisory authorities and self-determination, which manifested itself in the movement for the abolition of the position of principals or their election by the teachers; in some cases the same principle inspired pupils to demand participation in the administration of schools and even a voice in the selection of their teachers. In Hamburg a number of schools (*Gemeinschaftsschulen*) were organized on Tolstoyan principles, and teachers, pupils, parents, and any other persons who felt that they had anything to contribute were allowed a voice not only in the administration, but in the determination of what should be taught as well as when and how. Pupils participated as their disposition moved them. Anarchy, however, soon gave place to organization and cooperation.

More important than such radical ventures into the new was the change in the spirit of the authorities, who recognized the importance of freedom in the new political regime. Not only did they sanction the establishment of experimental schools (*Versuchsschulen*) in the public school system, but they realized that the day of uniformity and standardization had passed. The system of inspection was reformed, and in place of uniform, prescribed curricula and courses of study, the authorities issued Suggestions (*Richtlinien*), leaving to the teachers the responsibility for making their own courses of study with the help of the Suggestions and in the light of local needs; the duty of inspectors became one, not of control, but of sympathetic discussion and guidance. This change in administrative practices gave the teachers their opportunity; some could reconcile the Suggestions with established practices; others could now, alone or in coöperation with other teachers in their district, or through their associations, adapt them to the canons of the new theories. For standardized uniformity there were now substituted freedom and variety; for bureaucratic control, general standards and outlines and the professional responsibility of the teachers. The first four or five years of the new regime were years of feverish experimentation; gradually better understanding of the practical situation, and to some extent the effect of the economic crises which have meant increased size of classes and reduction in the funds available for school supplies and equipment, have produced more normal conditions. Variety of educational efforts still remains the characteristic of the new systems and the theories and principles which have been described continue to inspire teachers and schools, but there is less of the exaggerated interpretations of freedom which marked the earlier experiments.

THE SYSTEM OF ELEMENTARY EDUCATION

Provision of Schools

Pre-school education has not been fully developed. For children below the age of three there are available *creches (Krippen)* and children's homes (*kinderheime*). Children above the age of three may be sent to *Kleinkinderschulen* or *Kindergarten*, the majority of which are private and may only be opened with the approved of the authorities. In addition, young children as well as children of school age out of school hours may be looked after in *Kinderhorte*, which provide a variety of play and manual activities. The supervision of these institutions is, in Prussia, in the hands of the Ministry of Social Welfare (*Volkswohlfahrtsministerium*) in so far as the welfare side and organization of their work is concerned; instructional work is supervised by the Ministry of Education. All teachers and leaders in these institutions must be trained and hold state certificates.

Elementary education in Germany is provided in *Volksschulen*, which since the Revolution are divided into two sections, the foundation school (*Grundschule*) of four years and the upper section, also of four years. The *Grundschule* is the common four-year school which all children, irrespective of class distinction, are required to attend, unless they are enrolled in private schools or are educated at home under exceptional conditions. The *Grundschule* represents a compromise; a common six-year school was advocated by the sponsors of the *Einheitsschule*. The private schools are those which were in existence before the Revolution or are recognized as experimental schools. The preparatory school (*Vorschule*) for secondary education has been abolished, and private schools which are substitutes for public schools are tolerated, despite a constitutional provision (Article 147) for their abolition, only because neither the Federal nor the State Governments are in a position to compensate their owners, if they are closed. Pupils may be educated at home only if their physical condition, certified by a doctor, is such that they ought not to attend a public school.

The *Grundschule* is thus the foundation school in which the majority of German children receive the first four years of their education. By amendments to the constitutional provision, which were passed as a result of protestes from parents,[41] gifted children may complete the course of the *Grundschule* in three years.

From the *Grundschule* the majority of the pupils pass on to the upper section of the *Volksschule* for four additional years[42], the rest continuing their education in middle or secondary schools. In practice the *Grundschule* and the upper section constitute an unbroken unit under one administration. Only thirteen per cent of the elementary schools in Germany are fully organized with a separate class for each year; one third of the schools are single-teacher schools. The desire to provide better educational opportunities for children who remain in the elementary schools has led to the establishment in most States of advanced classes (*gehobene Klassen*), which enables pupils to remain in school for one or two additional years beyond the eighth; fees may be charged in these classes, which in some schools are organized into distinct units, and foreign language and mathematics may be added to the curriculum. For pupils who are retarded, there is a grouping of special classes (*Förderklassen*); pupils who are retarded in the last year before they leave school may be given special instruction in the fundamentals in concluding classes (*Abschlussklassen*); pupils who appear likely to fail to secure their promotions may be given additional instruction (*Nachhilfe-unterricht*). For backward but educable pupils there have been organized special schools (*Hilfsschulen*), which were first organized in Mannheim; to such schools pupils may be assigned, after spending one or two years in a regular school, on the recommendation of their teachers and after a medical examination; the curriculum of the *Hilfsschulen* is devoted mainly to training of hand and eye through a variety of manual activities.

Education and Religion

Religious instructions is given in all schools; the Constitution, however, provides that pupils may be exempted from it at the request of their parents and teachers may only give it, if they choose to do so. The relation of the religious question to schools and the organization of the schools on denominational or undenominational lines were discussed already. In Prussia the majority of the schools are denominational (*konfessionelle Schulen*)—that is, Protestant, Catholic, or Jewish; a few are interdenominational (*Simultanschulen* or *paritätische Schulen*) in which the pupils receive religious instruction from teachers or ministers of their own denomination. Since the industrial areas are in the main opposed to religious instruction, difficulties arose in some schools because of the large number of requests for exemptions, and the practice developed of organizing such pupils in collective classes (*Sammelschulen*), and of establishing special secular schools (*Sammelschulen*), to which were assigned, but at their own request, only teachers who refused to give religious instruction.

Compulsory Attendance

The Constitution (Article 145) required compulsory education to be universal with full-time attendance at school for at least eight years, followed by part-time attendance up to eighteen. This is not an innovation in Germany, but the proposed abolition of private schools has introduced school compulsion (*Schulpflicht*) in place of compulsory education (*Unterrichtspflicht*); the old laws compelled parents and guardians to have their children and wards educated, but left the choice of school to their discretion; under the constitutional provision and state laws, which require attendance at a *Grundschule*, the choice of school has been withdrawn.

Compulsory education in Prussia has been regulated anew by a decree of December 15, 1927, which became effective on January 4, 1928. All children who are physically and mentally mature must enter school at the beginning of the school year nearest to the sixth birthday and remain in attendance until the end of the year in which they reach their fourteenth birthday. Exceptions are allowed at both ends; children who are weak or mentally immature may postpone entrance by a year, and pupils who have already been assured of employment may, if they are fourteen years of age, leave before the end of the school year. Pupils who receive private instruction must be examined periodically to discover whether they cannot attend a public school. The census of pupils eligible for school attendance is prepared in each locality by the police and sent to the school authorities at the beginning of each school year; the pupils are then assigned to the school which they must attend. The responsibility for regular attendance falls upon parents or guardians, who are liable, in cases of unjustifiable absences of pupils, to a fine ranging from 1 to 25 Mark; employers who knowingly employ pupils of school age during school hours are liable to a fine up to 150 Mark. Absences are reported by the teachers through the regular channels to the police. Pupils who move from one school district to another or from one town to another must provide themselves with a certificate of dismissal and must enroll in another school within six weeks. Blind children must attend an institution from the age of six to fourteen; deaf-mutes from seven to fifteen.

Text and Schoolbooks

All pupils must be provided with textbooks and school supplies required for instruction at the cost of their parents; aid may be given to poor pupils unable to purchase them, or a loan library may be provided for their use. No textbook may be introduced into any school without permission of the county and central authorities. Pupils must have primers, readers, song-books, books for religious instruction (approved by the Ministry and the denominational authorities), slates and pencils (in lower classes), and exercise books for the different subjects. The single textbooks never played a very important part in class instruction in Germany; they were used as reference books after the lesson had been given by the teacher. With the introduction of activity methods the textbook as such is assuming a position of even lesser importance, while libraries and source materials become more appropriate than outlines and summaries.

Organization and Administration of Schools

Seperate elementary schools are provided in Prussia for boys and girls in all schools with more than three classes, and women teachers are not allowed to have classes in which there are boys. The large majority of schools in Prussia in 1927 had less than three classes; of 33,405 elementary schools in 1927, 14,076 were single-teachers, schools, 6492 schools had two teachers, 4529 three teachers, 1808 four teachers, 959 five teachers, 815 six teachers, and 4790 had seven or eight teachers.

The size of classes is determined indirectly by the method of state appropriation funds, which employs the basis of one teacher for sixty pupils; localities which desire to have smaller classes must bear the additional cost out of their own funds. Directly, a decree of May 24, 1922, set the maximum number of pupils in a class at eighty; a later decree of October 4, 1926, provided for an average class size of forty-five pupils; when the number exceeds fifty, an additional teacher must be employed. The economic conditions in Germany have prevented the effective realization of the movement for lower classes.

The schools are administered by principals (*Schulleiter*); in schools with at least three teachers and less than six, the principal is known as the head teacher (*Hauptlehrer*); in schools with six or more teachers he has the title of *Rektor*. The special examination for this position was abolished in 1920 and the selection is made on the basis of general qualifications, experience, and ability. The *Hauptlehrer* receive a remuneration in addition to their regular salaries as teachers of 500 Mark a year; the *Rektoren*, an addition of 1200 Mark. In schools with six teachers or more, one of the teachers may be designated as associate principal (*Konrektor*); a second associate is appointed in schools with fourteen teachers or more; the additional remuneration of a *Konrektor* is 500 Mark. The principals and assistant principals are not the superiors of the teachers, but are officials charged with certain administrative duties in addition to teaching (the *Rektoren* must teach at least twelve periods a week; the *konrektoren* have full charge of a class). The principal is responsible for the administration of his school to the authorities, keeps the records of the school, conducts its official correspondence, and is the intermediary between, the school and the parents or the public; beyond this, he has other duties which may be assigned to him by his council of teachers. The *Konrektor* is the deputy of the *Rektor* and is assigned special duties such as the care of the school library, social welfare work among the pupils, the administration of the school bank, special instruction, the organization of parents' councils and meetings, and any other tasks designated by the teachers' council.

The principal is not the superior of the teachers, but a peer among peers. The demands of the teachers for participation in the administration of schools were finally met by a decree issued on September 20, 1919, which provided for the creation of teachers' councils in each school

(*Lehrerkonferenz*). All teachers holding permanent appointments and other teachers with at least six months of service are eligible to membership in the councils. The functions of the councils are to look after the general welfare of their schools, to confer on and discuss methods of instruction, assignment of classes, promotions of pupils, use of school funds, the provision of school materials and supplies, and cooperation to secure unity of work. The principal is the chairman of the council; on its advice, he may visit older teachers in their classrooms, criticize, and discuss their work with them; under the regulations, he is expected to supervise young teachers, those who have not yet received their permanent appointments. The administration of schools has thus been placed on a collegiate basis with the principal serving as the executive officer of his council, a practice which is feasible in a system in which there are few schools' with more than twenty classes.

Curriculum

The curriculum and course of study in elementary schools are governed by state regulations, with the exception that general suggestions for the organization and work of the *Grundschule* were issued by the Federal Government. With legislation and suggestions for the *Grundschule* in 1920 and 1921, federal influence on elementary education came to a close; even these were supplemented by state suggestions. Federal legislation defined the scope of the *Grandschule* and required the closing of preparatory schools (*Gesetz betreffend die Grundschule and Aufhebung der Vorschulen,* April 28, 1920, amended by a law of April 18, 1925, making three years attendance at the *Grundschule* permissive); on July 18, 1921, a decree was issued giving suggestions on the aims and organization of the *Grundschule (Richtlinien für die Zielbesetzung und die innere Gestaltung der Grundschule)*, which served as a basis for the curriculum suggestions prepared by each State.

The significant changes which have taken place since the Revolution in the preparation of curricula and courses of study have been, first, that they are no longer issued by the central authorities as decrees or laws which are immutable, but as suggestions (*Richtlinien*) on the basis of which each school or locality prepares its own course of study; secondly, that to an increased extent teachers participate in their preparation through cooperative activity in each school, or through district committees, or through teachers' associations; from time to time experienced teachers may be invited to cooperate with inspectors or the central authorities. Thus, the Prussian decree of March 16, 1928 (*Richtlinien zur Aufstellung von Lehrplänen für die Grundschule*), specifically requires that:

In the construction of the courses of study for individual schools opportunity for cooperation in the widest sense must be granted to the teaching staff[43].

Aim of the Grundschule

The aim of the *Grundschule* as defined in the federal decree of July 18, 1921, is as follows:

The first four years of school have their own goal and unified sphere of activity. Their goal is the gradual unfolding of the child's abilities out of the instinct for play and movement toward a normal desire for work which manifests itself inside the school community[44].

This statement is further elaborated as follows in the Prussian decree of March 3, 1921:

The *Grundschule*, as the common school for all children in the first four years of school, has the task of giving to the children who attend it a basic training on which not only the *Volksschule* in its last four years can be built, but also the middle and secondary schools with their more extended instruction. Therefore, it must awaken and train all the spiritual and physical forces of the children and equip them with those knowledges and skills which as groundwork for every type of further instruction, are absolutely essential[45].

In detail the suggestions recommend the development of the abilities of the children through play and movement, leading gradually over to instructional activities which will introduce them to an understanding of their physical and cultural environment. Through practical activities they should receive a training of hand and eye and the foundation for the cultivation of various modes of expression; training in the mother-tongue should be cultivated through practical activity accompanied by drawing, modeling, cutting out, and observation; physical training should be developed through games, excursions, gymnastics, and sports. The materials of instruction should be related to and derived from the home and local environment of the children, and the choice of subjects and activities should be determined by the pupils' background, according to districts and localities, sex, ability, and interests. In other words, the basis of curriculum-making in the *Grundschule* should be *Heimatkunde* (the home, yard, garden, schoolhouse, street and market, the countryside, life and work at home and in school, and in the shop, factory, and on the farm). Such a background provides the materials for story-telling, dramatization of fairy and other tales, singing and recitation of folk and children's rhymes and poems, modeling, drawing and other manual activities. The study of the environment extended by excursions supplies the content for geography, history, nature study, local myths and traditions. The environment must be treated as a whole and out of the integrated instruction (*Gesamtunterricht*) in the first year there should be derived the subjects which constitute the work of the last three years. The *Grundschule* must not be a *Lernschule*, in which the pupils acquire information from the teachers, but an activity school (*Arbeitsschule*) which stimulates them to learn through self-experienced activity and through cooperation with their teachers and their fellow-pupils. Throughout the course the emphasis is to be placed on various forms of expression and activities. Unity and integration are to be observed by the provision, suggested in a decree of March 23, 1923, that pupils be taught by the same teachers for two year periods.

The time-schedule which follows is intended for a fully graded school; schools which do not have four separate classes for each of the four years are expected to conform to the time-distribution suggested. The work of the first year should be organized as an integrated whole (*Gesamtunterricht*); permission may be obtained to continue the integrated programme for one or more years beyond the first.

Time Schedule of the Grundschule

	Year	*Year*	*Year*	*Year*
Subject	1*	2	3	4
Religion		4	4	4
Environmental study (*Heimatkunde*) / German		9	10	11 (10)†
Writing		2	2	2
Arithmetic		4	4	4
Drawing			2 (1)	2 (1)
Singing		1	2 (1)	2
Physical training		2	2	3 (2)
Sewing			(2)	(2)
Total	18	22	26	28

* The work of the first year is organized as an integrated whole (*Gesamtunterricht*).

† The figures in parentheses are for girls only.

Aim of the Last Four Years of the Volksschule

The aim of the upper section of the *Volksschule* is determined not only by the general principles governing education—the interests of the pupils, close articulation with the environment (*Heimat*), and activity methods—but also by the special consideration that for most pupils this course will be the end of full-time education, and that they will enter immediately on practical careers and continue their education chiefly in vocational schools; a few will be found eligible for transfer to a secondary school (*Aufbauschule*) at the age of thirteen. In general, however, at this stage, too, the educational needs of the pupils and the objective of the constant and symmetrical development of their whole being, especially with reference to their emotions and will, must be the deciding factor[46]. Self-activity, intellectual as well as physical, must continue to be the basis of instruction.

The cooperation of the pupil must not consist chiefly, in the absorption of knowledge, but the objectives of instruction are to be worked out under the guidance of the teacher through observation, experiment, investigation, independent reading, and verification[47].

A wide range of concrete activities provides opportunities for a variety of forms of instruction and study—the preparation of sketches, drawings, and instructional materials—especially for geometry, geography, and nature study—the organization of collections, experiments in natural science, the care of animals, school gardening, and, for girls, sewing and home economics. School excursions (*Wandertage*), which serve primarily for physical education and must be arranged for one day each month and for shorter periods as occasion demands, bring the pupils into contact with a wide variety of experiences and materials of instruction—observation of plant and animal life, of earth and weather conditions, problems of business and labour, agricultural and industrial activities, and monuments and records of historical significance. In the promotion of reality in education and understanding of community and social life, every possible agency provided by the locality must be utilized, whether in city or in country. Direct experience must be supplemented by the use of books, schools and public libraries, and museums. The real contrast between the old and the new school lies in the fact that the walls of the schoolroom have been removed and the materials of instruction, instead of being provided through the cold, factual form of books or the teacher's exposition are derived from living contact with the environment. The school excursions as such are not an innovation in German education; it is their application in the new education which has acquired a new significance. With the establishment of a nation-wide network of youth hostels (*Jugendherbergen*) pupils can be accommodated at a very low cost in any part of Germany, an opportunity which is extensively used by whole classes accompanied by their teachers during the vacations.

The curriculum includes religion (or moral instruction for pupils exempted from religious instruction), German, history, and civics, geography, natural science, arithmetic, geometry, drawing, music, physical training and sewing for girls, with manual training for boys and home economics for girls where these can be provided. The Suggestions (*Richtlinien zur Aufstellung von Lehrplänen für die oberen Jahrgänge der Volksschule,* Decree of Ocober 15, 1922), issued by the Ministry are intended to suggest standards to be attained in each class rather than to prescribe details to be carried out. The responsibility for working out courses of study in accordance with the local environment devolves upon the teachers.

The guiding principles (of the Suggestions) determine and limit in general the materials that are to be treated. The choice and distribution in particular are matters for the courses of study to be drafted for the individual school, in the organization of which the principle of basing the instruction upon life in the community must be respected. The amount of materials to be chosen varies with the school. In all schools, however, care must be taken that the materials prescribed in the curriculum are not superficially treated, but may be thoroughly worked through from an intellectual point of view. Schools of few classes, in order to be able to secure a richer selection of materials, may organize their work on the basis of alternating year courses[48].

The time-schedule suggested is as follows:

Time-Schedule of Upper Section of the Volksschule

Subject	*Boys' School*				*Girls' School*			
	5	*6*	*7*	*8*	*5*	*6*	*7*	*8*
Religion	4	4	4	4	4	4	4	4
German	8	7	6-7	6-7	7-8	7	6-7	6-7
History and civics	2	2	2	3	2	2	2	3
Geography	2	2	2	2	2	2	2	2
Natural Science	2	3-4	4	3	2	2-3	3	3
Arithmetic, Geometry	4-5	5-6	5-6	5-6	3-4	4	4	3
Drawing	2	2	2	2	2	2	2	2
Singing	2	2	2	2	2	2	2	2
Physical training	2-3	3	3	3	2	3	3	3
Manual training	2	2	2	2	..	..	..	..
Sewing	..	..	..	..	2	2-3	2-3	2-3
Total	28-30	30-32	30-32	30-32	28-30	30-32	30-32	30-32

The Suggestions no longer define the course of study in detail or by years; they are, as they are intended to be, guides or principles for the teachers. Religious instruction varies with each denomination; since the schools are in the main denominational, beyond the common aim of religious and moral training stress is laid upon instruction in dogmatic tenets of each denomination. The aim in teaching of German is to cultivate mastery in the oral and written use of the mother-tongue, to develop an appreciation of the native language and literature, and to stimulate further reading with pleasure; as compared with the traditional practice, although it is not neglected, less emphasis is placed on the formal side of language study (grammar and spelling), while in the study of literature more attention is paid to variety and breadth in the selection of readers and books than on repetition and memorization which tend to kill pleasure in reading. Instruction in history has been completely revised, and, in place of the former emphasis on inculation of loyalty to the Hohenzollerns (whose portraits have been removed from all schools and classrooms) and on the study of war[49] there has been substituted the study of the development of the German people and the German State as illustrated in their political, social, economic, and cultural progress. 'The highest law of history instruction must be to come as near as possible to historical truth.' Love of the people and of the fatherland and a sense of civic and social responsibility must be aroused. Civic instruction is to be given through history first and must culminate in a study of the Federal and Prussian Constitutions.[50] Party politics must be avoided in the schools, and pupils in all schools must receive instruction in the nature, duties, and aims of the League of Nations (Decree, May 28, 1927).

For geography the local environment is the starting-point; its aim is to develop familiarity with the home district and Germany and to give a general knowledge of foreign countries. With the assistance of the meteorological Institute in Berlin, schools are encouraged to study meteorological charts and to establish observation stations. Germany's need of colonies is to be stressed; illustrative material for this purpose is provided by the Colonial Institute in Berlin; in the same way, through the *Verein für das Deutschtum im Ausland*, also in Berlin, the cultural bonds between Germans at home and abroad are cultivated. Through natural science the pupils are introduced in an elementary fashion to botany, zoology, physiology, physics, chemistry, geology, and agriculture; an important part of the instruction in this subject is assigned to physiology, hygiene, health, temperance, and care of infants. The number sense, the place of mathematics in life, the meaning of quantitative form and measurement are taught through arithmetic and geometry. Drawing aims to cultivate the use of form and colour as a means of expression, and through music joy in song, feeling for tone qualities, and training in singing as a leisure and cultural activity through membership in choral societies are cultivated. Manual training for boys is closely correlated with other subjects of the curriculum, as is also the study of home economics by girls.

Physical education has been given special attention since the War, partly to provide a substitute for compulsory military training, which has been abolished, and partly to repair the ravages of the War and post-War period on the health of the nation. Care is paid in the selection of principals and inspectors to discover their interest in and understanding of the importance of physical education, to which the attention of teachers and parents is directed. Pupils may be exempted from physical instruction only on a doctor's certificate which must be periodically renewed. The time assigned to the instruction may be supplemented by folk and other games, marches, skating, and sledding in winter, and swimming in summer wherever possible; for these activities one afternoon a week (*Spielnachmittag*) must be set aside. Information on the literature of the various aspects of physical education is supplied by the *Museum für Leibesübungen* and through the *Deutsches Archiv für Leibesübungen* in Berlin.

There are no examinations in the Prussian elementary schools at the end of each year or of the whole course. Promotions are made on the recommendations of the class teachers with the approval of the teachers council.

Conclusion

The reform of education in Germany since the Revolution closely parallels the reform which followed the defeat at Jena in 1806. Then, as now, the nation had been defeated and realized that national reorganization could only be achieved through educational reconstruction. In the early nineteenth-century reform, however, attention was devoted mainly to secondary education; in the reconstruction since 1916 the whole of the educational system has been affected, but the most thoroughgoing reform has been in the field of elementary education and the preparation of teacher for elementary schools. The principle of educational reform, accepted then as now, is that national unity and national solidarity can be attained only through loyalty to a common culture shared in by independent, responsible individuals;

the difference between the past and the present is that the former stressed the content of instruction, the latter, aided by the progress of educational theory, the method. In both periods the reforms were animated by a spirit of liberalism, but while in the first this spirit was gradually destroyed by the pusillanimity of the reigning monarchs, in the second the reaction is being caused more by the economic conditions which affect the rest of the world as well as Germany and by the failure of these powers whose destiny is bound up with the fate of Germany to strengthen the forces which are genuinely loyal to the development of democratic institutions in the spirit of the Weimar Constitution. The trend to narrow nationalism and the movement toward the Right wing in politics are the results, not of the will of the German people, but of world politics whose development the international mind has failed to inspire.

As a result of the new philosophy of education and as a protest against the pre-War system, German educators have begun to realize the meaning of freedom—in administration, in teaching, and in learning. Freedom, however, implies in education guidance by teachers who have themselves been trained to be free; the first radical reform which was undertaken was accordingly that in the preparation of teachers. The number of teachers who have had the advantage of the new preparations has been small up to the present, but liberalization of administrative practices, the organization of teachers' councils, the change in the spirit of methods of inspection as well as the system of preparation have given the teachers a feeling for the dignity of their work which can only be appreciated by members of a profession rather than servants of a machine-like organization. Added to this have been the contributions of theorists, the results of experimentation, and the guiding suggestions of the authorities, all of which have created a ferment disturbing to the calm indifference of a system whose operation is prescribed in every detail. Freedom and variety are today the characteristics of German elementary education; the exuberant license which prompted the more radical experiments, more striking as protests than as contributions to education, have given place to a reasoned reconciliation of freedom and responsibility. The claims of the child, the educand, as a developing human being are recognized, but they are not cultivated to the neglect of a common national end, the appreciation and understanding and advancement of German culture. Political, militaristic, and nationalistic indoctrination have been replaced by the development of the free, independent citizen, responsible for and inspired by the rich cultural forces of the nation of which he is a member.

These are the ideals which German education is striving to achieve and would achieve in a period of normal development. It must again be pointed out, however, that, unlike the Soviet Revolution, the German Revolution was not a complete break with Germany's cultural past and that the old and the new continue side by side; except by compulsion all teachers cannot be made over to one pattern. But, although schools can be found in Germany today which still bear upon them the marks of the old tradition, a new day has dawned in German education, and the responsible leaders will in the new era be the teachers; and, if the forces of reaction do not secure control, the German schoolmaster, trained to understand the child on the one hand and to interpret his environment on the other, will again win the victory, but this time for German democracy.

4. ITALY

History

The reform of elementary education in Italy, which took place in 1923, was inspired by discontent with its past development, by a new philosophy, and by Fascism. From its foundation by the Casati Law of 1859, Italian education had not suffered from neglect by the legislators, but educational laws, not motivated by any definite principles, were piecemeal and in general remained good intentions. The

Casati Law required the establishment of elementary schools, one for boys and one for girls, in every commune so far as local resources permitted the carrying out of the law. The Coppino Law of July 15, 1877, following the unification of Italy, sought through education to train Italians, and made attendance compulsory from the age of six at least for the lower course—that is, up to the age of nine or ten. Compulsory attendance was extended to twelve and state aid was introduced by the Orlando Law of July 8, 1904, which also required adult illiterates to attend school in the evenings on pain of forfeiting certain rights and privileges—the franchise, public employment, and permits to hunt and carry arms. The Sonnino Law, July 15, 1906, provided for the establishment of state schools in districts with scattered population. Finally, the Daneo-Credaro Law, June 4, 1911, recognizing the ineffectiveness of local autonomy in education, set up provincial organizations to establish schools at the cost of the State in poor or indifferent communities; the effect of state aid was to lead to the surrender of local autonomy, with the result that an investigation conducted in 1923 revealed that only 264 localities out of 8354 had retained the right to provide elementary education; the majority of the autonomous communes were in the North. The percentage of illiteracy ranged from 11 per cent in Piedmont to 70 per cent in Calabria. The proportion of pupils enrolled in the elementary schools varied from 90 per cent in the Northern provinces, mainly industrial, to 59 per cent in Sicily and 41 per cent in Calabria, while of those enrolled, 94 per cent attended schools regularly in the most progressive province, Venetia, and only 47 per cent in Sicily and 32 per cent in Calabria. The number of pupils who succeeded in passing the annual examinations and securing their promotion, and the uneven distribution in the size of classes, ranging in some places from one pupil to more than sixty in others, revealed the failure of the laws to secure any real progress[51]. Inefficient administration, inadequate preparation, and poor professional discipline were other causes which, besides an inert public opinion, militated against an adequate execution of even the low minimum prescribed by the laws.

On the educational side elementary education was dominated by the philosophy of positivism, which emphasized knowledge for its own sake, placed science on a pedestal, was rationalistic and tended to set up standards and ideals which did not correspond in any way with the customs, prejudices, and ideals of the people. Combined with an emphasis on secularism, positivism had the effect of making the schools unreal, divorced from life, and external. Influenced in part by German educational theory and methods and in part by French rationalism and the analytical trend, the curriculum of the Italian elementary schools had become encyclopedic in content and atomistic in methods. The teacher, under the direction of detailed prescriptions and relying on a professional preparation which emphasized methods, rules techniques, and devices, was set apart as a lay priest ministering knowledge and the sciences to the neglect of life around him and the real spirit and interests of the child.

Against the positivists trend in nineteenth century philosophy a new philosophy of idealism was opposed by Benedetto Croce and Giovanni Gentile, who with the establishment in 1903 of *La Critica,* a philosophical journal, gradually built a school to which the younger Italians flocked. The interpreter of this philosophy for educational purposes was Gentile, who began with an attack on the unreality of the work of all schools, elementary and secondary, and on the prevailing dualism between mind and reality. Between these Gentile would recognize no distinction; reality does not exists by nature, but is the creation of the mind, of the spirit by the pure act of thought. The only true reality is the human spirit education is philosophy in action and cannot be built up on the basis of biological analysis or of a psychology which separates the mind from reality and the world. Such a separation means the development of rules, techniques devices, and methods, which are posited on theories of how the mind works, and instruction becomes the process of filling the mind with knowledge, facts, and information. This process is all the more unsound in system which prides itself on being secular, neutral, agnostic, skeptical, and materialistic. Education under these conditions becomes a pseudo-science, abstract and divorced from reality, and in turn emphasizes, not the growth of man as man, the development of personality, experience as a formative factor, but informational and instrumental teaching, the tools rather than the spirit and culture. The traditional school set up three entities—the teacher, the content, and the pupil—and the intermediaries between the first and third consist of methods, which mechanize the process of education makes it pedantic and schematic.

What is then needed to bring about an educational reform? Not a revision of the curriculum or new courses of study with the addition of new subjects, but a fundamental change of outlook and acceptance of the philosophy of active idealism. True education is possible only through personal experience, not by imbibing doses of knowledge and information ladled out by the teacher. Hence the centre of the educative process is the child, not the teacher nor the content nor methods of instruction. Hence, also, the emphasis on the personality of the child as a human being with a spirit whose free growth must be encouraged and must be respected. What the child beings with him to school and his environment—his family, his religion, the folklore in which he has grown up, the dialect which he speaks, his nationality, and history of which he is a part—cannot be ignored. Education means, accordingly, the free development of the spirit and is a spiritual activity which is one and cannot be divided and atomized into a multiplicity of aims, purposes, and objectives; it is one, as that reality which is the creation of the mind is one. Breadth of mind does not come from rationalization or intellectual liberalism as ends in themselves, but from enlightenment which grows from breadth of experience and self-cultivation. The function of the teacher is not to transmit his wisdom to the child, a process which would still leave it as an external, unrelated thing, but to provide opportunities for enriched experiences flowing from and based upon the curiosity, interests, and emotional life of the child, his inner world, his recreational life, and his joy in the beautiful.

The mind is one, and its method is the act of creating reality; but three categories can be recognized in this creative activity of the mind which brings about unity between the Ego and the non-Ego, between the subjective and the objective. These categories are art, religion, and philosophy, which must be the points at which education becomes philosophy in action. By art Gentile does not mean instruction in art, but the way in which the mind of the artist operates in expressing his concept of the world; art is pure subjectivity, the expression of the self, and the formation of personality. Artistic or aesthetic teaching, accordingly, is not limited to one field, but it is the formation of personality through expression and activity in any field—penmanship, composition, and play as much as drawing and music. Religion is consciousness of the object and the idea of God, or the omnipotence and omnipresence of spirit as manifested in the world of man with which the individual spirit must enter into harmony. Man is a man to the extent that he becomes a man—that is to the extent that his spirit becomes a part of the human spirit and his will becomes will at the same time as it is the will of all. But by religion Gentile does not mean the teaching of a religious creed, but religion as the essence of the growth of the mind itself, applicable to the conquest of the sciences as of religion in the narrower sense. The reconciliation between art, the subjective, and religion, the objective, is brought about by philosophy which creates the unity between the two. Hence a theory of education for all teachers is this "clear, precise, and sincere concept of reality, which opens our eyes in philosophy and making us fully conscious of our nature realizes it in full by establishing in us that mind which is the only legitimate and effective teacher."

The essential principles of the reform from the point of view of this philosophy are freedom and activity—freedom for the schools, the teachers, and the pupils to follow the principles of their own development, and activity of teachers and pupils. The authority of the teacher depends upon his ability to promote the progressive human and spiritual development of the pupils and upon his own ability to grow and cultivate himself. Freedom, however, implies a responsibility to cooperate in the development of culture, "which is the progressive conquest of freedom," in the interests of the nation as a whole, for

> National cultures have never been more conscious than now of the higher needs of the mind, needs that are not only aesthetic and abstractly intellectual, but also ethical and religious. For a school without an ethical and religious content is an absurdity. The school is not the form and means of the elevation of the mind; but it is precisely that elevation itself; it is the formation of men and consciences. There is no conscience that has a form indifferent to its own content and to its own faith. Every faith is sacred; but it must be a faith. The Italian school which the State, the supreme conscience of the Italian people, must maintain with serious determination and a firm understanding of its own duty, must be a human school for its university faith; but also it must always be an Italian school of its national faith.

In this process of building a national culture, the school must remain free as a developing, growing institution changing the content of its work as the spirit changes. Such work cannot be defined by officially prescribed courses of study and regulations, which Gentile had already insisted in 1920, three years before his reform, must be abandoned.

> Away with preestablished programmes, then of every description! Spiritual activity works only in the plenitude of freedom...What we need to do is to wait, observe, and have faith. For God will reveal himself to us, and God is the very Spirit of ours which at every moment prescribes its law to itself and thus determines its own content[52].

In the development of his reform, Gentile as Minister of Education was assisted by Giuseppe Lombardo-Radice, who was Director of Elementary Education in his Ministry. Lombardo-Radice brought to the task the inspired enthusiasm of long years of experience with children and the training of teachers. A modern Pestalozzi, he had built up his philosophy of education by observation and practice. With Gentile he was opposed to the materialistic, positivist tradition in Italian education. The process of education should develop by intuition, not through presenting a mass of objects to be studied by the pupil, but as a manifestation of his life and the evolution of ideas which he derives from his own experience. This process can be promoted by encouraging free and frank expression whether in the use of dialect and the mother-tongue, or in composition, singing, and art, or in play and recreational activities. The child must be respected as an investigator, an explorer, a student of nature and the great documents of the human spirit in religion, science, history, and literature rather than as a learner of formal manuals and textbooks. Only in this way can the child develop his personality as an independent, self-respecting individual and not a tool of others; only in this way can his spirit grow into a realization of itself as at one with the spirit of humanity[53]. Education is growth through self-conscious activity, for the free man is the creator of his own personality through play and work.

In Ernesto Codignola, Director of the Royal Higher Normal School in Florence, Gentile found another active collaborator, whose influence has been exercises not only through his opportunities for training the higher officials in the educational service, but in his interpretations of the history of educations and philosophy, addresses to teachers, and the publications of educational and cultural journals. His influence has been especially strong in the emphasis which he has always placed on the reform of the preparation of teachers and in his attack on the exaggerated value attached to so-called professional subjects—theory and method, which in his opinion, as in that of Gentile, should be replaced by broad cultural training and philosophy[54].

Because Gentile's philosophy of idealism emphasized the absolute, the omnipotence of the spirit, and the significance of historical truth, it was accepted as the philosophy of Fascism, and Gentile was selected to undertake "the most Fascist of all reforms," the reform of education. There was nothing contradictory between his emphasis on the supremacy of the spirit and the Fascist emphasis on the supremacy of the State and of the nation, nor between his plea for individual growth and the organization of a hierarchical administration, for an individual's will and spirit realizes itself in the will and spirit of others. But while Gentile and his associates realized the essential importance of nationalism and of national culture as the environment for the growth of personality, their aims were remote from attempting to cultivate political nationalism. And yet the place which they assigned to the study of popular heroes as manifestations of the human and national spirit furnished a ready opportunity for those who wished to use the schools for political ends; hero-worship could conveniently be turned to advantage in favour of a dictator, and the affirmation of the ideal values of Italy could easily be made to start with Vittorio Veneto. Hence it is significant that after Gentile, on completing his reform, retired from the Ministry (Lombardo-Radice had already retired because of his opposition to the tendency to mix education and politics), the schools have become increasingly Fascist. The direction of physical education was placed under the control of the *Opera Balilla*, a Fascist organization, incorporated under the National Ministry of Education in 1929. In 1928, in a discussion with the Minister Public Instruction, Mussolini declared that his policy called for a new code of elementary education to educate the younger generation in the new atmosphere created by Fascism and to arouse in it a clear consciousness of (*a*) what the Italian people has been and hopes to become in history; (*b*) her contribution through discoveries and inventions to the knowledge, art, and civilization of the world; (*c*) the beauty and wealth of the Italian soil; and (*d*) the contributions made by Italians scattered over the world to the productive activity of diverse nations.

The aim must be the "Fascistization of all schools not only in their courses of study but in their personned." In an earlier address Mussolini had made the following statement:

> The Government demands that the school shall derive its inspiration from Fascism; it demands that school shall not be, I do not say, hostile but not even aloof from Fascism, or agnostic in the face of Fascism; it demands that every school in every grade and in all its instruction train Italian youth to understand Fascism, to ennoble itself through Fascism, and in the historical atmosphere created by the Fascist Revolution. (*Discorso all'Augusteo*).

Although teachers are not required to take an oath of allegiance to Fascism as are university professors, they do take an oath of allegiance to the Government. Early weeding at of anti-Fascist teachers and the presence in all schools of teachers who are members of the Fascist Party have had the same effect as direct compulsion. In the classrooms the portraits of the King and the Duce and the Crucifix on the walls, the presence of black-shirt teachers, who are members of the Party, and pupils in the uniform of the *Balilla*, and the Fascist salute[55] are ever-present reminders of the Fascist ideal of "work, discipline, and harmony." The control of textbooks and the publication of a series by the Government contribute to the same ends—the political direction of the schools. One of the strongest factors, however, has been the incorporation of the *Opera Balilla* in the Ministry of National Education, its control of physical education, and the influence which it exercises through its members, boys and girls, who are in the schools.

THE ORGANIZATION OF ELEMENTARY EDUCATION

The System of Schools

The system of elementary education, which is free, includes the preparatory stage (*grado preparatorio*) given in pre-schools (*asili d'infanzia, asili infantili, giardini d'infanzia, scuole materne*)[56] for pupils from the age of three of six, the lower stage (*grado inferiore*) of three grades, and the higher stage (*grado superiore*). Until 1930 these stages were supplemented by a prevocational course of two or three years, known as the *corso integrativo di avviamento professionale.* The Royal Decree-Law of October 6 No. 1379, transferred this course to the lower secondary level as a *Scuola secundaria di avviamento al lavoro,*[57] thus abolishing the distinction, which is still found in France (*école primaire superieure*), in Germany (*Mittelschule*), and in England (senior schools, central schools), between intermediate or higher elementary and secondary education.

Compulsory Attendance

Compulsory attendance begins at the age of six and continues up to the age of fourteen. The length of the school year is ten months; pupil who for economic reasons cannot attend school for the school year must have the same number of lesson periods as are required for the whole year. Schools are open every day in the week except on Thursday and Sunday. Pupils must attend the type of elementary school provided in their locality—that is, graded, unguarded, or aided school[58]—and must remain in such school until the completion of their fourteenth year unless there are available in the neighbourhood other courses and institutions of an educational and cultural nature. Responsibility for the school attendance of children of school age is placed upon parents, guardians, and employers, and, in the case of orphan children, on the directors of institutions or private individuals to whose care they are assigned. Parents and guardians who undertake to provide for the education of their children or wards in their own may must prove their technical and financial ability to do so. Private schools may be opened and maintained by persons who have the same qualifications as teachers in public schools. Pupils who are educated privately at home or in schools must be submitted to the regular examinations conducted for public school pupils. Blind and deaf-mute children, who are not abnormal in other ways, are also compelled to attend school, deafmutes up to the age of sixteen; for such pupils special schools, public or private, having, if they wish, infant sections, are recognized as schools to which state aid may be given and in which the principals and staff must have special preparation; the same requirements of examinations are set up for these defective as for normal children.

A list of children who reach the age of compulsory attendance is prepared each year by the mayor (*podesta*) of each locality and submitted to the government inspector. The names of such pupils who are not in attendance at the annual opening of the schools is posted on official notice-boards and, if a satisfactory explanation of their absence is not given by those responsible for their attendance, proceedings may be begun against them. The penalty which may be imposed rises from a fine of two lire, increasing for repeated non-observance of the law of fifty lire; these amounts are doubled in case of employers who knowingly employ children of school age. A similar procedure is followed against parents and others for unjustifiable absences of the children for whose education they are responsible.

Pre-school Education

All pre-schools for children between the ages of three and six are recognized legally as the preparatory stage of elementary education. Attendance is not compulsory nor is the establishment of such institutions compulsory. The *asilo d'infanzia* is an old established institution in Italy; the first *asilo* was opened in Cremona in 1827 by Ferrante Aporti (1781-1858), a priest, philanthropist, and educator, whose activities, inspired by Pestalozzi and Pere Girard, on behalf of young children and whose educational writings set a stamp on the pre-school which survived even after the introduction into Italy of the Froebelian methods. Another influence on the development of the *asilo* was that of the sisters Rosa and Carolina Agazzi, who, in 1894, reorganized an old *asilo* at Mompiano in Brescia and were supported in their work and theories by Professor Pietro Pasquali. Their contribution lay in the utilization of a real environment for the enrichment of the lives of young children. Here they developed their own equipment, devised special methods for teaching singing, emphasized instruction in the mother-tongue and training of the senses, and through play and natural activities promoted the mental, moral, and physical advancement of the pupils; a sense of responsibility was cultivated in the older pupils, who were required to take care of the younger. The Agazzi system, which attracted attention at the Educational Congress held at Turin in 1898, was adopted by the city of Trieste in 1910. In 1915 it was pronounced as a model for pre-schools by the Minister of Public Instruction, and after the War was adopted for the *asili* established by the *Opera Nazionale di Assistenza per l'Italia redenta* (National Association to Assist Liberated Italy). A third direction from an Italian educator has been given to pre-school education by Madame Maria Montessori, who in 1907 established the first *Casa dei bambini* and there developed her theory of auto-education and the use of didactic materials. It is difficult to gauge the influence of Montessori in her own country; by those educators who have been influenced by the new philosophy of education her system is criticized as narrow rigid, formal, and mechanical on the one hand, and as lacking in social purposes and vitality on the other.

The provision of pre-schools for children between three and six has increased rapidly. This increase has been due both to the interest of the Government and the activity of the *Opera Nazionale per l'Assistensa e la Protezione della Maternita e dell'Infanzia* (National Association for the Assistance and Protection of Maternity and Infancy) which has sponsored child care, nursery schools and *creches*, as well as the pre-schools of the type of the *asilo*. From 4587 *asili* in 1915 the number rose to 5902 with over 400,000 children in 1922, to 7076 in 1926-27 with an enrolment of 607,891 children, and to 9546 with 749,876 children in 1929-30. In the last year, 1043 provided free meals to all children in attendance, 2431 free only to the poor, and 912 made a charge for them. Distributed according to methods employed, 422 used those of Montessori, 1283 those of Aporti, 1458 those of Foebel, and in 6383 the methods were mixed. The schools in 1929-30 were in charge of 5903 directresses, 10,851 teachers and 4061 assistants.

Teachers in the preparatory stage must have special qualifications and hold a certificate of capacity of teach in this stage. They may be trained in six government schools of methods (*scuole di metodo per l'educazione materna*) which offer three-year courses, or in summer and other special courses, or in other institutions which provide the necessary preparation. Since 1926 the Ministry has been authorized to sanction and aid recognized associations in conducting experiments to differentiate the methods of instruction in the preparatory and elementary stages and to train teachers.

As defined by the regulations, "the preparatory stage is recreational in character and aims to train the first manifestations of intellect and character to the pupils." Besides simple prayers the curriculum includes singing of simple nursery and patriotic songs and music, free gymnastics and rhythmic games and exercises, simple exercises in manipulation, plastic and manual work, gardening and care of domestic animals, elementary general information and correction of popular prejudices and superstitions, and reading, recitation, and dramatization. The time-schedule, divided into thirty-five brief periods per week is as follows:

Subjects:	
Religion	1
Singing, free drawing, calligraphy, recitation	4
Elementary information and recreative intellectual occupations	6
Gardening, manual activities, domestic activities, physical activities and games, meals and hygienic care	24
	35

The absence of formalism, the opportunities for experimentation, and the interest of the committees of patronage (*patronati scolastici*) have placed the *scuole materne* among the most attractive institutions in Italian education. It is in these schools that Lombardo-Radice's insistence on the cultivation of the spirit of childhood, joy in life, and joy in play is best illustrated. At present, however, only about one-fourth of the children between the ages are provided for in preschools.

Elementary Schools

Elementary education until 1930 include the lower stage of three years (*corso inferiore*), the upper stage of two years (*corso superiore*), and the prevocational stage (*corso integrativo*) of two or three years. In 1930 the last stage, as already stated, was transformed with the *scuola complementare* into the *scuola di avviamento al lavoro* and transferred to the secondary level. The first two stages are given in the graded schools (*scuole classificate*); the *scuole non classificate*, or ungraded schools, are found mainly in rural areas and offer, as a rule, only the lower stage. The maximum size of a class according to the regulations is sixty; if this number is exceeded for a period of two years, an additional teacher must be appointed or the class divided and taught in alternate sessions.

The work of elementary schools is governed by the Royal Decree of October 1, 1923, No. 2185, incorporated in the *Testo Unico* (1928), the regulations on the time-schedule, courses of study, methods of instruction for elementary schools (*Ordinamento*, November 11, 1923), and the regulations on the courses of study in the mixed elementary rural schools (*Ordinamento*, January 21, 1924). The curricula are defined in general terms in the Code; that of the lower stage includes the following subjects:

1. Prayers and fundamental ideas of Christianity,—short and clear sentences and stories of immediate bearing taken from the Scriptures and especially from the Gospels; stories from sacred history; illustrations of the Pater Noster.
2. Reading and writing.

3. Elementary arithmetic and the metric system.
4. Oral exercises in translation from dialect; easy exercises in written composition; recitation of national hymns and poetry.
5. General information with special provision for direct experiences in agricultural and industrial work; knowledge of works of art, records, and monuments.
6. Elementary geography.
7. In schools which do not have a higher stage, the history of the Risorgimento up to the present.

The curriculum of the upper stage continues to develop the work begun in the lower and includes:

1. Readings on Catholic morals and dogma based on the Ten Commandments and the parables in the Gospel; principles of religious life and worship; Sacraments and rites according to the Catholic creed and practices.
2. Reading of books useful as guides in the problems of home and society.
3. History and geography, particularly of Italy; elementary notions and reading about the structure—geographical, administrative, agricultural, industrial, commercial, banking, and employment conditions—of those countries to which the immigration of the locality is directed.
4. Elementary study and reading of the political organization, administration of justice, the duties and rights as man and citizen; elements of economics.
5. Elementary arithmetic and geometry.
6. Elementary science; formation of collections of specimens obtained on school journeys; hygiene.
7. Applied design.
8. Physical education.

The prevocational course (*corso integrativo*), which is retained pending the reorganization introduced in 1930, continues the general studies, and adds applied design, plastic work, elements of mechanical work, elementary knowledge of electrical appliances for the home, theory and practice of agriculture, fundaments of some manual trade, elements and practice of seafaring, cooking, and domestic arts, repairs, bookkeeping and any other course approved by the *provveditore* (superintendent).

The courses of study and time-schedules issued on November 11, 1923, were published, not as prescribed requirements, but as suggestions (*indicativo*), leaving to the teachers the task of drawing up the courses for their own schools and classes.

The courses of study are intended to be suggestive only. They suggest to the teacher the result which the State expects from his work in each school year, leaving him free to use appropriate methods to attaint it. For a number of reasons these are always diverse and variable according to the real situation in which the teacher finds himself in a given school environment, and according to the personal culture of the teacher and the special stamp which he will have succeeded in the course of a watchful experience in giving to his own spirit as an educator.

This freedom imposed upon the teachers the responsibility "of constantly renewing their own culture, not with the aid of petty manuals in which are collected the crumbs of knowledge, but at the living fountains of the true culture of the people." And so too with reference to the methods of instruction:

Each teacher must discover the methods of instruction, as a living norm, in himself aided by the study of those authors who have mediatated on education, or have given accounts of their spiritual experiences, or have developed suggestive activities through the children, in whom the norms, though not expressed, are at all times implicit. Above all, the teacher will perfect his own instructional activity, living with warm enthusiasm the life of his people, listening insatiably to the voices of the Great, already studied in the years of professional preparation, and looking for new guides for his thinking in good books not previously read. In this way he will succeed in realizing his process and will bring into the school the vibrant echo of his study.

The three important features which the reform has sought to emphasize are religious instruction, aesthetic training, and self-expression and self-activity of the pupils. According to the Code, "instruction in the Christian doctrine according to the form handed down in Catholic tradition is the foundation and crown of elementary education in all its stages." Gentile's emphasis on religious instruction as the search of the spirit for the eternal, the beginnings in the elementary stage of philosophy, has been explained earlier. Neither he nor his associates intended to emphsize dogmatic teaching: this was brought about later as a result of the Concordat with the Vatican in 1929. Teachers are not required to give religious instruction unless they can do so with a clear conscience. In any case, those who do give it must be approved by the ecclesiastical authorities, whose approval is also required for the textbooks which are used.

Esthetic education is not limited to art instruction, but must inspire every lesson. From the point of view of the philosophy of Gentile and of Lombardo-Radice, it means the slow groping for perfection through self-expression. It dominates in particular the work in language and literature, in singing and music, in play, and, of course, in art. Perhaps the most characteristic feature in all Italian elementary schools today is the illustrated diary which pupils above the first class are required to keep, and the illustrated monthly and annual composition. The suggestions for diaries of pupils in the third year (ages 8-9) include the following topics. Descriptions of all events in the life of the school with free comments, such as notes of lessons, excuses for absence, praise and reproval received, difficulties overcome, records of stories told by the teacher, descriptions of games, interesting facts about the school, notable events and celebrations. In the higher classes this content is supplemented with accounts of books read. The diaries must be illustrated. One form of diary which is widespread is the *Calendario alla Montesca*, or daily illustrated records of observations of nature (weather, plants flowers, farming, etc.) which was first elaborated in the schools of *La Montesca* and *Rovigliano* in Città di Castello (Umbria), established for the children of farmers on the estates of Alice and Leopold Franchetti in 1901. The *Calendario*, because it is more systematic, provides for a closer relation to life than the diary which is left to the spontaneity of the pupils and which too frequently becomes formal and inept through repetition and uncritical in selection. The *Calendario*, without encroaching on the free expression of the pupils, has the advantage of defining the scope of their observation and activity.

Instruction in singing progresses from simple nursery and folk and patriotic songs to the study of music, intonation, proper use of the voice and expression, and choral singing. Art work is closely associated with all other subjects with a strong emphasis on free expression in line and colour; in the last three classes the study of artistic masterpieces is introduced. The same principle is followed in the teaching of language and literature; while grammar and the study of words are not neglected, the free expression of the pupils is encouraged in oral and written practice; in the selection of reading, teachers are urged to introduce the pupils to the "voices of the Great," to the masterpieces of literature, "for the greatest authors are always the most simple" and bring the reader into harmony with the spirit of humanity; but his does not mean that the literary expression of the people, their folklore and dialect, should be ignored. As was pointed out, every school is required to have a library maintained by the contributions of the pupils, the communes, and other associations. History and geography are limited in the main to the study of Italy and the region in which the school is located: in the fifth year the course in history includes the study of the great heroes of Italian history—painters, sculptors, architects, scientific discoverers, the Italian army and navy, the World War, the development of public services in Italy, the condition of labour, and the national resources as compared with other countries.

Two other courses leave room for a variety of activities and the introduction of the elementary sciences—there are *nozioni varie* (general information) and *occupazioni intellettuali recreativi* (recreational intellectual activities). The former give a large place to hygiene and relations to parents, to the school, to fellow-pupils, and much of the information included under the term "social studies" in American schools. In the fifth class the *nozioni varie* are divided into *scienze fisiche e naturali e nozioni organichi di igiene* (physical and natural science and organic notions of hygiene) and *nozioni di diritto e di economica* (elements of government and economics). The first of these courses is intensely concrete and practical, including in hygiene simple descriptions of the anatomy and physiology of the human body and lessons on health, with visits to laundries, bakeries, factories, hospitals hygiene laboratory, and athletic clubs. The course in physical and natural sciences is more concerned with giving the pupils some notion of their place in modern society—the mineral resources of the country, hydro-electric power, climate and thermal stations, application of chemistry to industry, and botany and agricultural development.

Recreative intellectual activities aim to train the pupils in the art of play and healthy leisure occupations—indoor games, charades, niddles, story-telling, folklore and traditions in dialect. Every subject of the curriculum—geography, history arithmetic, manual activities—is drawn upon and their recreational uses are indicated. The development of school journeys and of regional studies contribute to the same end and help to keep the work of the schools in close touch with realities.

Educational Experiments

Not only are freedom of adaptation and activity of the pupils emphasized in all the regulations, but schools may obtain special permission to undertake experiments. By the Royal Decree-Law of February, 1926, No. 206, the Minister of Education may authorize associations, which are in his judgment competent for the task, to organize semi-annual or annual courses to experiment with different methods in elementary education. Such courses may be granted state subsidies. Teachers who wish to take such courses must already hold the official certificates of capacity to teach and must also have had a number of years of experience. Those who receive the diplomas granted at the end of such courses may receive appointments in experimental schools. Many such schools have been officially recognized and conduct their experiments under the supervision of inspectors. Educational experimentation is not new in Italy; that of the Sisters Agazzi has already been mentioned, while Montessori's work is known all over the world. The schools of *La Montesca* and *Rovigliano* in Città di Castello, established in 1901 by Alice and Leopold Franchetti for the children of agricultural labourers, developed an interesting programme especially adapted to children living in a rural environment. *La Scuola Rinnovata* or *La Rinnova* (known also as *Ghisolfa,* from the district in Milan where the school is located) was established by Madame Giuseppina Pizzigoni in 1911, as a public experimental school built upon the activities and experiences of the pupils, emphasizing work in the open, manual occupations, play and games; the school carries the pupils from the preparatory stage up to the close of the compulsory attendance period and in the last years provides prevocational training in well-equipped shops. Madame Pizzigoni succeeded in developing a real school colony with spacious buildings, extensive playgrounds, and a swimming-pool; besides providing a hygienic environment and supplying meals to the pupils, Madame Pizzigoni added an adequate system of medical inspection. The various cultural associations and other private organizations have been responsible for experimentation in rural schools. Open-air schools, the earliest of which was the Trotter School in Milan, have been increased in numbers not only for physically defective children but for all[59].

The spirit of experimentation and innovation is undoubtedly in the air in the Italian elementary schools, inspired not only by the new tendencies in educational theory, which in a sense Italy shares with other countries, but also by a realization of the new task imposed upon the school by the Fascist Revolution. Educational experimentation requires, however, teachers who are better prepared than those whose task is prescribed by government regulations. Despite the emphasis on the new spirit in education, on freedom for the pupils, the discipline still remains formal and mechanical; except in the preparatory stage, there is not that freedom of movement which is expected in the new schools. There is in fact a real conflict between the new theory and the Fascist emphasis on discipline. The teacher brought up under one tradition changes to the new with some difficulty, with the result that even the "free" diary and composition become stilted, formal, and mechanical.

Textbooks

The Italian teacher's freedom is still restricted in two directions. He has no voice in selecting textbooks and state examinations have been retained. No textbook may be used which has not been approved by the Ministry of Education and included in its official list. All publishers and authors are required to submit five copies of each book for examination by special commissioners; the fee for such examination is 120 lire. The critical reports on books which are approved are published; unfavourable reports are transmitted on request to the publishers and authors concerned. The influence of this system was particularly noticeable in the new and revised editions of the history textbooks which were published about 1928; all contained additional chapters written in almost identical form on the part played by Italy in the World War, her victories, the Fascist Revolution, and the work of *Il Duce*. In other words, textbook-writing is governed by the suggested course of study issued by the Ministry. In 1927 the Government undertook to publish its own series of elementary school textbooks, on the plea that in this way the cost of books could be kept down at a time of economic stringency. At the opening of the twenty-eighth session of Parliament the King pronounced the *libro del Stato* as the "indispensable instrument for the revival of culture and national education." The pupils purchase their own textbooks, poor pupils receiving assistance from the *cassa scolastica* and the *patronato scolastico*. The fact that uniformity of textbooks militates against the development of freedom of instruction does not seem to have been raised. Copies of approved textbooks must be deposited in the office of the *provveditore*.

Examinations

During the five years of the elementary course (*Crso inferiore* and *corso superiore*) pupils are promoted to the second, third, and fifth class on the basis of their records (*scrutinio*), and tests conducted by the teachers in the last week of the school year; promotion to the fourth—that is, from the lower to the upper stage—is based on an examination conducted by a committee consisting of the supervisor (*direttore didattico*) or a delegate appointed by him, the class teacher, and another teacher specially selected for the purpose. Pupils who on their records or in the examinations are deficient in more than two subjects may take another examination at the beginning of the following school year and be promoted if they pass. Pupils who are educated at home or in private schools are required to submit to examinations, also conducted by special committees, for the certificates of elementary education, which consist of (1) certificate of promotion or admission to the different classes; (2) certificate of the lower grade on completing the third year; and (3) certificate of elementary studies (*certificato di compimento*) at the end of the fifth year. Where the *corsi integrativi* (sixth to eighth year) are provided, pupils are promoted to the sixth year by examination, and on the successful completion of the course, receive a certificate indicating that they have complicated the period of compulsory attendance required by the law; this certificate (*certificato di adempimento dell' obbligo scolastico*) serves as a labour permit (*di speciale ideonità al lavoro*). Pupils who reach the age of fourteen without having completed the whole course may receive on request a certificate indicating the stage that they have reached. Every pupil, whether in public or private schools, is required to provide himself annually with a record book (*pagella scolastica*) in which are recorded his attendance, promotions, and success in examinations. In the *scrutinio* and in the examinations, pupils are given one of four marks; unsatisfactory, satisfactory, good, praiseworthy (*insufficiente, sufficiente, buono, lodevole*), and are passed on the last three marks only.

Time-Schedule

The time-distribution of subjects in the elementary school suggested in the regulations is as follows:

	I	*II*	*III*	*IV*	*V*	*Prevocational*
Religion	1½	1½	2	2	2	2
Singing, free drawing, calligraphy, recitation	2½	2½	4	5	5	3
Reading, writing, and language	7	6	5	5	4	3
Spelling	...	2	2	...	...	...
Arithmetic, geometrical design, bookkeeping	4	4	4	3	3	2
General information, and recreational activities	4	4	4	1	1	1
Gardening, manual work, household arts, physical training and play, meals, and hygiene care	6	5	4	4	4	...
Physical and natural sciences, hygiene	...	...	...	2	2	3
History and geography	...	...	...	3	3	2
Elementary government and economics	...	...	...		1	1
Vocational work	...	...	...	...	...	8
Total	25	25	25	25	25	25

Physical Education

It will be noticed that physical training and play are not given a separate place in the time-schedule. The promotion of physical education, which is strongly stressed by the Fascist authorities, was at first placed under the supervision of a special association (*Ente Nazionale di Educazione Fisica*); by a decree issued in 1927 its organization and administration were placed under the care of the *Opera Nazionale Balilla,* which in turn became an official branch of the Ministry of National Education in 1929. Under the regulations issued by the *Opera Balilla* four periods of half an hour each were assigned to physical exercises in the third, fourth, and fifth years, and two periods a week of an hour each in the sixth, seventh, and eighth years and in secondary schools. The organization and supervision of physical training were placed in the hands of the provincial and communal committees acting through a director and office of physical education and sports, which draw up courses and train elementary school teachers for this branch of the school work. In addition, special teachers of physical education and sports are trained in a three-year course in the *Scuola Superiore Fascista* in Rome. In addition to direct physical training, the directors are required to see that facilities for sports and athletics are made accessible in every locality, that school excursions and exercises in the open are arranged, and that pupils are entered for athletic and gymnastics competitions and exhibitions.

Opera Balilla

It is through the far-reaching work of the *Opera Nazionale Balilla* perhaps more than through direct instruction in the classroom that the synthesis between education and nationalism as defined by the Fascist authorities is accomplished. For besides being the recruiting and training organization for the Fascist party, the *Opera Balilla* through its members and through the great variety of its activities, in and out of school, exercises a determining influence on the patriotic and national development of youth. Open to boys from the age of eight to the age of eighteen, the *Opera Balilla* recruits the majority of its members from pupils in the elementary schools. Thus in 1930 there were 981,947 boys between the ages of eight and fourteen in the junior branch technically known as *Balilla* and 371,529 youths between fourteen and eighteen in the senior branch, *Avanguardisti*. The section for girls had in the junior branch, *Piccole Italiane*, girls from six to twelve, had 670,183 members and 98,000 girls in the senior branch (*Giovani Italiane*). From the point of view of national education, the *Opera Balilla*, with its symbolism, its uniform, its military organization and discipline, its provision of the many-sided opportunities for outdoor life, and its emphasis on religious devotion moral character, and duty, is a powerful instrument for national unity, which in many respects, transcends the influence of the schools. On the surface, the organized and disciplined activities of the *Opera Balilla* seem to be diametrically opposed to the philosophy with which Gentile sought to inspire Italian education. Actually, the contradiction is only superficial and the difference is one of methods. What Gentile and his collaborators hoped to secure by free activity and expression—the reconciliation of the spirit of the individual with the spirit of the absolute, for practical purposes the State, and of his will with the will of others, defined in Italy by the Fascist Party—the *Opera Balilla* as the active agent of the Party secures by direct action, training, indoctrination, and discipline. Gentile directed his attention to the process, *Opera Balilla* to the result, and with both man becomes free is so far as he recognizes the authority of the State.

Conclusion

The significance of the Italian reform in education lies in the congruence of the two directions upon which it is based—the philosophical and the political or national—which give education a unity which it never enjoyed before 1923. Despite the control of a strong political ideal, the Italian system illustrates how much scope can still be left for free experimentation and differentiation. One may disagree with the critical attitude of contemporary Italion leaders on what are regarded as the essential of professional preparation—time will indicate the modifications which must be introduced—but the reform has already shown what a body of teachers, inspired by a potent ideal, can accomplish. As contrasted with those countries in which scientific experimentation in education is regarded as holding the key to progress, Italian education stands out because of its emphasis on the educand as a whole personality or a spirit in process of development and growth rather than as a bundle of nervous connections to be trained; against the analytical method which claims to experiment without a clear concept of a goal defined by the environment in which it serves, Italian education is a constant protest. By a curious paradox, the process of education is defined in terms which are almost similar by the idealists in Italy and the pragmatists in the United States; they part company, however, when the pragmatist refuses to define the ends of individual growth and the idealist find them in the Fascist State.

5. RUSSIA

Theory of Soviet Education

The educational reform of the Soviet Revolution represents a blend of revolutionary educational theories which had already been current in Russia for at least half a century earlier, of the new educational philosophy of freedom and activity, and of the control of education in the interests of the new social order. Many of the ideas which have been put into practice or incorporated into theory since the Revolution had been enunciated by the leading Russian educational theorists of the nineteenth century: V.V. Belinsky and N.I. Pirogov, with their emphasis on educating the individual as a man; K.D. Ushinsky, who insisted on the importance of national culture as the basis of instruction, suggested the outlines of the "complex" method, and laid the foundations of a science of education; Leo N. Tolstoy, who preached the doctrine of absolute freedom in education;

and S.N. Kuvenko and P.A. Kropotkin, who placed labour in the centre of the educative process. In 1905, S.T. Shatsky inaugurated an experimental school in Moscow based on his observations in the United States, and six years later, having moved the school to the country, he reorganized it on the basis of domestic and agricultural activities, close relationship to economic life, and self-activity and responsibility. The control of education by the State and by the Orthodox Church prevented any extensive application of the new education in the schools. Something else, however, was lacking—a social order in which the new education would have real meaning.

This meaning was provided by the Revolution and the principles upon which it was based. Its permanent success depended upon a close articulation between the schools, the new order, and the Communist ideology. In the first place, all education must be politicized; in the words of Lenin, "Our task in the school world is to overthrow the bourgeoisie, and we declare openly that the school, apart from life, apart from politics, is a lie and Phypocrisy." For educational purposes this principle was elaborated by the educational leaders of the Revolution, Lunacharsky, Pokrovski, Pinkevitch, Shatsky, and Krupskaya, and in a measure by others, such as Blonsky and Kalashnikov, who were not so clearly identified with Communism. Education can only have meaning, is the central contention of this group, in so far as it is identified with the social environment in which it functions and to which it contributes. The dominant interests of the Revolution are those of the workers, soldiers, and peasants. The function of the school is to prepare the future builders of socialist society and champions of the ideals of the proletariat, and this function can only be carried out successfully to the extent that the educative process is directly oriented toward labour, nature, and society, which provide the content of instruction. Only through looking at these three elements as a complex can the unity of education be preserved, a principle which is synthesized in Marx's definition of education:

By education we mean three things: first, mental education; second, physical training as given in schools by means of gymnastics and military training, and third, technical education which introduces the prospective worker to the general principles of the processes of production and at the same time gives to children practical information regarding the use of various working tools.[60]

Only through labour, nature, and society can the school give reality to education and direct in to the ultimate aim, the acceptance of the ideology of the new order, which rests upon productive activity and collectivism of the proletarita. Hence the school is definitely an instrument of indoctrination, a vehicle for inculcating the principles of Communism. To the extent that this principle is accepted can freedom in working out the aim of education be tolerated and the development of the individual through his own activities and participation be permitted. The aim of education is thus defined, not in terms of an abstract philosophy, but in accordance with the paramount claims of the social order.

The major aim of general instruction [says Pinkevitch] is the development of an outlook upon the world. This involves the introduction of the individual to an understanding and evaluation of the entire culture heritage of the present time. Our socialistic understanding and Marxian evaluation will of course differ fundamentally from those of the bourgeoisie. We must educate warriors for socialism who clearly understand the problems of their class and are able to evaluate independently all of the most important expression of the contemporary culture. This does not mean that we make no allowances for the needs of individual development. We dreams of a man fully equipped with all the knowledge of the present day and to whom all that is truly beautiful is near; we dream of an active, strong man, struggling through the revolutionary classes of contemporary society for a realization of ideals which throughout the world will bring peace and happiness to all mankind. Such a conception of the aim of general instruction in no way contradicts the aim of professional instruction...A man must have an allround education and at the same time know well some particular specialty.

The ideal Communist citizen, which it is the task of education to mould, is thus described by Professor Thomas Woody:

The new citizen believes in, and can justify by Marxian dialectic, the *dictatorship* of the Communist Party, or as is generally said, the dictatorship of the Proletariat. He is *militant* in his defense and advocacy of it. He must be an *activist*. Though it seems a paradox at first glance, he is to be class-conscious; yet he is to become, at the same time, a *classless* mind. He believes in *universal labour*, holds the labourer in his regard, and the exploiter in greatest contempt. His mind must be secular (dominated by science) and atheistic, *political, collectivistic, and non-nationalistic,* and positively *international*. He must be healthy in the physical sense, a sound mind in a sound body. It is to be a sexless mind, i.e., reorganizing no preferences based on sex. He who possesses these is the new man.

Here are enunciated clear, definite, and unmistakable aims and ideals to be attained, by comparison with which the aims of education as usually stated, "development of character," "training of personality," "training of citizens," "imparting of culture," and even the innumerable objectives which are set up by American education without relation to a dominant aim, pale into insignificance as vague and intangible.

Soviet education sets up a definite pattern according to which the individual is to be moulded, and because the school is constantly kept in close touch with its environment and is constantly under the supervision of the official and unofficial control of the constituted authorities and of members of the Party. From this pattern are derived all the ends—cultural, spiritual, intellectual, moral, and physical—of education, and in turn unity of purpose is derived from it. Religious training has, of course, been banned with religion and the schools are dominated by another form of orthodoxy—the politico-economic. Moral and ethical training based on religious and absolutist concepts has been discarded as bourgeois practice, and its place has been taken by "proletarian class norms in the way in which we see them in the concrete historic environment of today" (Pinkevitch).

The whole of education is dominated by dialectic materialism, the concept that the history of mankind can only be explained in terms of its economic development and changes in the methods of production and exchange. An existing society cannot be changed through the school, but the school must reflect society as it is and be intimately related to contemporary life, which in the new social order derives its significance only in the light of the collective activity and production of the proletariat.

From the point of view of a science of education, to which Russian educators have made extensive contributions through the centres for scientific research in Moscow and Leningrad, corroboration is furnished in the emphasis which is placed upon nurture or environment as a potent educative force. Education thus becomes the process of "conditioning" the pupil. And this the Soviet school has undertaken to achieve by surrounding him with an environment, material and intellectual, to which he can respond only in one way. The strength of Soviet education lies in the absence of a break in gauge, in a consistency of methods and ends, which was only partially achieved in the Jesuit and in the pre-War Prussian systems.

ORGANIZATION OF ELEMENTARY EDUCATION

Pre-schools

Since education is regarded as one of the strongest influences in the development and perpetuation of the new social order, it should begin at as early a stage as possible. Infancy and childhood are the most important periods in the life of the individual. Unable to carry out one of the fundamental ideas of Communism, the training and education of children from their earliest infancy in state institutions, the new order has sought to achieve the same end as nearly as possible by establishing institutions—*creches*, children's homes, nurseries—in which infants can be left during the day. Such institutions serve two ends—the early physical and social training of children and the emancipation of women of the working classes to take their place side by side with men. Here the infants are provided with a healthy environment, are fed, are surrounded with didactic materials, acquire their first social training through their playmates, and begin to engage in socially useful labour in so far as they can help to keep the school clean, to look after themselves, and develop certain habits of responsibility.

In the kindergartens, which follow the infant stage, the children begin to participate actively in building to their own lives through socially useful labour and the establishment of close associations between the school and contemporary life. At this stage, the formal education influences begin through labour, nature, and society. The pupils engage in activities which are imitative of the work of adults, are trained in collectivistic habits, and develop their powers through creative pursuits. Fairly tales have been banned as relics of bourgeois class conflict and folk stories as survivals of superstitions, and their place has been taken by an extensive children's literature closer to the realities and the materialism of the day. Even toys have been transformed into miniature reproductions of tools and instruments used by adults. The curriculum includes nature study, talks, and stories which give the pupils concrete understanding of the life about them, reading, writing, arithmetic, play, music, and art.

Before the close of the pre-school period, at about the age of eight, children become eligible for membership in *Oktiabrata* (Octobrists), the organization which represents the first stage in the training of future members of the Communist Party and which links the young child with the organizations for his older brothers and sisters, the Pioneers and the Komsomols (League of Communist Youth). But membership in the Octobrists means more than this; it means, so far as the intelligence of the children permits, the recognition of consecration to a cause and active work in the school and out of it in its interests. The task set before the Octobrists by Lenin was as follows: "First, and most important, constantly help the workers and peasants in their struggle; second, study; third, and last, make strong your own organization."

Elementary Education

Compulsory education, where schools are available, begins at the age of eight and continues up to the age of twelve. Elementary education is given the first four years of the unified labour school of seven or nine years, which, it is hoped, will in time be attended by all children between the ages of eight and seventeen. The unified labour school is free, secular, and co-educational, and it is required by law to be open 190 days in the country areas and 205 days in the cities for form four- to six-hour periods a day; in 1928 the average number of days on which schools were open in twelve countries was 155.5 days in the rural districts and 180 days in the cities.

From what has preceded, the aim of the elementary school is clear; it is to give instruction in knowledge and habits and education in the broadest meaning of the term—sense training, development of native abilities, intelligence and will, the cultivation of an outlook on the world definitely based on class consciousness. Knowledge and information are, however, not the main ends but incidental outcomes from the study of labour, nature, and society directed to the social revolution. At the centre of all activities stands socially useful labour, both in and out of school, which gives the Soviet school its polytechnical nature, thus defined by Krupskaya:

This does not mean a school in which one studies several trades, but rather a school where children learn to understand the essence of the labouring processes, the substance of labour activity of the people, and the conditions of success in work. It is a school where children learn to know the extent of their powers.[61]

The programme of the labour school was indicated in 1918, worked out by the State Scientific Council in the Commissariat of Education, and issued in 1923. The method of organization of the course of study is that known as the complex (*Gesamtunterricht* in Germany, integrated instruction in the United States), but differing from the German and American practices in being directly related to those major phases of human life—nature, labour, and society. In other words, instead of organizing the curriculum in the traditional fashion, by subjects, the course of study is developed round central themes related to the phases indicated. The general outline of the curriculum is indicated in the following scheme:[62]

Grade	*Nature*	*Labour*	*Society*
1	Seasons.	Immediately surrounding labour life of both village and city family.	Family and school.
2.	Air, water, soil. Nature and care of cultivated plants and animals which surround man.	Labour life of village or city block in which child lives.	Social institutions of village and city.
3.	Elementary observations (information) in physics and chemistry, nature of local region; life of human body.	Economics of local region.	Provincial social institutions. Picture of past of one's own country.
4.	Geography of Russia and other countries. Life of human body.	State economy of Russian Republic and other countries.	Organization of State in Russia and other countries. Pictures of past of humanity.

The curriculum is centred around the three major themes, which, when divided into a large number of themes and topics, become the course of study, as illustrated in the following analysis:[63]

Country School	*Town School*
First Year	
1. The first steps in school.	1. The first steps in school.
2. Family work in autumn.	2. The protection of health.
3. The protection of health. Participation in the celebration of the Anniversary of the October Revolution.	3. Life and labour of a family in the autumn.
4. Preparation for the winter and winter work. Participation in the celebration of Lenin's Day.	4. Preparation for the winter, and life and labour in the winter.
5. Life and labour in the winter.	5. The coming of spring, and spring work.
6. The approach of spring and preparation for spring work. Participation in the May Day celebration.	
7. Spring work. Participation of the children in spring work.	
8. Participation in the examination. Exhibition of the school.	
Second Year	
1. Children's life and labour in the summer, and the beginning of autumn work in the school.	1. Children's life and labour in the summer.
2. Autumn work in the village. Participation in the celebration of the October Revolution.	2. The town in the autumn.
3. The protection of health in the family and in the village.	3. The protection of health in the family and in the town.

Contd. . .

Second Year (Contd. . .)	
4. Village life and labour in the winter.	4. Life and labour in towns.
5. The beginning of spring work and preparation for spring work. Participation in the May Day festivity.	5. Spring, and spring work.
6. Spring work in villages. Account of work done during the school years and plans for the summer.	
Third Year	
1. *The village:* Harvest and agricultural produce; the village and environs; local trades, village life and village organizations.	1. *The town:* The town and its environs. The labour of the town; commerce and cultural life of the town.
2. *Town and village:* Factories and works, city life. The cultural life in town and village.	2. *The village:* Cultivation of fields manure, seasons, of fruit, sowing.
3. *Spring in the village and the work of the peasant:* Tilling land; rivers and lakes in the spring; the meadows; beehives. Participation of the school in the May Day festivity. Account of the work done during the year.	3. *The work of the group during spring and summer:* Work on the piece of land belonging to the school. Rivers and lakes; the woods in the spring; the meadows.

Fourth Year

1. The Union of Soviet Republics. The earth as a sphere. Climate. The place of nature and labour in rural economy in our country. Rural economy in different localities of U.S.S.R. Accounts of agriculture in other countries. The northern borders of U.S.S.R. The southern borders of U.S.S.R. The industries of U.S.S.R. The origin of U.S.S.R. The government of U.S.S.R. The Communist Party. The relation between important foreign states (Germany, England, France, and the United States).
2. The care of the Soviet Government for improvement in the standard of life of the workers of U.S.S.R.
3. Topics from other work done during the four years.

In the earlier suggestions for carrying out the work of the unified school on the basis of the complex, it was intended that the so-called fundamental subjects—reading, writing, and arithmetic—be taught incidentally. As it was proved in practice that this would not be done or that these subjects were taught surreptitiously, the time-schedules were modified and special lessons in them were introduced. The "complex" scheme does, however, provide for social education through labour and the study of contemporary life, for music and rhythmic activities, for art, and for physical training. The study of nature leads over gradual, to the study of science as furnishing the materialistic expansion of life and the instrument of social and industrialization progress.

The most effective influences of the school are exercised, not so much through actual instruction, which is important in itself and follows the methods of the new education, but through the provision of opportunities for self-organization and self-government, school excursions to factories, museums, public institutions, and the intimate relationship with the junior organizations of the Communist Party—the Pioneers and the Komsomols. Commissions of the pupils are organized for sanitary, economic, cultural, and record purposes in each class and for each school and culminate in student councils responsible for the general interests of the school as a whole. Clubs and circles may be established for a variety of purposes. The most active spirits in the schools from the point of view of the Communist order are the Pioneers, members of the Children's Organization of Young Pioneers, who are admitted into the organization at the age of ten and continue until they are sixteen. Before admission to membership they must serve a period of probation and prove their sincerity and understanding of Pioneer ideals. In relation to the school of which he is a member, the Pioneer is a recognized leader. Distinguished by his badge, tie and salute, the law of his group calls upon him to assume such leadership and be an example to his comrades:

He will not avoid those who stand apart but go to them, try to draw them into his work and acquaint them with the organization. In school the Pioneer must actively share in school life, support discipline, and draw others into club activities, circles and games; arrange meetings and explain the tasks and purposes of Pioneers—and especially the commands of our leader and teacher, Comrade Lenin.[64]

As leader, he must stand out as an example in his studies, in his physical life, and in helpfulness to others; as a future Party member he must be an activist. Constantly under the eyes of his comrades and under the direction and leadership of a member of the next higher organization in the hierarchy, the Komsomols, the Pioneer is an active instrument of socio-political education in his school and a constant reminder that the school must be a part of contemporary life, an institution which is an extension of the new social order of government in the interests of the proletariat.

It is this social status of the school in the Soviet Republic which gives it life and meaning. In theory, at any rate, it seeks to carry out the principle that education is life and not a preparation for life in a more real sense than in other countries where this principle has been adopted. In practice and school may lag behind the theory, but only because the teachers until recently have either been lukewarm in their allegiance to the new education or inadequately prepared for the new task assigned to them. This much may, however, be said, that the Soviet ideology and Soviet educational theory constitute an unbroken circle; that it does not shrink from the acceptance of education as indoctrination, even while it accepts the principle of freedom and respect for individual development; that recognizes and utilizes every formative influence which will mould the future citizen into a loyal member of the social order. That school practices may be open to criticism may be true, but the magnificence of the whole concept upon which education is based and which takes one back to Plato's *Republic* can only be criticized when democracies have set before themselves the concept of social education which will be the moral equivalent of the Soviet Republic.

6. UNITED STATES

History

The elementary school in the United States is today what it has always been intended to be—the common school of all the people, with the exception of the very small number whose children attend private schools. The idea of a public elementary school had been incorporated in American traditions as early as 1642 when in Massachusetts parents and masters were required to teach children to read, a provision which was changed in 1647, by the "Old Deluder Satan" Law, into a requirement that every town of fifty householders must appoint a teacher to give instruction in reading and writing. After many vicissitudes and amendments increasing the penalty for failure to establish schools, the law was virtually a dead letter when the Republic was established. From this time on the political motive for providing schools was substituted for the religious; the schools were to promote solidarity, freedom and good citizenship.

Although seven States provided in their constitutions for the creation of systems of public education, nearly a generation elapsed before public elementary schools began to be established in considerable numbers. Public consciousness was aroused as in England by the development of Sunday schools, the organisation of philanthropic associations for the establishment of schools, the rise of Lancasterian schools, and the creation of societies to conduct propaganda in favour of public education. No small part was played in arousing public opinion by workingmen's associations and by public-spirited citizens—DeWitt Clinton, Lyman Beecher, Calvin E. Stowe, James G. Carter, Horace Mann, Henry Barnard, and many others. The characteristics of the public school were that it must be free, common to all without class distinctions, non-sectarian, supported by public taxation, and supervised by the public authorities.

The task which confronted the leaders was not always simple. Opposition had to be overcome to the idea of the non-sectarian schools, to the abolition of tuition, to the levy of taxes for education, and to the introduction of state control over education. The rise of the common people during and following the Jacksonian era, the development of urban centres consequent on the expansion of industrial enterprises, and the gradual increase in the number of immitants were factors, which, besides the active propaganda of educational and civic leaders, gradually broke down the opposition. By the middle of the century in some States, and after the Civil War in others, the principle of the public elementary school was generally accepted.

During the first stage in the evolution of the public elementary school there were no definite principles governing either the length of the course of its content. Starting with the three R's, the curriculum was gradually expanded; as the pupils increased in number and age, the elementary school was divided into primary, intermediate and grammar schools or into primary and grammar schools. To the earlier subjects there were added geography, grammar, composition, history, and music. Following the division of schools into stages, the grades themselves were slowly divided into classes until by the middle of the century there emerged the public elementary school with seven (generally in the South), eight (the normal type), and nine (in New England) classes or grades. This development was, however, possible only in the larger centres of population; the survival of the district system and the large rural population have militated against the universal adoption of grades schools until the present day, although efforts were made to grade the work of the ungraded schools into eight divisions.

The progress of elementary education was determined in the second half of the nineteenth century by the expansion of industry, the gradual conquest of the frontier, the rapidly increasing number of immigrants, and improvement in the means of communication. On the educational side changes in the curriculum were influenced by the development of normal schools, the introduction of Pestalozzian methods, and the spread of Herbartian and Froebelian philosophy. The curriculum continued to expand by the accretion of new subjects—drawing, manual work for boys and domestic arts for girls. In general, however, there had not yet been formulated a distinctively American philosophy of education adapted to the distinctively American idea of the public elementary school.

It was not until the last decade of the nineteenth century that a characteristically American attack on education began to be made. To this there contributed the establishment of chairs of education in universities and the development of departments or schools of education, the organisation of educational associations like the National Education Association and the National Herbart Society, the beginnings of the child-study movement, and the work of such leaders in Francis Parker and John Dewey. The rise of national consciousness following the Spanish-American War and the rapid increase in national wealth combined with criticism, which were levelled against every aspect of education from within the professional groups, led to a period of unrest and transition which has not yet closed. From the point of view of organization, it was felt that the break at the close of eight years of elementary education was unsatisfactory in so far as it postponed the beginning of secondary education to the age of fourteen; this led to a movement for a six-year elementary school, to be followed by three years in the junior and three years in the senior high school. At the other end, the kindergarten, which was rapidly being established as a part of the public school system, was not integrally articulated with the early grades of the primary school. The curriculum and methods of the elementary school were also subjected to the criticism that they were formal and perpetuated anti-quoted processes, utterly unadapted to the life and needs of the child. It was out of this setting that there emerged the problems which still surround the development of the elementary school.

THE PRESENT SYSTEM

Provision of Schools

It was pointed out above already that the control of education is vested in each State and that the Federal Government, with certain reservations, does not exercise any regulative authority over education. Each State delegates to the local areas—districts, towns, townships, and cities—the power to provide educational facilities under the supervision and with its financial aid, the extent of which varies considerably in different parts of the country. The provision of elementary schools is mandatory in every State by legislative enactment, but the extent and duration of elementary education varies from State to State and in different parts of the same State; the elementary school may give a six years' course articulated with the junior high school; more generally the course is eight years in length; in the South the length of the course is still seven years; in parts of New England nine years. It may or not be proceeded by the kindergarten. There are still about 160,000 schools, in which the pupils are unguarded and are taught by a single teacher; this situation, which means a denial of equality of opportunity, has been remedied by the establishment of consolidated schools to which the pupils are transported daily. Between the ungraded and the graded schools—six classes or more with their own teachers—there are schools with two or more teachers. There thus exists a great variety in the opportunities even within the field of elementary education: magnificent buildings in one area may be matched by hovels in others; in one area the public school system may provide opportunities from the kindergarten up to entrance to college or even beyond, while another has only an ungraded, one-room school taught by a teacher with slight qualifications; the average number of days of school attendance in 1928 ranged from 98.1 days to 171 days in the year, and the percentage of average attendance from 67.1 per cent to 92.3 per cent; the average cost for current expenditures per pupil in average daily attendance varied from $34.35 to $144.56, while the amount per pupil for capital outlays ranged from $2.77 to more than $30 for the country as a whole, and in city systems from $25-57 per pupil for all current expenses to $216.77. There is thus an absence of uniformity in standards, quantity, and quality in the American elementary schools and in the further absence of a central controlling agency. All that can be attempted in a study of elementary education is to present a general picture of the present status and of the tendencies in the future.

Compulsory Attendance

Compulsory attendance laws are now found in all States, but there is no uniformity of practice either in the ages of the pupils or the duration of the period of attendance. The first compulsory attendance law, requiring attendance at school for twelve weeks a year between the ages of eight and fourteen, was passed in Massachusetts in 1852. The example of Massachusetts had been followed by twenty-five States by 1889, but according to a report of the United States Commissioner of Education, the laws were inoperative except in Connecticut and Massachusetts. Some provision for compulsory attendance had been made by all but six Southern States by 1914; in 1920 the enactment of a compulsory attendance law by Mississippi made attendance compulsory throughout the country. The adoption of the principle of compulsory attendance does not signify uniformity of standards, as may be seen from the following summary showing the age requirements:

6-18 Ohio; 6-16 New Mexico; 7-14 Lousiana, North Carolins; 7-15 Arkansas and Virginia; 7-16 Connecticut, District of Columbia, Florida, Illinois, Indiana, Iova, Kansas, Kentucky, Massachusetts, Michigan, Mississippi, Missouri, Nebraska, New Jersey, Rhode Island, Tennesse, West Virginia, Wisconsin, Wyoming; 7-17 Delaware, Maine, Maryland,

North Dakota; 7-18 Nevada; 8-14 Georgia, South Carolina, Texas; 8-16 Alabama, Arizona, California, Colorado, Minnesota, Montana, New Hampshire, Pennsylvania, Vermont, Washington; 8-17 South Dakota; 8-18 Idaho, Oklahoma, Utah; 9-15 Oregon.

The variations in length of attendance required is as follows:

No minimum laid down, Alabama; 3 months, Oklahoma; 4 months, Florida, Mississippi; 5 months, Utah; 6 months, Arkansas, Colorado, Georgia, Indiana, North Carolina, 7 months, Idaho, Illinois, Kentucky, Louisiana, Michigan, Minnesota, New Mexico, North Dakota, South Carolina, Virginia; 7½ months, Maine; 8 months, Arizona, California, Delaware, Iowa, Kansas, Massachusetts, Missouri, Nevada, Ohio, Oregon, Pennsylvania, South Dakota, Tennessee, Washington, West Virginia, Wisconsin, Wyoming; 8½ months, Vermont; 9 months, District of Columbia, Maryland, Montana, Nebraska, New Hampshire, New Jersey, New York, Rhode Island; 9½ months, Connecticut.

These variations are still further aggravated by the inadequate methods of enforcing compulsory attendance laws. Except in cities and in the larger units of administration, such as countries, enforcement is unsatisfactory. In the larger areas special departments of school attendance have been established charged with the duties of drawing up and keeping the school census up to date and of encouraging and enforcing attendance. The work of the attendance departments in some larger cities is supplemented by visiting teachers, whose function it is to investigate, not only cases of irregular attendance, but their causes, and on the basis of such investigation to make appropriate recommendations to the classroom teachers or to the parents to ensure the proper scholastic or physical adjustment of the pupils concerned. Beyond this, difficult cases of irregular attendance are met by the establishment of special classes and special schools; habitual truants may be committed to parental schools which are either day or residential and in which the work and discipline are adapted to meet the peculiar needs of the pupils so committed.

Poor attendance is particularly characteristic of the rural schools and may be the result of climatic conditions, distance, inadequate means of transportation, illness, or in many cases, an unsuitable curriculum or poor teaching. Much depends in such schools upon the influence of the teacher, perhaps more upon the adaptation of the curriculum to the rural environment.

Religious Education

The American public elementary school was established as a non-sectarian, secular institution in which sectarian instruction is not permitted. The establishment of denominational or "parochial" schools is nowhere prohibited; the attempt made in Oregon to require all children up to the age of sixteen to attend public schools was declared unconstitutional in 1924. Denominational elementary schools are not given aid from public funds anywhere in the country, nor are they supervised or inspected, although inspection by state authorities is provided for in twenty States. In Nebraska, South Carolina, and South Dakota denominational schools must be approved by the public school authorities; in a number of other States standards are set up in the curriculum and quality of instruction, but are rarely enforced. Perhaps the only general requirement is that denominational schools must report the attendance and enrolment of pupils.

Although sectarian schools, sectarian instruction, and sectarian control of public schools are prohibited, religious instruction is not forbidden directly and in Virginia is actually permitted by law. Where found, however, religious instruction in elementary schools consists merely in the reading of the Bible without comment. Beyond this, religious instruction does not form a part of the regular curriculum and does not appear on the time-schedules. There has, however, recently begun a movement to permit pupils to attend religious instruction provided by denominational or interdenominational groups during school time.

Pre-schools and Kindergartens

The large majority of American children are found in the public elementary schools. A smaller number, between the ages of four and six, attend kindergartens where they are available, and a still smaller number are sent to pre-schools which have recently be introduced into the United States and are still mainly private in character. Although the pre-school or nursery school was established under the influence of similar schools is Europe, the motives are somewhat different. They have been promoted in the interests of psychological and educational research rather than for the philanthropic desire to provide for the children of the poor opportunities similar to those enjoyed by the children of the well-to-do. A number of organizations interested in the study and physical welfare of children and in the promotion of better care of children in the home have contributed to their development; among these are the Child Study Association, the National Committee for Mental Hygiene, the American Child Health Association, and the National Congress of Parents and Teachers. Their promotion has been based on the principle that the first six years of the child's life are the most important for physical development, mental growth, the acquisition of language and other habits, and emotional adjustments, and that many of the ills of later life may be attributed to faulty training in childhood. Hence the nursery schools must be centres not only for research, but also for the training of parents.

The nursery school is accordingly to be distinguished from day nurseries, of which there are about 600 provided by philanthropic, religious, and welfare associations, run for profit, or attached to social settlements, industries, and public schools (Los Angeles is the only city maintaining the last type). The interests of the day nurseries are promoted by the National Federation of Day Nurseries. The nursery schools have been established by cooperative groups of parents (Chicago, Boston, Smith College), or in connection with clinics (Yale Psycho-Clinic Guidance Nursery), or attached to departments of education (Teachers College, Columbia University; Iowa State College of Agriculture; University of Iowa; University of California in Los Angeles; and a number of teachers colleges), or by private endeavour for research purposes (Bureau of Educational Experiments, New York, and Merrill-Palmer School of Home-Making, Detroit). Two nursery schools are provided in the public school system in Los Angeles (Normandie Nursery School) and Chicago (Franklin Public School Nursery). In 1928 there were 121 nursery schools in the country.

The aim of the nursery school is to discover the best conditions for meeting the needs of growth. The work of the nursery schools is by no means standardized, but in general they admit children from the age of about sixteen months and keep them up to the age of four years. The character of the buildings varies and there is an absence of that standardization which in England is due to the influence of Margaret and Rachel McMillan. The common aim of the nursery schools is to promote simple healthful living, cleanliness, planned diet, and a variety of activities, through play, music, story, and rhythm. Many schools keep careful records, not only of the health but the conduct and experiences of the children. The schools receive the children at about 8.30 in the morning and keep them for half or a full day, up to 5.30 in the afternoon. There is still great variation in the work of the nursery schools in the types of buildings, length of session, size of groups under one teacher, fees, and work. Some schools have a flexible programme; in others there is a fixed timetable. The present status of nursery schools was clearly summarized in the following statement:

There has been no crystallization of the programmes of education for young children in nursery schools. Questions which are still controversial include the size, kind, and quality of play materials and of physical apparatus; the amount of independent personal care and care for property to be expected of children at two, three, and four years age levels; the size of group which a nursery school can handle, and the desirability of conducting organized group work; the amount of indoor and outdoor play; adequate provision of food for mid-morning, noon and afternoon lunch; the values of conducting nursery schools a full day or a half day; types of records to be kept each day, each week, and at other times during the school year; the details of physical examination considered essential and methods of preventing contagion; adequate methods of giving mental and social tests. Even this list of controversial questions does not complete the problems continually arising in nursery schools.[65]

The kindergarten was introduced into the United States by German immigrants; the first school of this type was established in 1855 in Watertown, Wisconsin, by Mrs. Carl Schurz, who had studied with Froebel. In 1860 Miss Elizabeth Peabody established a kindergarten in Boston and encouraged the opening of a private training school for kindergartners by Madame Matilde Kriege and her daughter in 1868. Four years later Miss Marie Boelte opened a training school in New York; a student of this school, Miss Susan Blow, was invited by William T. Harris to establish the first public kindergarten in St. Louis. From that time public and private kindergartens continued to be established, but are still found most generally only in the larger cities. In 1928 the enrolment of children between the ages of four and six was 700,000.

Originally conducted wholly on the principles laid down by Froebel, the modern kindergarten has today discarded almost all of them. The chief emphasis is placed upon the development of good habits, training in social behaviour, formation of character, and sound physical progress. The programme of the kindergarten consists in the main of a variety of activities which may serve partly as a means for socializing the child and aiding the child to adapt himself to his environment, and partly to provide an accumulation of experiences which will furnish an enriched environment and may later serve as a foundation for beginning formal subjects—language, reading, writing, and numbering. The aim of the kindergarten has been defined as the provision of "a happy, colourful, and joyous environment, where children may really live together." The activities developed to attain this aim are play, dramatization, constructive and creative work (music, art, handwork), and games.

The kindergarten in its origin was an addition to the elementary school, attached to but not a part of it. Different in origin and governed by different aims and principles, the two departments were generally not articulated satisfactorily, with the result that the transition from the kindergarten to the first grade was too abrupt. There has accordingly developed a movement to correct this defect by extending to the first, and in some cases, even to the second grade, the organization of the school work on the basis of activities and by introducing formal subjects very gradually. The whole period so organized from a unitary point of view has come to be known as the kindergarten-primary stage and in many school systems has administratively been placed under one supervisor.

THE ELEMENTARY SCHOOL

Organisation

The elementary school is the school attended by the majority of children of school age. Normally children are admitted at the age of six, even in those States where the compulsory attendance laws specially a later age of entrance. The duration of the elementary school period is in most systems eight years, except in the Southern States, where it is seven years, in some New England States, where it is nine, and in those areas when the junior high school, admitting pupils after six years of elementary education, have been established. Schools which have several teachers are administered by a principal, appointed by the local board of education on the recommendation of its superintendent from candidates who generally must bold a special certificate for the position or have qualifications higher than those required of classroom teachers.

The responsibility of the principal extends to the general administration of his school and the supervision of the teachers under him. One of the most general criticism of the work of elementary school principals is that so much of their time is devoted to routine details, keeping of records, and other clerical duties that little is left for educational leadership and supervision of classroom instruction. Since the administration of education tends to be centralized in local systems, leadership and direction come too frequently from the superintendent and his staff, and schools bear the impress of these leaders rather than of the principals and teachers. Principals are rarely expected to construct a curriculum of course of study for their schools, since these are made out by the central offices and passed on. A certain amount of initiative is, however, left to each school for the preparation of the time-schedule, the assignment of classes to teachers, and adaptation of the course of study to the peculiar needs of a school. In schools with more than two hundred pupils, the principal is generally relieved from teaching. As the administrative and supervisory official, he has the right to supervise his teachers and to use whatever methods he may consider desirable.

Promotion and Classification of Pupils

Schools vary in size from the small rural school with less than ten pupils to the large city school with more than one thousand pupils. The question of the optimum size of school has not been considered. The size of classes varies from thirty to forty; on this question a number of investigations have been conducted, but have not yielded conclusive results—some studies point to a class of thirty or less, others seem to indicate that the size of class is immaterial so far as results are concerned. The promotion and classification of pupils constitute one of the important functions of the principal in a graded school, but even here he may be limited by a plan determined by the administrative staff of the system in which the school is located.

With few exceptions the usual practice is to divide the work of each year into two sections (A and B), and to promote pupils every six months; hence the nomenclature of classes generally found goes from the lowest class, 1B, 1A, 2B, 2A up to 8A. In larger schools parallel classes are provided which render classification and promotion more flexible, an end which is attained in other systems (e.g., St. Louis) by quarterly promotions. Pupils are classified on the basis of ability, which is tested either by examinations or by tests. Recently this method of homogeneous grouping has been challenged on the ground that it is artificial and does not provide for the intermingling of different types of ability found outside the school and that labelling of classes as fast or slow, or advanced or backward, is unust to the pupils.

Various plans have been adopted to create systems of classification and promotion which will be most appropriate to individual ability. Detroit divides each grade into X, Y, and Z classes for the bright, normal, and slow pupils respectively; for the slow group, the curriculum is limited to the minimum essentials; the curriculum of the normal group is modestly enriched; and for the bright group, it is greatly enriched. Where parallel classes have been adopted, as in Cambridge, Massachusetts, Portland, Oregon, and Norfolk, Virginia, the pupils are divided into fast and slow groups, the latter taking eight years and the former six years to complete the course; the work of each group is so synchronized that pupils may be transferred from one to the other as occasion arises. In Batavia slow pupils are given special assistance by an extra teacher to enable them to keep up with the others of their class, a plan similar to that of Pueblo, where slow pupils are sent to a special teacher. Other variations which seek to adapt the work to the ability of each pupil are special or extra promotions, which are not regarded with favour, vacation schools in which retarded pupils may catch up with their classes or accelerated pupils may gain time, and special or ungraded rooms in which the special difficulties of backward pupils are investigated and corrected.

The recognition of individuals differences has led to the construction of diagnostic tests and of practice materials whereby defects may be discovered and corrected.

The most radical departure from normal practices has been introduced in Winnetka, Illinois, where Superintendent Carleton Washburne has adopted a modified form of the Dalton Plan of individual instruction. Recognizing individual differences and variation in abilities, Washburne has divided for curriculum into the commons essentials and group and creative activities. The former consist of the fundamental processes which require practice, speed, and accuracy. For these subjects there have been developed carefully graded tasks at which each pupil works at his own pace; definite goals are set and the pupil tests himself from time to time before proceeding to the next stage; he may, when necessary, seek the help of his teacher. The group and creative activities include literature, history, geography, music, art, play and assemblies, and manual work, which are studied by the class as a whole. Another form of the experiment which enables pupils to progress at their own rate is the Dalton Plan, which differs from the Winnetka Plan in that it is not limited to certain subjects, in the monthly assignment system, and in other details. Although developed by an American educator, Miss Helen Parkhurst, the Dalton Plan, except in modified form and with limitations, has not had a wide following in the United States.

While it does not bear directly on the question of classification and promotion, the "platoon" school is an experiment in the reorganization of school activities. Originating primarily as a device to provide adequate accommodation for a rapidly increasing population (in Gary, Indiana), the idea of the "platoon" school has been elevated to the status of an educational principle. Since the home provides decreasing opportunities for worthy educational activities, it is the duty of the school to add to its existing programme those activities which were formerly provided in the home. Further, in view of the large cost of modern school buildings, there is economic waste in leaving any part on them unused not only after the school day, but also during the regular sessions. Accordingly, the platoon plan aims to make the maximum use of the school. Each school under this system, which has been adopted with more or less modifications by nearly 120 cities, divides the pupils into two or three, but generally two groups or platoons; while one group is receiving class instruction or study, the other is engaged in work (music, drawing, nature study in the laboratory, or library), or play (physical training or assemblies in the auditorium). The characteristic of the platoon school on the curricular side is according its division into "work-study-play." The platoon school, it is claimed, can provide better equipment, specialized teachers, special rooms, and an enriched curriculum, and the pupils can be kept busy at a variety of activities during the whole school day. Since they are taught by specialist teachers, the community of each group is retained by providing "home rooms" under a teacher charged with its supervision.

The Aim of Elementary Education

The aim of the American elementary school has been determined by a number of factors. The first of these is the heterogeneous character of the population, occupying a vast area and made up of individuals and groups drawn from all parts of Europe and differing in language, customs, and standard of values. The second is the democratic form of government which implies an absence of distinction and demands an education which will prepare for the responsibilities of a common citizenship. The third factor is the contribution of psychology to better knowledge of the child and of the methods of his growth through the learning process. The fourth is derived from the philosophical consideration of the relation of the individual to society and the State with a strong emphasis on his right to free growth and development. The fifth is the characteristically American emphasis on adaptation to changing needs, a tendency to look to the immediate present and future, and a refusal to be bound by traditions. All of these factors have led to the development of a pragmatic point of view which sets up values in terms of direct utility either to the individual or to society. The traditional aim of imparting a certain amount or kinds of knowledge, knowledge as power, or knowledge for its own sake, is no longer accepted as a defensible aim of education. The strongest influence in the development of a new aim of education in the United States has been the philosophy of John Dewey, with its insistence that "the school should be life and not a preparation for life" and that "the school cannot be a preparation for social life except as it reproduces conditions of social life."

The integrating and socializing aim of elementary education has been defined by Professor T.H. Briggs as follows:

> In such an organization of education as exists or will exist, in the United States, the most important purposes of the elementary school are conceived to be, first, to furnish the common training necessary for all children "regardless of sex, social status, or future vocational"; and, second, by means of this common training, to integrate the future citizens of our democracy.

In discussing the aims of education in other countries, it was possible to cite the statements found in the official publications of the respective ministries. The absence of such a central authority in the United States renders it impossible to cite aims which are generally accepted; of theoretical statements there is no end; the nearest analogy to an official definition of aims is to be found in the statements issued from time to time by committees appointed by the Department of Superintendence to investigate the reorganization of the curriculum. In general, American education is seeking to distinguish between (1) the *aims* which determine the whole process of education or of instruction in a single subject, (2) *objectives* which should determine the organization of the curriculum for the attainment of various ends, and (3) *outcomes*, or the expected results of instruction.

Thus there may be one large comprehensive aim governing elementary education and within elementary education there may be included arithmetic; in the organization of this subject there are innumerable objectives within the four fundamental processes; the outcomes of instruction are skills and techniques in and knowledge of numbers and their relations. This method of attack, it is claimed, has the advantage of specificity and of clear adaptation of ends to means. It is derived from the method of job analysis in industry where every process has its own operation and all the processes yield a clearly defined result. It is based scientifically upon the stimulus-response theory (the S-R bonds) of mechanistic psychology, which emphasizes specificity of learning. In this process it is sometimes forgotten that in education the whole is greater than a combination of its parts.

In the studies of curriculum organization, which have been conducted since 1924 by the Department of Superintendence and which are summaries of current practices, this is the method which has been pursued. The *Fifth Yearbook* of the Department begins with an analysis of the common aim of American education:

What are America's educational ideals? Education for life and service in a democracy cannot rest upon capricious or indefinite theories. It must have for its basis a sound and reliable philosophy. Fortunately, the founders of the Republic planned a nation in accordance with definite purposes, to achieve which they framed the Constitution.

Officially they promulgated these six purposes in the preamble: (1) a more perfect union, (2) justice, (3) domestic tranquillity, (4) the common defence, (5) general welfare, (6) preservation of the blessing of liberty. They held the conviction that these should be secured by education. Since that time the States have provided for schools at public expense, taxing all for the general welfare. In tax-supported schools these American ideals are permanent. Upon their realization depends the perpetuity of our government which is composed of citizens. The progress of the Republic is conditioned by the development of its citizenry. To keep the citizenry at a rising level, schools have been established at public expense.[66]

On the basis of this statement the following common aim was formulated:

The common or ultimate purpose of American education is the development of the kind of citizenship that will guarantee both the preservation and the promotion of public welfare. To carry out this common aim, the four following general objectives have been set up:

1. To promote the development of an understanding and an adequate evaluation of the self.
2. To promote the development of an understanding and an appreciation of the world of nature.
3. To promote the development of an understanding and an appreciation of organized society.
4. To promote the development of an appreciation of the force of law and of love that is operating universally.

Another statement of "the main objectives which should guide education in a democracy" was published in 1918 in a *Report* of the Commission on the Reorganization of Secondary Education, appointed by the National Education Association. Although issued under the title of *Cardinal Principles of Secondary Education,* the following objectives have been accepted as applying equally to elementary education: (1) health; (2) command of fundamental processes; (3) worthy home membership; (4) vocation; (5) citizenship; (6) worthy use of leisure; and (7) ethical character.

These statements of aims apply to all education; the specific objectives of elementary education were defined in these terms:

(1) Advance the child, although by no means perfect him in his ability to read, write, and speak correctly

the English language, and to know and to use intelligently the elementary process of arithmetic.

(2) Advance the child in his ability to know and to observe the laws of physical and mental health and well-being and to appreciate the meaning of life and of nature.

(3) Advance the child in his ability to know and to appreciate the geography and history of his own community, state, and nation, and of the world at large; to sense his share in the social, civic, and industrial order of such a democracy as ours, and to meet the full obligations which such knowledge and appreciation should engender, to the end that justice, sympathy and loyalty may characterize his personal and community life.

(4) Advance the child in his ability to share intelligently and appreciatively in the fine and musical arts as they are related to the three great universal needs of food, clothing, and shelter.[67]

Social efficiency and good citizenship are, then, the chief ends of education. Starting from this point, the objectives may be derived. These may be analyzed simply as by Superintendent H.B. Wilson on the occasion of the revision of the course of study of the Berkeley Public Schools into vital or physical efficiency, vocational efficiency (right use of leisure), civic efficiency, and moral and religious efficiency, with outcomes in knowledge, habits, and skills, and attitudes in each. The job-analysis method has, however, gone much farther; Professor Franklin K. Bobbitt, in his *Curriculum-Making in Los Angeles,*

listed over one thousand definite, particularized objectives in human abilities, habits, attitudes, appreciations, skills, powers, and judgment, personal characteristics, etc. These were all classified under the following ten divisions:

(1) Social intercommunication, mainly language.

(2) Physical efficiency, the development and maintenance of one's physical powers.

(3) Unspecialized practical labours, such as repairing simple mechanical devices used in the home, driving a motor car, etc.

(4) Occupational objectives, the labour of one's calling.

(5) Efficient citizenship, the activities of the efficient citizen.

(6) Social efficiency, activities involved in one's general social relationships and behaviour.

(7) Leisure occupations—recreations and amusements.

(8) General mental efficiency—its development and maintenance.

(9) Religious attitudes and activities.

(10) Parental responsibilities—activities, the upbringing of children and the maintenance of home life.[68]

Into the more theoretical discussions of the aims of education, it is impossible to enter here, not only because of their variety, but also because for the present they do not represent the actual situation in America except in some experimental, public and private schools. In general they concentrate more on the free development of the individual, his needs, interests, and capabilities, and on creative activity rather than on the social aim, which is expected somehow to be the ultimate outcome. The contrast between the old and the new theories of education is well pointed out in the following exposition of the *Opposite Poles in Educational Theory:*

Opposite Poles in Educational Theory[69]

Theory of Repression	*Theory of Expression*
1. Education is preparation for adult life, it ends when maturity is reached. It is primarily a reshaping, reformatory process for the child, who is looked upon as a bundle of original sin.	1. Education is life; it continues throughout life. It is an unfolding process. Spontaneous self-expression is the means employed; and unrepressed child nature is its own best guide.

2. The aim of the curriculum is to prepare for future opportunities and responsibilities. The curriculum necessarily involves much that is distasteful and foreign to the child's immediate interests.	2. The aim of the curriculum is to stimulate and encourage children to grow by providing for them, through a rich and suggestive environment, activities in which they joyously engage.
3. The method of teaching is formal drill on set assignments logically arranged. Rigid discipline moulds the child into adult conformity.	3. The method of teaching is following the inner urge of the child which results in spontaneous activity. Freedom and self-expression best develop latent talent.
4. Training results from acquiring, through memorization, the facts that make up the social heritage of the race.	4. Training results from meaningful activity growing out of the child's needs and interests.
5. Learning is a cold storage process by which the child stores up facts and skils for future use.	5. Learning is the acquisition of facts and skills essential to the fulfilment of the child's immediate interests.
6. Through education the child is inculcated with accepted doctrines and imbued with the sanctity of established institutions and vested rights.	6. Through education the child is imbued with a spirit of irreverence for blind tradition and a critical attitude toward things as they are.
7. School equipment is simple—a room, a teacher of the drill-master type, a rod, and a book.	7. School equipment is varied and attempts to duplicate life situations. The teacher is a sympathetic observer of childhood.
8. Child activity in itself has no justification. Childhood is merely a period of intensive preparation for successful participation in adult life.	8. Childhood is its own justification. It should be a period of carefree self-expression untram meled by the demands of adulthood with its unfulfilled anticipa-tions.
9. Too much education is feared. Education beyond one's station is to be deplored. Early entrance into industry and the early assumption of adult responsibilities should be encouraged.	9. The more education the better. Through education every child can be brought to a higher level or station in life. The period of youth and school attendance should be extended.

Curriculum and Courses of Study

The outstanding preoccupation in American education during the past ten years has been the study of curriculum problems, which arose out of a feeling of discontent with the traditional programme of the elementary (and secondary schools). This programme is criticized as a purposeless and unorganized accretion of subjects which emphasize the acquisition of more or less useless facts, information, and knowledge, stress discipline and intellectual training, and neglect the development of the total personality of the individual in relation to his present environment. In the task of curriculum revision have participated not only the official agencies for the administration of education, state and local but national organizations like the Department of Superintendence of the National Education Association, the National Society for the Study of Education, individual leaders in the field of education (both general and "curriculum experts"), and research divisions of university departments of education.

The movement for the revision of the curriculum and courses of study has resulted from a number of different factors. So far as the content and aims of the curriculum are concerned, each State in the country and in most States each local district has been a law unto itself, and this variety has manifested itself also in great diversity in the amount of time devoted to the different subjects. These differences are shown in the accompanying table in which the amount of time given to the elementary subjects in the schools of Seattle is compared with the average amount of time given in forty-nine cities of over 100,000 population.

In spite of this diversity, which from one point of view is desirable, it is felt that there are certain national ideals that need to be cultivated. So much time has been devoted to methods that the realization of purposes and the improvement of subjects have been disregarded. On the other hand, the making of curricula and courses of study has been too much dominated by convention and traditions to the neglect of the demands of everyday life. The curricula have grown by the accretion of subjects and subject-matter without any careful synthesis or interpretation. Courses of study have been imitated and copied, while the influence of textbooks has been detrimental to freedom and local adaptation.

Comparison of the Time Allotments in Number of Minutes per Week by Grades in the Seattle Schools with the Average Allotments in Forty-nine Large Cities*

Subjects Taught		*Grades*								
		I	*II*	*III*	*IV*	*V*	*VI*	*VII*	*VIII*	*TOTAL*
Language	49 Cities	130	141	167	176	187	194	207	215	1417
	Seattle	0	50	75	110	200	225	225	225	1110
Reading	49 Cities	421	404	332	245	182	141	142	136	2003
	Seattle	600	525	425	310	135	135	225	212	2567
Spelling	49 Cities	39	82	87	85	82	78	72	73	598
	Seattle	0	75	100	100	60	60	60	60	515
Penmanship	49 Cities	67	72	77	78	77	75	63	58	567
	Seattle	50	75	75	75	60	60	60	60	515
Arithmetic	49 Cities	64	143	193	206	211	211	212	211	1451
	Seattle	0	150	250	240	225	255	250	200	1570
History	49 Cities	17	19	30	54	84	97	148	167	616
	Seattle	100	30	50	75	135	135	250	125	900
Civics	49 Cities	9	12	11	12	14	15	23	27	123
	Seattle	0	30	25	25	35	30	0	75	220
Geography	49 Cities	11	14	59	137	156	162	137	84	760
	Seattle	0	0	50	100	180	180	0	112	622
Science	49 Cities	22	23	23	23	21	21	22	26	181
	Seattle	38	20	25	25	25	40	40	40	253
Hygiene	49 Cities	16	16	16	22	27	27	25	22	173
	Seattle	37	20	25	25	25	25	35	35	227
Physical Training	49 Cities	90	67	89	90	90	89	98	104	737
	Seattle	0	0	50	50	50	50	50	50	300
Supervised Play	49 Cities	22	19	18	14	16	16	16	15	136
	Seattle	150	150	100	50	50	50	50	50	650
Recess	49 Cities	105	106	106	96	91	90	84	74	752
	Seattle	100	100	100	100	100	100	100	100	800
Industrial Arts	49 Cities	22	22	25	30	50	65	90	106	410
	Seattle	25	50	63	60	60	0	0	0	258
Drawing	49 Cities	87	88	87	86	82	75	77	79	661
	Seattle	75	50	63	75	75	75	75	75	563
Music	49 Cities	71	74	74	77	76	74	70	75	591
	Seattle	75	75	75	80	80	80	80	80	625
Miscellaneous	49 Cities	97	93	99	97	99	98	88	87	758
	Seattle	0	0	0	50	50	50	50	50	250

* Department of Superintendence, *Second Yearbook,* p. 140 (Washington, D.C. 1929).

There is today "a great need for a scientific determination and general acceptance by both educators and laymen of the aims and objectives of modern elementary education. If education is to be placed on a thoroughly scientific basis, outcomes must be considered in the determination of processes. Selection of objectives is the first step toward putting education on a firm foundation."[70] Accordingly, the questions that are being asked in the present survey of the curriculum are as follows:

Is the present course of study in harmony with present social and individual needs? Is it in harmony with advancing educational practice based upon the rapidly developing science of education? .... How shall a programme of revision be organized which will result in the best possible course of study? How should provision be made for continuous modification and improvement of this course? How may the teaching corps be stimulated actively to participate in the revision and intelligently to corporate in its interpretation in the classroom? How may the community be brought into sympathetic understanding of the whole programmes?[71]

Underlying the movement is a new attitude which has developed in the twentieth century, opposed to the narrow conception that the function of the school is to provide training in a few simple tools. Modern life has become so complex, the number and diversity of pupils in schools so great, that the curriculum calls for a new orientation; not merely pruning of dead material and the addition of new topics, but a complete, thoroughgoing revision is necessary if the school is to contribute to successful life in society.

Determination of Content

The general trend of aim in curriculum making having been discovered, the next problem is to devise methods for determining the content. Professor Bobbitt thus summarized the steps in curriculum construction:

(1) Determination of objectives; (2) Formulation of guiding principles; (3) Selection of pupil experiences; (4) Selection of needed materials; (5)

> Placing experiences in proper sequence as determined by maturity; (6) Experimentation to test placing of experiences; (7) Welding the experiences found suitable for any particular year or term in a thoroughly correlated instruction; (8) Constant revision in the light of experience and experimentation.[72]

Somewhat similar were the suggestion of Professor W.W. Charters:

> (1) Determine the ideals and activities which constitute the major objectives. (2) Analyze these and continue the analysis until working units are obtained. (3) Arrange them in order of importance. (4) Raise to positions of high rank in these lists those ideals and activities which are of great value for children even though low in value for adults. (5) Determine the number of most important ideals and activities which can be mastered in the time allotted to school, after eliminating those which can be learned outside of school. (6) Arrange the material in proper constructional order, according to the psychological nature of children and the texture of the materials.[73]

Professor Otis W. Caldwell, formerly Director of the Lincoln School of Teachers College, Columbia University, emphasized the importance of considering the needs of the pupils for whom a curriculum is being made.

I wish to state certain principles which it seems should be clearly defined for use in any reorganization of the school subjects of a study.

1. *Pupils' attitude toward school subjects.* Children learn best, retain longest, and find learning most stimulating and most usefully available, when the subject matter and methods of school work are engaging and genuine, not repulsive and artificial... Subject-matter should be so selected and used that more should be gained than has been in the past from its inherent significance to pupils.

2. *Pupils must succeed in school subjects if they are to be educated.* Subjects should be so selected and used, and pupils and subjects should be so graded that more pupils will succeed, in order that later achievement may also be had.
3. *The rate and quality of learning are improved by an increase in the number of senses used.* There is too large an omission of fundamental experiences which involve touch, taste, sight...the experiences of the daily life for which we say we are preparing our pupils...We have fallen into a conventional education of words.
4. *The subjects should be organised and used so that pupils may teach one another.* Education has never made adequate use of the fact that children learn much from one another, and our present subject organization does not favour such mutual teaching...The topics and content of studies should be such that pupils can come into mutual and cooperative mastery of them.
5. *The school's organization is a legitimate and necessary part of the subjects of instruction.* School is training for social effectiveness, the school instritution must itself be socially effective. To be so the educational processes must be cooperative, and the activities and procedures which enter into the school's organization must be used as true subject matter material... This means that school curricula and methods and building organizations must be participated in by pupils, and that the school's own organization is a part of the school's curricular possession, not a personal possession of the administrative officers...Ideas will never be carried out unless they are embodied in the machinery.[74]

The Making of Courses of Study

The universal practice in the United States has been until recently that the curriculum and courses of study have been prepared in great detail by the superintendent of education himself, or with the aid of his administrative staff, and handed on to the teachers. The methods of preparation have varied—in some cases the curriculum and courses of study have been mere imitations of others recognized as standard; in other they have been based on and followed the textbooks which were prescribed. To some extent, the subjects and the curriculum have been prescribed in legislative enactments; among these are flag exercises, fire prevention, temperance, health, physiology, history from certain national points of view, and so on.[75] The past ten years have witnessed the beginnings of a movement to enlist the participation of teachers in the preparation of the curriculum and courses of study. Starting in Denver, the movement has extended to other large cities, among these Detroit, Cincinnati, Dayton, St. Louis, and Houston. In Denver the curriculum revision was the result of the cooperative activity of teachers, principals, supervisors, and university and other agencies which were engaged in curriculum investigations; experts were invited for consultation, criticism, and advice. Teachers and principals were organized into separate committees for each subject and special arrangements were made to enable members of such committees to attend meetings during school time. Following the publication of the courses of study, a department of curriculum revision was established to maintain a continuous revision.

The Denver experiment and the continued unrest in curricular matters not only stimulated other cities to undertake similar revisions, but led to the creation of departments of curriculum research as a part of the administrative organization in a number of cities or attached to schools of education in universities; it led at the same time to the emergence of the "curriculum specialists" available for consultation and advice. Among the studies undertaken in this connection are the following, given in an account of the work of the Bureau of Curriculum Research of Teachers College, Columbia University:

(1) Analyzing the outstanding courses so as to determine: (a) general trends and tendencies, (b) the overlapping of content and experience materials, (c) the best projects in various subjects as well as those which disregard subject-matter lines entirely, (d) the best drill devices in the various phases of different subjects.

(2) Studying, by various methods, classroom teaching in outstanding school systems and experimental schools, in order: (a) to compare the work as outlined in the courses of study with actual practice, and (b) to note wherein the work in the classroom differs from ideal and theoretical schemes.

(3) Analyzing textbooks.

(4) Making curriculum materials more usable by setting up tentative suggestions for adaptation to various communities. Some of the factors which should be considered in this study are size of the community, preparation of teachers, individual differences of pupils, types of administrative organization and the like.[76]

Not only is this a period of transition, but there is inevitably a gap between theory and practice. Hence, while theory stresses that education is life and not a preparation for life, that the curriculum should consist of experiences and activities which represent real "life situations" or actual problems as they arise in the social environment of the school, in actual practice published courses of study range from detailed prescriptions of facts, information, and skills to be imparted to suggestive outlines of activities meaningful and significant to the pupils at their particular stage of development.

Not only are courses of study, in the preparation of which teachers have had no part, prescribed, but supervisors are employed to guide the teachers is carrying out these prescriptions, and, while external examinations have generally been abandoned, standardized tests or achievement tests tend to lead to the same result, which is further promoted by the use of prescribed textbooks. Knowledge, facts, and information at one end of the scale contrast with the revision of courses of study based on analyses of contemporary American life and its needs on the one hand, and the study of pupil capacities, interests, needs rates of learning, and other individual characteristics on the other; the methods of arriving at this revision are measurements, statistical records, analyses, and controlled experimentation.

The great variety of education practices throughout the country has already been illustrated above (see Table, pages 162-63). It may be further amplified by the accompanying which tables give at the same time the lists of subjects found in the elementary schools of the country; although the tables present the figures for 1920, there has probably not been any substantial change in the general situation.

There are thus no established norms either as to the subjects taught or the time allotted to them. There is still less uniformity in the courses of study despite the nation-wide discussion of the problem by a large number of agencies. Some courses prescribe the details which are to be taught in each subject; others are textbooks and guides on educational theory and methods. The Wisconsin Course of Study, for example, in the section on geography discusses the aims, gives general suggestions in methods and organization, a general statement of content by grades, a summary of the standards of accomplishment to be reached, and a list of books on content and method to be used by the teachers. This procedure is followed in all subjects. The Denver Course of Study in arithmetic may be cited as another example of a course which is at once a textbook in subject-matter, general and special methods, standards, and reference material. Opening with a General Introduction, it discusses general aims, how the course of study meets general aims, relation between content and method in achieving the end, value of knowing the course as a whole, development of character traits, and a concluding summary. This is followed by Suggestions Relative to Instruction (development, methods of presentation, drill, motivation through interest, application—the thought side of arithmetic), the Elimination of Difficulties in Reasoning, Individualization—Suggestions for Diagnosis of Difficulties and Remedial Instruction, General Suggestions, Tests and Results of Scientific Investigation: Relative Value of Subject-Matter. Each of these sections is illustrated by practical examples. The remainder of the volume (376 pages) is devoted to the distribution of the course in the grades, which further statements of aims, suggestions, standards of attainment, and examples for each of the six grades. The same procedure is followed in volumes of the other subjects of the curriculum. More usually the courses of study, after a few general suggestions, give itemized lists of the topics to be treated in each class. Another form of course of study, which is gradually disappearing, is that which directly follows a selected textbook both in organization and content.

Textbooks

Despite progressive movements in curriculum, it is still true that the textbook method of instruction (the "recitation" method) and of subject-matter organization is the dominant practice throughout the country. In its origin the textbook was introduced into American schools to compensate for the poor preparation of teachers and in time it has become difficult to dislodge. Free textbooks were introduced in Philadelphia in 1818 and in Massachusetts in 1844. In 1927 twenty States required by law the free distribution of textbooks to pupils, twenty-three States had permissive laws, and five had no regulations on the subject. The practice of providing free textbooks is almost universal and particularly to pupils in elementary schools. In twenty-five States uniform textbooks are adopted in all parts except the independent cities, six States permit county adoption, and seventeen allow local adoption. Textbooks are selected in eleven of the States which have uniform adoption by the state board of education; in other States special textbooks commissions are appointed;

in the localities the selection is made by the boards of education; rarely do teachers participate in the selection. Not only is there uniformity of textbooks in many States, but the period of adoption is over a long-term of years, three for four years, twenty-one for five years, nine for six years, two for eight years, and one for ten years.[77]

The extensive market and the competition for adoption have resulted in the production of textbooks which are superior in many respects to the European in form, make-up, binding, print, and illustrations. Textbooks are prepared by teachers at all levels of the system and leading experts in subject-matter and in theory have participated either individually or in cooperation. Selection committees, advised by their officials, are guided generally by certain standards for measuring both the material and scientific character of books submitted to them. The aim in the preparation of textbooks is to base them upon the latest contributions from the side of theory, methods and curriculum principles and in certain fundamental subjects of tests and measurements. So far as textbooks are concerned, they are in general beyond criticism; difficulties arise, however, when the single textbook rather than the teacher's mastery of the subject of instruction becomes the sole reliance both of teacher and pupils. This is what is meant by the "recitation" methods, which, despite all theoretical discussions of progressive methods, prevails very widely—the teacher assigns a certain number of pages in a textbook to be "studied," and on the following day the pupils must be ready to answer questions on them; hence much depends on the quality of the textbook and the extent of instruction and guidance that the pupil may derive from it. Changes in methods of instruction are proceeding rapidly; the single textbook is gradually being replaced, not only by the use of several or by supplementary books, but also by the development of library methods. The extensive use of the textbook has been a corollary of poor preparation of teachers, and, as professional preparation improves and a proper balance between the attainment of mastery of content and methods is secured, the textbook method, but probably not the textbook, will be relegated into the background for purposes of consultation and reference as in most European countries.

Methods of Instruction

The textbook or recitation method still continues to be the characteristic method of instruction in American elementary schools. It has been subjected to severe criticism as emphasizing only the acquisition of knowledge, of dead cold facts, and of information unrelated to the life and needs of the learner. After the five formal steps of Herbart had been discarded, efforts were made to supersede or to supplement the recitation method by training pupils in how to think and how to study, a training which was accompanied by library work. But this method still seemed to imply the study or reorganisation of what was regarded as the cut and dried material of one or several textbooks. Training in how to study was a step in the direction of wider range of activities than were possible under the recitation methods, but the activities were still scholastic and did not arise out of life situations which should determine the proposes of the pupils activities. Accordingly, there developed out of the ever-widening influence of pragmatic philosophy in education, combined with the laws of learning, based on the mechanistic psychology, a new general method, the "project method." "A project is any unit of purposeful experience, any instance of purposeful activity, where dominating purpose, as an inner urge, (1) fixes the aim (or end) of the action, (2) guides the process, (3) furnishes its drive, its inner motivation for its vigorous prosecution." Psychologically this means that learning is based on three laws: (1) law of readiness; (2) law of exercise (use and disuse); and (3) law of effect or the satisfactory attainment of the purpose. The project method has on the whole been more discussed than practiced except in a few experimental schools and with younger children.[78]

The project method, if not carried out according to its definition, combined with the criticism of subject-matter prescribed merely as content to be learned, has led to a new approach to both curriculum and methods. The curriculum, according to the advocates of the new philosophy, should consist of activities and experiences arising out of the lives of the pupils and methods should vary according to the ends attained. This means, in turn, a complete change from the traditional subject organization of the curriculum to integrated subject-matter. The child does not distinguish between subjects and subjects; his experience at any one time is whole and integrated; so, too, his school activities and subjects, as they have been known, should be introduced as the need for them emerges. This is, of course, the American analogy for the German *Gesamtunterricht,* but appears to have been arrived at independently. At present, it is found in public schools more frequently in such integrations as "social studies," a blend of history, civics, geography, and hygiene, or "general science," a course based on study of the science of everyday life and drawing upon hygiene biology, botany, chemistry, and physics. In its more general form the integrated curriculum is found in the kindergarten and early primary grades and more often in experimental schools.

Into a discussion of the development of special methods of teaching the different subjects of the elementary school curriculum, it is impossible to enter here. On the whole, much of the time in the courses of professional preparation has been devoted to the study of special methods which inadequate attention to the mastery of the subjects themselves. This emphasis has tended to restrict professional growth and to militate against freedom and flexibility in the classroom. The movement for the revision of the curriculum and for the development of training of teachers through professional subject matter are helping to reduce the emphasis hitherto placed on special methods.

Control of the Teaching Process

Only in a limited sense, however, can it be said that education in the United States is characterised by freedom and flexibility. There is variety in so far as each State is responsible for its own system of education and each local unit—whether town, township, county or city—enjoys a certain independence. But within each local unit every school tends to be dominated by the same principles and functions. The character of a school is determined not by its principal and staff, but by the policy of the superintendent in charge of the whole system of which it is a part. Through the prescribed courses of study and sometimes prescribed methods, through teacher-rating schemes (in some areas), through teachers' institutes held at the beginning of each school year to discuss the work of the year, through supervision, and through tests and other forms of standardization, the freedom of the teacher tends to be limited. On the other hand, there are distinct evidences of a change. The participation of teachers in the preparation of courses of study, which has already been mentioned, is an advance in the right direction. Scientific tests and measurements are no longer accepted as having the infallibility of the yardstick and are regarded as valuable mainly for diagnostic purposes. Teachers' institutes are changing in character and are becoming more practical with opportunities for discussion by the teachers. The mobility of teachers and the pursuit of further study in summer sessions or during a longer term are helping to create professional attitudes which will in the end result in greater professional freedom and flexibility. Finally, the nature of supervision, which at one time was directed to securing uniformity of practices, has changed; the function of the supervisor is to help the teacher and through the teacher to improve instruction; the supervisor no longer exercises the authority of a policeman, but rather that of a special expert, ready to guide, assist, and advise. Despite these advances, American elementary education suffers from the impermanence of the profession, which means a constant change of personnel. From this point of view, it is not feminization of the teaching profession which is the weakness of American schools, but the fact that neither men nor women enter the profession as a permanent career, women leaving for marriage and men for more remunerative careers either within the profession of education itself or elsewhere.

Private Schools

The establishment of private schools is virtually unrestricted; public authorities may in some States have the right of entry, but in general the only limitations are that enrolment and attendance must be reported. According to the figures for 1927-28 there were enrolled in private schools of all kinds 2,134,999 pupils (1,002,336 boys and 1,132,663 girls) the majority attending parochial schools of the Roman Catholic Church. The only influential private schools are those which are definitely established for experimental purposes. Of these, some are entirely private, others are attached to university schools of education. It would be difficult to gauge the influence of private experimental schools; in the development of new curricula, courses of study, and methods, they have played a part which public schools, with their emphasis until recently on mass education and uniformity, were not able to undertake. The contributions of such private schools range all the way from the absolute concept of freedom to more moderate experimentation with such materials are used in the public schools. In general, they have adopted the following principles enunciated by the Progressive Education Association:

The following is a statement of the goals toward which the new education is tending. It is safe to say that no school has attained them all, nor are they put forth as the specific aims of any one group or organization. Rather they are a general summing up of such characteristics as find expression in some part throughout all forward-looking education.

The child's physical well-being. One of the most important considerations of the school is the health of the pupils. Space in which to move about, light and air, clean, well-ventilated buildings, attention to proper nutrition, access to the out-of-doors and greater use of it, are all necessary. There should be frequent use of adequate playgrounds The school should observe closely the physical condition of each pupil, and, in cooperation with the home, make abundant health available to every child.

Opportunity for Full Development

Opportunity for initiative and self-expression should be provided in an environment rich in interesting material, the free use of which will release the creative energies of the child.

Social Development and Discipline

Group consciousness is developed in children through participation in the school as a community. Discipline should be a matter of self-mastery rather than external compulsion, and character development the result of social experience, and of the recognition of spiritual forces and resources underlying all nature, life, and conduct. A co-educational student body, and a faculty of both men and women, constitute a normal life situation for character and development.

Beauty of Environment

The school should furnish an environment that is simple, natural, and beautiful.

Interest the Motive of All Work

Interest should be satisfied and developed primarily through (1) direct and indirect contact with the world and its activities, (2) use and application of knowledge thus gained, (3) correlation between different subjects, (4) the consciousness of achievement.

The Curriculum

The curriculum should be based on the nature and needs of children and youth, with the idea of acquiring knowledge as far as possible through the scientific method of first-hand observation, investigation, experiment, and independent search for material. Through these activities the world of books and abstract ideas is entered. The school should increasingly widen the circle of the child's world, leading him not only to appreciation of national ideals, but also to a realization of the interdependence of peoples and international good-will.

The Teacher as a Guide

The teacher should guide the pupil in observing, experimenting and forming judgments that he may learn how to use various sources of information including life activities as well as books, and how to reason about the information thus acquired, and how to express logically and effectively the conclusion reached. The teacher should be given latitude to express his own initiative and originality.

Scientific Study of Pupil Development

The school should study and endeavour to meet the individual needs and capacities of each child. School records should not be confined to the marks given by teachers to show the advancement of pupils in their study of subjects, but should also include both objective and subjective reports on those physical, mental, emotional, and social characteristics which concern both school and adult life, and which can be affected by the school and the home. Such records should be used as a guide for the treatment of each pupil and should also serve to focus the attention of the teacher on the all important work of child development.

Cooperation Between School and Home

Since the child's life at school and at home is an integral whole, the school cannot accomplish its purpose without the active support and intelligent cooperation of the parents. Reciprocally the school should aid the home in problems concerned with the child.

The School a Contributor to Educational Progress

The school should be an educational laboratory, where new methods are encouraged, and where the best of the past is leavened by the discoveries of the present, and the result freely added to be sum of educational knowledge.[79]

Conclusion

In view of the wide extent and variety of the country, it may be rash to present any general conclusion on elementary education in the United States. Variety marks the compulsory attendance laws and their enforcement, the length of the school year, the character of the buildings, the quality of the teachers and of teaching, the nature and scope of the curriculum and the courses of study, and the expenditure. If approached from this point of view, the country is far from providing equality of opportunity. Certain general tendencies do, however, stand out. The elementary school is the common school of all the children, and not only the common foundation, but the lower stage of a system which reaches from the kindergarten to the university. In the absence of a central educational authority for the whole country and of strong central authorities in all States, the burden of educational progress is borne by local systems, which are free to experiment, by institutions for the study of education, and by the societies for the scientific study of education. To some extent, the mobility of teachers and educators tends to the spread of certain norms for the whole country, and in the same way the use of the same textbooks over a large area has the same effect. But more characteristic than these facts are the vigour and imagination which are applied to the advance of educational progress. From this point of view the American school systems constitute a veritable laboratory. The very qualities, however, which are the strength of American education, as contrasted with education in other countries, are at once its weakness. There is on the whole too strong a tendency to develop education as an autonomous science, or, in other words, to found education on scientific theory to the neglect of the social environment in which it functions. The reason for this is to be found, not in a lack of vision (there is perhaps too much of this), but in the absence of any strong, dominating, cultural tradition. Hence the cult of the individual and of individual success; hence the reference in all curriculum discussions to the needs and abilities of the child and in more radical circles to the activities and experience of the child as the only guides worth considering. American education—and what is said of elementary applies equally to other branches of education—unlike education in other countries, does not grow out of, and does not merge into, a consciously recognized culture. Because it lacks this solid foundation, there is a tendency to experiment in every direction with a native faith that the cannos of science can be applied to human affairs.

REFERENCES

1. In this "Message on a New Step in Education"; *see Educational Yearbook, 1928*, of the International Institute, Teachers College, Columbia University, p. 39 (New York, 1929).
2. On administration of education in England.
3. The School Attendance Bill, which proposed to extend full-time compulsory education to fifteen, was passed in the House of Commons, 1931, with an amendment which provided that the bill, if enacted, was not to become effective until provision was made to assist voluntary organizations with grants for buildings; the bill was rejected in the House of Lords.
4. The latest edition was issued in 1927.
5. *See Handbook of Suggestions for the Consideration of Teachers and Others Concerned in the Work of Public Elementary Schools*, p. 8 (London, 1927).
6. *The Primary School*, p. xvi.
7. *The Primary School*, p. 93.
8. *Our Public Elementary Schools*. p. 8 (London, 1926).
9. *Handbook of Suggestions*, pp. 38 f.
10. *Handbook of Suggestions*, p. 13.
11. *Handbook of Suggestions*, p. 16.
12. *Report of the British Association, 1923*, p. 267. See also a similar statement by Sir Percy Nunn in *Report on Examinations*, pp. 54 f. (New York, 1931).

13. *The Primary School,* pp. 152 f.
14. *Handbook of Suggestions,* pp. 55 f.
15. See Meader, Emma Grant. '*Teaching Speech in the Elementary School* (New York, 1928).
16. *Handbook of Suggestions,* p. 120.
17. *Handbook of Suggestions,* p. 132.
18. *Handbook of Suggestions* contains an *Appendix on the League of Nations.*
19. *See The Syllabus of Physical Training for Schools (1919), Syllabus of Physical Training for Public Supplement for Older Girls (1927), Reference Book of Gymnastic Training for Boys (1927) and Handbook of Suggestions on Health Education* (1928), all issued by the Board of Education.
20. *See Report of the Consultative Committee on Books in Elementary Schools* (London, 1931).
21. At Kearsely, near Bury, Lancashire.
22. Education Pumphlet No. 60 (London, 1928).
23. *School Government Chronicle,* Jan. 16, 1928, p. 60.
24. *Report on the Education of the Adolescent,* p. 73.
25. One of the serious criticisms of the American system is that in the zeal to provide identified opportunities for all the interests of the able students have been sacrificed. See Thorndike E. L. "The Distribution of Education," *School Review,* May, 1932, pp. 335 ff.
26. See the *Annual Report of the London County Council* on the Elementary Schools of London, 1925, Appendix 1 (London, 1925), and *The London Education Service,* pp. 52 ff. (London, 1927).
27. Auguste Comte's philosophy of positivism and its educational interpretation would, of course have to be excepted. Emile Durkheim is known outside of France as a sociologist by many students who do not know that he was professor of education at the Sorbonne.
28. Nitlean, Cloudesley, *Studies in Foreign Education,* p. 219 (London, Harrap, 1913).
29. *Educational Yearbook, 1929,* p. 141. This and the other quotations in the above paragraphs are taken from Felix Pécaut's article in

this volume on "The Philosophy Underlying the National System of Education is France."

30. *Educational Yearbook, 1929,* p. 171.

31. Quoted by Albert Thomas in an address on *La Prolongation de la Scolaritié et ses Repercussions sociales.* See *L'Hygiene par l'Exemple,* January-February, 1928, pp. 11 ff.

32. According to a report quoted in the *Living Age* (January 12, 1924, p. 50), from *L'Intransigeant,* out of 700 recruits at one army station, two out of every ten could be classed as educated in the ordinary sense of the term; of the remaining eight, five on the average could read and write a little, two could spell with great difficulty, and the eighth was quite illiterate. In justification it may be stated that these recruits had passed through the period of compulsory school age during the War.

33. See further, Chapter VII

34. See further, Chapter V.

35. From the *Instruction, 20 Juin 1923, relative nouveau Plan d'Etudes des Ecoles Elemutaires.* See Kandel, I. L. *French Elementary Schools, Official Courses of Study,* p. 54 (New York, 1926).

36. Kandel, *op. cit.,* p. 45.

37. Kanded, *op. cit.,* p. 51.

38. Prudhommeaux, J., *Pour la Paix par l'Ecole* (Nimes, 1928); German translation, *Der Kumpf um das Geschichtsbuch in Frankreich* (Leipzig, 1920).

39. Gay, P. H. and Morteux, O., *Programmes Officials des Ecoles Primaires Elementaires, 1923, Texte officielle, Repartition Mensuelle et Hebdomadaire, Emploi du Temps—Documents Annexes* (Paris, 1924). A translation of this work will be found in Kandel, I.L., *op. cit.,* pp. 121 ff.

40. Alexander, T., *Prussian Elementary Schools,* Chapter XVII (New York, 1918).

41. The requirement of four years' attendance in the *Grundschule,* followed by nine years in a secondary school, would have extended the period of education by one year beyond the traditional twelve.

42. In Bavaria three years.

43. Kandel, I.L. and Alexander, T., *The Reorganization of Education in Prussia,* p. 193 (New York, 1927).
44. *Ibid.,* p. 191.
45. *Ibid.,* p. 193.
46. Kandel, I.L., and Alexander, T., *op. cit.,* p. 203.
47. *Ibid.,* p. 204.
48. Kandel, I. L. and Alexander, T., *op. cit.,* pp. 205 f.
49. The use of textbooks which glorify war and false interpretation of the World War and its curses are forbidden.
50. A common decree was issued by the Ministers of Education on July 19, 1922, containing suggestions for the cooperation of schools and universities for the protection of the Republic. See Kandel, I. L. and Alexander T., *op. cit.,* pp. 213 ff.
51. See Ministers della Pubblica Istruzione. Direzione generale per l'Istruzione Elementare. *Relazionc sul Numcro, la Distribuzionc ed il Funzionamento delle Scuole Element* (Rome, 1923).
52. Gentile, G., *The Reform of Education* translated by D. Bigongiari, Chapter X (New York, Hartcourt, Brace & Co. 1922).
53. Lombardo-Radice's most important works are his *Nuovi Saggi di Propaganda pedagogics,* (Turin, 1922); *Educazione e Diseducazione* (Turin, 1923); and *Vila nuova della Scaida Popolo* (Rome, 1925).
54. Codignola's writings include *La Reforma della Coltura magistrale* (Catania, 1917); *La Pedagogia rivoluzionaria* (2nd ed., Florence, 1925); and *II Problema dell Educazione nasionale in Italic* (Florence, 1925).
55. The Fascist salute, a revival of the ancient Roman salute with outstretched arm (*Salute Romano Fascista,* is justified as a same Fascist and hygienic practice. "destined to exercise the most beneficent influence on the formation of the character of the young." The Fascist salute was required in the schools in an official circular of January 2, 1926 (*Bolletino Officials,* January 5, 1926).
56. The last name, *scuale materne,* is the title used for the pre-school in the Code for Elementary Education (*Testo unico delle Leggi e Norme giuridiche sulla Istruzione elementare, a sulla sue Opere d' Integrazione,* 1928). The official name has not succeeded in ousting the traditional use of *Asili d'infanzia* or *asili infantili.*

57. Chapter VIII.
58. The variety of types of elementary schools is given in Chapter IV.
59. For other ėxperimental schools see Ferriere, A., *L'Aube de l'Ecole sereine en Italic* (Paris 1927).
60. Quoted in Pinkevitch, A.P., *The New Education in the Soviet Republic* p. 193 (New York, John Day Co., 1929).
61. Quoted in Pinkevitch, *op. cit.*, p. 200.
62. As given in Pinkevitch, *op. cit.*, p. 305.
63. *Educational Yearbook, 1927,* of the International Institute, Teachers College, Columbia University, pp. 324 ff. (New York, 1928).
64. Quoted in Woody, Thomas, *op. cit.*, p. 110.
65. U.S. Office of Education, Bulletin, 1920, No. 16. *Biennial Survey of Education,* 1920-1928, pp. 286 f.
66. Department of Superintendence, *Fifth Yearbook,* p. 9. (Washington, D.C., 1927).
67. This and the other quotations will be found in the Department of Superintendence, *Seventh Yearbook,* Chapter IV, pp. 79 ff. (Washington, D.C., 1920).
68. Department of Superintendence, *Second Yearbook,* p. 87 f. (Washington, D.C. 1929).
69. National Education Association, *Research Bulletin,* Vol. III, Nos. 4 and 5, Sept.-Nov., 1925 p. 118.
70. Department of Superintendence, *Second Yearbook,* p. 94 (Washington, D.C. 1929).
71. *Ibid., Fourth Yearbook,* p. 28.
72. *Ibid.*, Second Yearbook, p. 102.
73. Department of Superintendence, *Second Yearbook,* p. 102.
74. Department of Superintendence, *Second Yearbook,* pp. 103 f.
75. See Flanders, J., *Legislative Control of the Elementary Curriculum* (New York, 1925).
76. Stratemeyer, F., and Bruner, H.E., *Rating Elementary School Courses of Study,* pp. 170 f. (New York, Teachers College, Columbia University, 1926).

77. See Tidwell, C.J., *State Control of Textbooks* (New York, 1928).
78. The laws of learning have been subjected to criticism as an inadequate explanation of learning except at the lower levels by Professor B.H. Bode in his *Conflicting Psychologies of Learning* (New York, 1920).
79. It is not yet clear how the progressives plan to reconcile these principles with the mean recent movement sponsored by the Progressive Education Association for "social reconstruction through education"

2

Preparation of Elementary School Teachers

History

The preparation of elementary school teachers began simultaneously with the rise of public systems of elementary education. Its history thus begins in the nineteenth century, although the necessity of providing some preparation had been frequently recognized earlier. Richard Mulcaster, John Lily, John Brinsley, and Charles Hoole in England and Ratke and Comenius were among the first leaders of educational thought who advocated the training of teachers. To Duke Ernst the Pious belongs the honour of recognizing its importance as the basis of a sound system of education, and although he was himself unable, owing at depleted treasury, to organize institutions for the preparation of teachers, he left an injunction for their development in his will, drawn up in 1654. It was not until 1694 that his grandson, Frederick II of Gotha, established a number of *seminaria scolastica*. The experiment was short-lived and was soon overshadowed by the efforts of leaders in the pietist movement for the extension of education, with which the names of August Hermann Francke, J.C. Schienmeyer, and J.J. Hecker were associated. It was, however, the Pestalozzian movement which exercised a permanent influence on the development of institutions for the preparation of elementary school teachers in Germany at a time when, following the disaster at Jena in 1806, the importance of education as an essential instrument of national reconstruction was recognized. Though the efforts of disciples who were inspired by Pestalozzi, among whom were Plamann, Zeller, Henning, Denzee, Dinter, Harnish, and Diesterweg, the idea of preparing teaches in special institutions (*Lehrerseminare*) became firmly established in Germany by 1825.

In France the first institution for the training of elementary school teachers was established by the Convention in 1794 and opened in the following year in Paris as the *école normale* which became the prototype of similar institutions in other parts of the world and gave its name to the characteristic institution later established in the United States. The first beginnings of a system of teacher training in England were associated with the monitorial system developed by Andrew Bell and the National Society for the Education of the Poor in the Principles of the Established Church (1811) and by Joseph Lancaster and the British and Foreign School Society (1814). It was not until some twenty years later that an active movement began for the establishment of normal schools or training colleges. In 1835 John Arthur Roebuck unsuccessfully introduced a bill in Parliament for the creation of normal schools on the model of the French. One of the first proposals of the Committee of Council on Education, set up in 1839, was to establish a national normal school with a model school attached; owing to the opposition of the two societies mentioned, the funds already voted by Parliament and later increased were used to assist these and other denominational societies to erect training colleges. Side by side with this development there was introduced in 1846 the pupil-teacher system of training; the two systems have continued up to the present time. In the United States the preparation of teachers for elementary schools was first undertaken by the academies, the earliest of which was established in Philadelphia as a result of proposals made by Benjamin Franklin in 1749. The contribution of the academies, although widespread and adopted by the Legislature in New

York State, was not regarded as satisfactory. A campaign for the establishment of special institutions began to be promoted actively about 1825 by W.E. Russell, Thomas Gallaudet, Samuel R. Hall, who opened the first private normal school at Concord, Vermont, in 1823, and James G. Carter who later came to be known as the "Father of Normal Schools." Carter's efforts were crowned by the first legislative enactment in favour of normal schools in Massachusetts in 1838 and by the opening of the first public normal school in the United States at Lexington, Massachusetts, in the following year. The legislation and the normal school set the pattern for the country and displaced the preparation of teachers in academies. By the middle of the nineteenth century both the principle and the practice of preparing teachers were definitely established in the four countries considered here and began to exercise a profound influence in other parts of the world.

Changing Status

The subsequent development of systems for preparing teachers has been determined largely by the changing character of public elementary education in each country and by the progress of educational theory. So long as the emphasis of elementary education was mainly upon literacy and the teaching of the three R's, an adequate training in these subjects and in simple methods of instruction were regarded as sufficient and the test of an education consisted in evidence of mastery of these subjects. The social status of elementary education as the education of the masses helped to confirm this point of view, so we illustrated in the reactionary legislation passed in 1854 in Prussia through fear that too much education had inclined the elementary school teachers toward liberalism in politics. The development of compulsory and universal elementary education and the gradual social changes towards the end of the nineteenth century led to demands, not only for more education, but on the part of teachers for a type of preparation which was not limited merely to training in ability to give instruction in the rudiments. The movements for enriching the curriculum of the elementary schools and the rise of strong professional organizations combined to lead to an agitation for the preparation of teachers on a higher level than was provided. Secondary education as a minimum preliminary education and the organization of teacher-training institutions on a university level began to be demanded. Progress was slow; in some cases political, in others economic reasons were obstacles to reconstruction. The gradual recognition at the beginning of the twentieth century of the enlarged scope of the elementary school as an institution to give not merely instruction but an education in the broadest sense, the development of educational theory and psychology, which carried the conviction that the teacher's task consists of more than merely imparting information, the gradual movement toward the acceptance of the elementary school as the common school for all not for the masses alone, and the realization of the meaning of education as an instrument of social and national welfare—all these factors have helped to support the movement for better systems of preparing teachers for elementary schools.

This movement, however, represents inherently something more than a mere increase in the number of years of preparation or the organization of teacher-training institutions on a university level. It involves a change from an apprenticeship to a professional basis of preparation. So long as the function of elementary education was looked upon as the imparting of a knowledge of the three R's and perhaps history and geography, the acquisition of subject-matter and rules for imparting it—tricks of the trade—was regarded as an adequate preparation. The increasing complexity of the task of education, the recognition of each pupil as an individual, and the increasing recognition that an educational institution cannot be run as an institution in which the teacher's sole function is to carry out orders from above, whether in the form of prescribed curricula, courses of study, and methods of instruction, or of standardized examinations, all pointed in the same direction, that the teacher's preparation must be on a professional basis and that the teacher must be trained to teach through mastery not of rules but of principles. In other words, if the task of education, as Sir John Adams has described it, is to teach John *x*, then the teacher must know, not only *x*, but John, and his probable reaction to *x*. But he must know more than *x*, the subject; he must understand its significance in the environment in which he teaches, its educative value, and its relation to all other subjects, its pertinence for John's development, as well as the methods by which John's interest can be aroused to master it. The same holds true if, as in the "new" or "progressive" education, the teacher seeks to start with John's interests and to organize his environment for their growth.

There is, too, a further change which is taking place. So long as the school was conceived in its original sense as a place of leisure, an institution, sheltered and divorced from the main currents of life, in which certain subjects were to be imparted, an emphasis on subject-matter and methods still constituted an adequate preparation. The school cannot, however, be divorced from "politics," and literary or mental training alone do not give an adequate preparation for the complex demands of modern life. Without necessarily accepting the theory of Soviet education, that the school must be an institute on for indoctrination in the ideology on which the State is founded, educational theory in general accepts the principle that the school must inevitably be colored by the environment in which the school functions. The teacher must accordingly be not only a master of the subjects which he professes, but he must understand the relation of the school to social and national welfare as expressed not only on its cultural side but in its everyday manifestations—social, political, and economic.

The expansion of the scope and significance of the teacher's position implies as a natural corollary an extension of the period of preparation. Throughout the nineteenth century the vision of the intending elementary school teacher was restricted to his future occupation; selected at an early age from an elementary school, he was prepared either in an elementary school or in an institution administered by the authorities responsible for elementary education. As a consequence he was never able to shake off what the French call *l'esprit primaire,* a tendency to worship primary facts and information rather than ideas; narrow intellectual contacts inevitably resulted in narrow points of view. The tendency today is to postpone the early choice of teaching as a vocation by providing a complete general education in a secondary school followed by preparation in an institution on the university level.

The Problems of Teacher Preparation

The prolongation of the period of preparation does not, however, simplify the problems involved. While it is true that the introduction of a preliminary general education gives the teacher-candidate a broader background than is possible when the training institution is a direct continuation of the elementary school, the professional preparation of the teacher must include the methods of teaching the subjects which make up, as it were, the tools of his trade. Further, the time is passed when the claim that he who knows can teach can be justified; this means that preparation must include not only what to teach but how to teach. In the United States the emphasis tended for a long time to be on methods, on how to teach, as the most important part of professional preparation; in England both aspects were included, but subject-matter was taught by one group and methods by another group of instructors, the student often being expected to integrate and synthesize the two sides himself. The practice of the German *Lehrerseminare* was to synthesize the two, the teacher of arithmetic, for example, being responsible for the content of the subject, the study of its place in education, and the methods of teaching it as well as demonstration and supervision of practice in it. In other words, the teaching of each subject was professionalized; the German practice, however, was open to the criticism of devoting too much time to an extended review of the subjects of the elementary school without providing adequate opportunities of introducing the students to the standards of a higher education.

The problem of organizing adequate systems for preparing teachers is still further complicated by the recognition of the necessity of providing differentiated training for different stages of elementary education and for different environmental conditions. Provision must now be made for the preparation of teachers for nursery schools, for infant schools and kindergartens, for primary grades, and for intermediate schools, which for the time being still hover between elementary and secondary schools. A larger problem is the adaptation of teacher-preparation to the needs of urban and rural areas, a problem which has been directly attacked only in the United States and indirectly in England by the retention of a lower level of training for prospective rural school teachers.

In the reforms which are taking place in the preparation of teachers an attempt is being made to prolong the general, all-round education of the students, to give them a deeper and broader insight into the content and significance of the subjects which they are to teach, and at the same time to associate special methods simultaneously with the study of each subject. The tendency is thus to professionalizes subject-matter. Beyond this, the preparation of the teacher involves the study of the so-called professional subjects—the history and theory of education, educational psychology, and general theory of method; these traditional subjects are gradually being increased by the addition of tests and measurements, sociology, and special aspects of psychology. Finally, the practical aspect, induction into teaching, constitutes the third important phase of the problem. This problem is beset by difficulties more of an administrative than of a theoretical character due to the inadequacy of practice institutions directly under the control of the training institutions. These difficulties, combined with the increased responsibilities which have fallen on the teacher, have led to the recognition that the few years devoted to professional preparation could not be relied upon to produce a finished teacher and that a period of probation is necessary before a young teacher can be given a permanent appointment.

The rapidity it with which educational reforms are taking place and the growing recognition that the school must be adapted to social progress have in turn directed attention to the fact that the training of the teacher cannot be restricted to the years of preparation, but must be continued through out his career. For this purpose some countries have relied upon staffs of inspectors or supervisors to keep teachers up to the mark; elsewhere active professional organizations have helped to keep teachers in touch with educational progress; generally the tendency is to organize more formal methods for training teachers in service by means of conferences, study groups, and summer courses. A teacher who does not grow tends to stagnate and to become mechanical. Again the change in the character of education is demonstrated: when education was largely instruction in a somewhat fixed round of subjects, the initial training with occasional further study was adequate for the situation; the new place of the school in society, the necessity of overhauling subjects and curricula periodically, the participation of the teachers in the making of courses of study, the constant expansion and progress of educational theory which in turn are the results of experimentation, have so broadened the professional equipment of the teacher that two or three years of initial preparation are no longer sufficient to keep the teacher abreast of the times.

The changing character of the school, involving as it does an extension of the period of preparation, has begun to exercise another influence which is economic and social in character. Although the idea was gradually discarded in the nineteenth century that anybody was competent enough to teach in an elementary school, the low esteem in which the education of the masses was held attached to the teachers in the schools intended for them. Salaries were also commensurate with the esteem of the school and with the length of preparation required for teaching in them. The development of a professional consciousness which led to the creation of teachers associations the changes which have taken place more recently in the status of elementary education, and the gradual prolongation of the period of preparation have resulted in a slow but definite improvement in the status of elementary school teachers and in increased remuneration. In other words, the profession of teaching is not exempt from the general principles which govern supply and demand in other occupations. In addition to improvements in the remuneration of teachers which open up a genuine career, there have been provided protection against disability and retiring allowances. There are still difficulties to be overcome on the economic side; in some countries there is the problem of equal pay for men and women, or of the adjustment of salary scales to family responsibilities or to variations in the cost of living. The extension of the period of preparation which may in time, and in some places has, become almost as long for elementary as for secondary school teachers, may bring in its train a demand for single salary scales with which some American authorities are now experimenting. Tenure, on the whole, has not been a serious problem in European countries or in England, except occasionally in voluntary or non-provided schools, but in the United States there is still room for improvement. For the present, however, the important point is that there has been an appreciable improvement in the status of elementary school teachers such as could hardly have been anticipated at the beginning of the century. Progress will depend to some extent on the general acceptance of the elementary school as the common school for all and on the increased recognition of the significance of the school for social and national welfare. Improvement of status will have the further salutary effect of directing the attention and interest of teachers away from preoccupation with their economic condition toward closer study of the more fundamental and important problems of education.

The tendencies described above will be found exemplified more or less in the accounts of the systems for the preparation of teachers presented in the following pages. At one end is the Italian reforms of 1923, which, providing for the preparation of teachers in schools at the secondary level, is based on the assumption that the successful teacher is he who is thoroughly imbused with the cultural and spiritual aspirations of his country and for whom preoccupation with methods and educational theory, rather than a broad philosophical understanding of life, is a hindrance rather than a help. France has still retained the nineteenth-century attitude to teachers as servants of the State trained to carry out prescribed regulations. England is in a stage of transition and reform which represent a tendency to place the preparation of teachers on a university level with an emphasis on genuine professionalization; at the same time the traditional pupil-teacher system is retained for the training of rural school teachers. The United States represents every type of teacher-training from training in high schools to preparation in teachers' colleges and schools of education in universities. Germany again sets the standard, as she did at another level in the nineteenth century, by organizing the preparation of teachers on a university level either in independent institutions, in institutions affiliated with universities, or in universities. Soviet Russia stands outside of the general stream in training teachers for elementary schools in institutions at the secondary level and in he intimate association of this training with the polytechnization of all schools.

1. ENGLAND

History

The preparation of elementary school teachers was strongly influenced until recently by its dual origin in the purpil-teacher system and in training colleges. The former was introduced in 1846 by a Minute of the Committee of Council or Education for which Sir James Kay-Shuttleworth, who had seen the system at work in Holland, was responsible. It was definitely an apprenticeship system in which boys and girls were indentured at the age of thirteen to the headmaster of an elementary school for five years; the pupil-teachers taught during the day and after school hours continued their general education under the direction of their headmasters. At the close of the period they were submitted to the examination for the Queen's Scholarships, a competitive test by which the best candidates were selected to continue their preparation in training colleges.

The apprenticeship practice began to decline gradually after the Act of 1870 established a system of public elementary schools and the need of a broader academic preparation began to be recognized. The age of pupil-teachers was raised to sixteen in urban centres and to fifteen in rural areas; centre classes were established in 1874 and were gradually organized towards the close of the century into pupil-teacher centres; academic preparation was emphasized and for one year the pupil-teachers were required to obtained practical teaching experience. Those who passed the Queen's Scholarship Examinations proceeded to training colleges; those who failed became uncertificted teachers, but might later obtain certificates by examination without training, a practice introduced in 1847.

Training colleges began to be established first by the two leading educational societies, the British and Foreign School Society and the National Society, with the help of grants for buildings allotted to them in 1839 by the Committee of Council on Education; other denominational societies—Wesleyan, Congregational, and Roman Catholic—began to open their own colleges. The Borough Road School, in which monitors had been trained since 1805, was reorganized in 1842 and became a training college, but had already been preceded by one institution opened in 1836 by the Home and

Colonial School Society to train female teachers and another established in 1840 by James Kay (later Sir James Kay-Shuttleworth) to train teachers for pauper schools. With the help of building and per capita grants from the Government, the number of training colleges increased rapidly in the next twenty years. They were assured by the pupil-teacher system of a supply of adequately prepared teachers.

The dual system—pupil teacherships and training colleges—continued to provide the large majority of elementary school teachers. From 1846 to 1861 salaries were paid directly by the Government and teachers virtually enjoyed the status of civil servants. In the absence of publicly maintained secondary schools, the system was the only one practicable under the circumstances; its chief weakness was that it was wholly unrelated to any other branch of education—the students came from elementary schools, were pupil-teachers in elementary schools, were trained by teachers whose sole experience had been in elementary schools, and returned to elementary schools. The only opportunity open to the more ambitious teachers was to prepare for the external degree of the University of London. Despite the limitations of the practice, which became still more restricted when the vicious system of payment by results was introduced in 1861, the elementary school teachers performed a notable service in the progress of education. The desirability of introducing another spirit in elementary education began to be recognized and in 1888 the Cross Commission recommended the establishment of day training departments in universities and university colleges which had by that time begun to flourish in increased numbers. Two years later the recommendation was embodied in the Code, and a third method of preparing teachers was thus adopted at the university level.

The Education Act of 1902 created new possibilities and opportunities. In the first place, the Act permitted the larger local education authorities (counties and county boroughs) to provide secondary schools out of local rates with the help of government grants. Secondly, the same authorities were allowed to establish their own training colleges, for the building of which the Government began to give grants in 1906. The establishment of secondary schools created a new route by which intending teachers could obtain their preliminary training. Pupil-teacher centres were retained, especially in the rural areas, but gradually the majority of intending teachers, who were given free tuition and maintenance allowances, began to pass through the secondary schools. The difference between the two methods was that a candidate who entered a pupil-teacher centre remained up to the age of sixteen and then became a pupil-teacher up to the age of eighteen, when on passing an examination he might become an uncertificated teacher or enter a training college. The candidate who entered a secondary school pursued a general course also up to the age of sixteen, and then, if recommended by his headmaster and on signing a declaration to become a teacher, received a bursary or grant to continue his education for another year; at the end of this period he might, if he had passed an examination qualifying him for entrance to a training college, continue his studies there or become a student-teacher. The student-teacher year was divided between observation and practice in an elementary school and further study in a secondary school; at the end of the year the student teacher, if he had passed the necessary examination, might enter a training college or training department of a university or become an uncertificated teacher. The training colleges gave a two-year course, the university training departments originally a three-year course and after 1911 a four-year course, the first three in preparation for an academic degree, the fourth devoted to professional training.

This system continued until it began to be subjected to criticism which led to the appointment of a Department Committee in 1923

> to review the arrangements for the training of teachers for public elementary schools, and to consider what changes, if any, in the organization or finance of the

existing system are desirable in order that a supply of well qualified teachers adjustable to the demands of the schools may be secured, regard being had to (a) the economy of public funds; (b) the attractions offered to young persons by the teaching profession as compared with other professions and occupation; (c) the facilities afforded by secondary schools and universities for acquiring academic qualifications.

The Committee in its *Report*, published in 1923, in considering the problem of recruiting teachers, expressed itself as opposed to the practice of aiding intending teachers before the age of sixteen, and was of the opinion that the most effective method of securing a qualified supply of teachers is through satisfactory salaries, tenure, and pensions, improved conditions of school life, and freedom from undue administrative control. It recommended the ultimate elimination of supplementary and uncertificated teachers and the discontinuance of the acting teachers' certificate, whereby an untrained teacher could obtain a certificate by examination. It deprecated the system of student and pupil-teachership, but admitted that the latter might have to be retained in rural areas, where secondary schools were not accessible. The Committee rejected as not practicable the suggestion that all teachers should be trained in universities, but recommended a closer connection between training colleges and universities.

The Committee thus attacked some of the defects of the system of preparing teachers which had been accumulated in the course of its development. Among these were the premature recruiting of candidates for the teaching profession, the retention of the student-teacher year, the segregation of candidates in separate centres, and the isolation of the training colleges. The improvement of salary scales and the provision of a sound superannuation scheme had already made the teaching profession sufficiently attractive to dispense with artificial aids to secure a supply of candidates. The student-teacher year had been taken over from the pupil-teacher system on the assumption that a period of practical experience in elementary schools was desirable as a basis for testing the suitability of candidates and for the subsequent professional study. In practice some school principals devoted attention to the student-teachers assigned to them; in general the student-teachers without guidance picked up habits which they had later to unlearn. The training colleges had developed in isolation in the nineteenth century and in the twentieth had been left suspended without constituting an integral part of the system of higher education; academically and professionally they enjoyed little independence, since they were controlled by the prescription of courses and examinations in the *Regulations* of the Board of Education.

The Board of Education at once proceeded to take steps to put the recommendations of the Committee into effect. In 1925 a Circular (1372) was issued by the Board announcing the intention of discontinuing its practice of conducting the final examinations in training colleges; this was followed in 1926 by an invitation to universities and training colleges to consider plans for cooperation between them. The *Regulations for the Training of Teachers,* issued in 1926, omitted any reference to the student-teacher year and Circular 1383 (1926), while confirming the Departmental Committee's recommendation against its retention, permitted such local authorities as wished to do so, to continue the practice. The detailed syllabus and examination requirements were replaced by a general statement that

> The course of education and professional training in a training college must be in accordance with a suitable curriculum and must include systematic study of the principles and practice of teaching. Satisfactory arrangements must be made for the examination of students at the end of their course. In the case of training colleges other than those for domestic subjects, adequate provision must be made in approved schools for practice in teaching under proper supervision, and students who

have not had practical experience as teachers in an approved capacity must spend at least twelve weeks of their course in such practice.

In thus releasing the institutions for the preparation of teachers from its control, the Board of Education looked to the adoption of the practice which prevails in the preparation for other professions in England. The preparation of lawyers and doctors, for example, is controlled entirely by the organizations which represent these professions—the Incorporated Law Society and the Inns of Court and the General Medical Council; only those who have obtained certificates granted by such bodies are permitted to engage in the practice of the professions concerned. Accordingly, the control of the preparation of teachers would, under the continued supervision of the Board, because of its general interest and the grant of financial aid, be transferred to those organizations directly concerned with the preparation and employment of teachers—the universities, training colleges, local education authorities, and teachers' associations.

To carry out the recommendations made on this point by the Departmental Committee and the Board of Education, a Committee on Universities and Training Colleges was appointed and issued its recommendations in 1928. The Committee suggested the division of the country into twelve regional groups to promote contacts between the universities and training colleges. In each of these groups a joint board was to be set up, consisting of representatives of the universities, training colleges, and local education authorities, and charged with the duty of defining standards, curricula, courses of study, and examination requirements. To coordinate the work of the regional boards it was recommended that a Central Advisory Committee for the Certification of Teachers be created, consisting in turn of representatives of the institutions concerned, to consider standards, curricula, and the scope and range of examinations.

THE PRESENT SYSTEM

Preliminary Education

The main lines of the present system can now be described. The recommendations of the Departmental Committee and of the Board of Education have already begun to bear fruit and a full-time secondary education up to the age of eligibility for entrance to a training college or university training department has been adopted as the requirement for preliminary training. In 1930 the number of pupil-teachers in centers had fallen to about one quarter of the number in 1927; of the total number (1160) 761 were rural pupil-teachers. The number of student-teachers was about one third of the number in 1927. The class of teachers known as "supplementary" still survives; the only qualification required for appointment as supplementary teachers is that candidates shall be suitable women over eighteen years of age and in good health; there are no requirements of academic attainments or of training. They may be employed, if the Board's inspectors certify them as having teaching ability, but always upon a temporary basis, in the infants' or lower classes in rural schools. They are never, as is sometimes the case in the United States with teachers with scarcely better qualifications, in sole charge of a school. The normal practice will henceforth be that boys and girls will enter a secondary school between the ages of eleven and twelve and will there pursue a general academic course without being ear-marked for teaching or any other occupation. At the age of sixteen they may become candidates for bursarships offered by a number of local education authorities to suitable students who intend to become teachers in public schools. The bursarships carry free tuition and maintenance allowances for one or two years.

Whether candidates for the teaching profession obtain scholarships or bursarships, they are expected to pass the First Secondary School Examination and to have reached the age of eighteen, if they wish to be admitted to a training college, or, if they intend to apply for admission to a university training department, they must be seventeen years of age and must have passed either a matriculation examination or the First Examination with sufficient credits to be exempted from the matriculation requirement. Owing to the limited accommodation, admission to training colleges and university training departments is selective; the age and examination requirements are the minimal; beyond these candidates must submit a certificate of good health and testimonials as to character and promise, and in most cases are interviewed. Admission to a course of preparation is thus in a sense competitive; the best students find their way into the university training departments, the next best into training colleges; those who fail to secure admission still have the opportunity of becoming uncertificated teachers, or they may enter some training institution as non-recognised students, in which case they assume the total cost of preparation themselves. The new system guarantees an adequate academic and general education such as is required in general for admission to preparation for other professions. The able student may even continue this general education and pass the Second School or Advanced Examination, which overlaps to some extent with the first year of work required for an academic degree. A candidate who enters a training institution as a recognized student must sign a declaration of intention to complete the course and to follow thereafter the profession of teacher in a public school, with the understanding that preparation for the teaching career is the sole purpose of his taking advantage of the public funds provided for the preparation of teachers.

Training Colleges

Unlike institutions devoted to the same purpose in other countries, the training college is not a state institution; it is supported by the State, but since 1928, when the new system was introduced it is no longer state-controlled. It may be provided—that is, established and maintained by a public education authority—or non-provided or established and maintained by a voluntary, usually a denominational, society.

In 1930-31 there were 74 two-year training colleges provided as follows: (a) by a university, 1; (b) by a local education authority, 22; (c) by other bodies, 51 (Church of England, 29; Roman Catholic, 8; Wesleyan, 2; and undenominational, 12). The colleges are residential or day or both day and residential institutions.

The Board of Education bears a share of the cost of building training colleges, in the case of local education authorities up to half of the cost. The contributions for maintenance, salaries, and scholarships are paid to local authorities up to half of the cost of the approved expenditures; to non-provided institutions the annual grants are paid on a per capita basis as follows: for tuition, £28 for men and £26 for women students; for maintenance, £43 for men and £34 for women; for non-resident students, £26 for men and £20 for women (these sums may be paid through the colleges direct to students in cases of need).[1] In the provided colleges there are as a rule no tuition fees; in the non-provided colleges students pay the difference between the actual cost and the income derived from grants and other sources. Needy students is provided institutions may receive monetary assistance. Since only a small number of the local education authorities maintain training colleges, whose graduates may accept employment anywhere in the country, the Board of Education raises a fund of £70,000 annually by deducting from the grants made to those authorities which do not maintain colleges and distributing it to those which do.

The staffs or faculties of the training colleges include in increasing numbers men and women who have had a university preparation and hold an honours degree (that is, they have specialized intensively in some one or two subjects) and some experience in teaching, although not necessarily or always in elementary schools, a defect frequently criticized by those who detect a certain divorce between the work of the training colleges and the needs of elementary schools. The old distinction between subject-matter and methods, which used to be marked by the presence on the staffs of masters or mistresses of method, has disappeared. Each lecturer is responsible both for courses in the subjects in which he is a specialist, and in methods of teaching them, as well as for the organization of periods for observation and demonstration in the schools. Professional subjects—principles and theory, history and psychology of education—are taught by lecturers in education who are in general responsible for the arrangements for the practical teaching of the students. The salaries of lecturers in training colleges are slightly higher than those provided by the Burnham Committee for secondary school teachers.

Courses in Training Colleges

Until 1929 the Board of Education prescribed the curricula and courses of study in training colleges. Since that time the system recommended by the Departmental Committee, the Board of Education, and the Committee on Universities and Training Colleges has been adopted, and twelve regional groups, including universities and training colleges, have been counted to set up standards of courses and examinations. Each group is administered by a representative body variously known as a delegacy, joint board, or board of administration. Thus the Board of Administration for Yorkshire Training Colleges includes representatives of the governing bodies and principals of training colleges, of the two universities (Leeds and Sheffield), and the University college (Hull), and of local education authorities in Yorkshire. The Board is assisted by three agencies: (i) an advisory council representing all types of schools, universities, training colleges, and local education authorities to discuss and make recommendations on suggestions for the development of the training of teachers; (2) boards of studies to consider courses of study and the selection of examiners; and (3) boards of examiners to approve questions drafted for examinations, and to consider the reports of the examiners, both internal and external. Each regional group is permitted to charge fees for examinations, part of which is paid by the candidates and part (£1.10.0 per candidate) is contributed by the Board. In order to secure a certain uniformity of standard and to provide a medium for the discussion of common problem, a Central Advisory Committee has been created of twenty-five members, as follows: eight representing universities, four local education authorities, for training colleges, four training college staffs, four the teaching profession, and one domestic subjects.

Since the whole system of joint boards is recent and is regarded as experimental, there has been a tendency in the framing of courses of study and requirements for examinations to cling to the traditions established by the Board of Education during its period of control in these matters. In general the aim of the training colleges is to approach their problem from a single point of view, that of giving professional preparation, and, while the teaching of subjects is on a standard in advance of that of the secondary school, it is expected that they will be taught with a view to their use in schools; beyond this opportunity is to be provided to students to select one subject and to pursue it to an advanced standard. The courses are divided into three groups—professional, general or academic, and practical.

The Board of Administration for the Yorkshire Training Colleges prescribed the following Regulations for the final examination in 1931:

Professional Subjects

1. Principles and practice of teaching
2. Hygiene
3. Physical training (theory and practice).

General Subjects[2]

Group A

1. English
2. History
3. Geography

4. Mathematics
5. General elementary science (ordinary standard only)
6. French (advanced standard only)
7. Physics (advanced standard only)
8. Chemistry (advanced standard only)
9. Biology (advanced standard only)

Group B

1. Music (theory and practice)
2. Drawing
3. Needlework and handwork (for women)
4. Handwork (for men; advanced standard only)
5. Gardening (advanced standard only)

All students are examined in the professional subjects;[3] in the general courses they may offer four subjects at ordinary standard, or two subjects at ordinary and one at advanced standard, or one subject at ordinary and two at advanced standard. English must in all cases be one of the subjects taken, and whatever selection is made, subjects must be chosen from both Groups A and B. The examination does not as a rule include papers in general elementary science, drawing (ordinary standard), needlework, handwork for women, the practice of teaching, or the practice of physical training, which are tested chiefly by inspection, supplemented by written papers, if desirable; in practical music, gardening, and advanced science, the written papers are in all cases supplemented by inspection. The grouping of subjects and the standard taken are in general determined by the type of work in which the student intends to engage—ordinary work in the elementary school, work with children over eleven, and work with infants. There is accordingly an opportunity for differentiation which until recently has been somewhat empirical. The proposed reorganization of the system into infants, junior and senior schools will provide a better opportunity for specialized preparation than in the past. Specialization for work in rural schools is not provided except that where possible observation and practice in such schools are arranged.

Under the *Regulations* of the Board, all students who have not already had some experience are expected to devote twelve weeks to teaching practice during their period of preparation. The provisions for practice teaching vary; few training colleges have their own schools, but all arrange for the use of public schools, some of which may be specially designated as demonstration schools, other for observation and practice only. But even where schools are selected as demonstration schools, the staffs of the training colleges do not have complete control of their management and courses. In general, observation and demonstration are looked after by the subject-matter lecturers, and the continued practice by the lecturers in education. It cannot be said that the situation is satisfactory; with the elimination of the student-teacher year, the situation may, indeed, become worse, for unreliable as the results of the student-teacher year were, it did bring the intending teacher into close contact with elementary schools. A remedy for the situation was found several years ago by the introduction of a year of probation; originally introduced as a measure of economy to save a year's salary increment, a few authorities have realized the opportunity provided by this year if the probationers were placed under careful and sympathetic guidance; as a general rule, however, the success of the probationary year as an induction to the practical problems of teaching depends upon the ability and interest of the head teacher under whom the probationer secures her first appointment.

Candidates who pass the final examination conducted by one of the regional boards are granted a certificate, provided that they satisfy the inspectors of the Board of Education as to their ability in practical teaching. The Board has retained this connection with the certification of teachers because of its interest in the quality of teachers throughout the country; where desired by an examining body, the Board's inspectors will also test candidates in practical subjects. Candidates who obtain the certificates of the regional boards and satisfy the inspectors in practical teaching are recognized as certificated teachers after a year of probation. There has thus been developed a system of teacher preparation governed by standards which the profession will determine for itself with the advice of the Board of Education. The result which has been attained is best expressed in the words of former Prime Minister Stanley Baldwin:

The new entrant to the profession is no longer regarded as a government trainee for a government job, segregated in a special institution, meeting none but his own type. The crown of his work no longer takes the form of a government licence to teach. By converting the certificate into a diploma granted by a joint body representing both the university and the training colleges, the Board are enabling students to train alongside men and women destined for other careers. The teacher is thus being drawn out of a backwater into the main stream of the liberal profession, and sees life from more than one angle.

University Training Departments

Since the requirements for admission to university training departments connected with universities and university colleges are higher than for entrance to a training college, the more able students obtain their preparation by this route which was introduced in 1890. In 1930-31 there were twenty two training departments in universities and university colleges. It became obvious, soon after the introduction of this system and the rapid increase in the supply of secondary schools after the Education act of 1902 was passed, that students who obtained degrees preferred to look for appointment in secondary schools. For some time the period of preparation was three years, during which the student devoted his time to the courses required for the academic degree and to professional courses required for the teacher's certificate, a heavy burden which was lifted in 1911 by the introduction of a fourth year. The time was now divided, three years being devoted to the attainment of a degree (pass or honours) and the last year to professional training. Since this practice virtually removed any distinction between preparation for teaching at the secondary and elementary level, the Board of Education, in its *Regulations* of 1926, accepted the situation and dispensed with administrative distinctions between elementary and secondary training colleges and between university training departments and other training colleges.

University training departments receive grants from the Board of Education as follows: £35 for each recognized student in the fourth year of the course, a grant to cover the cost of fees for the degree course and an additional £5 per student for general supervision, and a grant paid to each recognized student (£26 for men and £20 for women living at home; £43 for men and £34 for women residing in hostels).[4]

The students in university training departments devote the first three years to academic courses leading to a degree either on the pass or ordinary level, which is characterized by extensive study of a number of subjects, or on the honours level, which implies specialization in one or more subjects closely allied (e.g., classics, Latin and a modern language, modern languages, history, mathematics and physics, physics, chemistry, etc.). On the professional side little difference is made in the work of the students, except that those who have a clear intention of teaching in the elementary schools must take courses in practical subjects. Teaching practice provided for according to the *Regulations* of the Board is arranged in both elementary and secondary schools. The course terminates with an examination conducted by the university, or in the case of university colleges by a degree-granting university which provides for the examination of external students; while there are variations in the character of this examination, it generally includes the professional subjects and methods of teaching special subjects. Successful candidates are awarded a diploma in education which entitles the holder to the elementary teachers' certificate, if the holder has had practical experience in an elementary school; candidates who fail to reach the requirements for the diploma may be recommended for a certificate.

As the reorganization of the system of education proceeds, it seems probable that candidates who complete a four-year course will be employed in secondary, central, or senior schools, and graduates of training colleges in infants or junior schools. Such an arrangement may result in a more general recognition of the need of more carefully organized differentiation of courses along functional lines. The four-year system, besides providing a supply of teachers with a thorough academic training and professional preparation, has also furnished the group from which head teachers of elementary schools have been drawn, since a degree has become a general requirement for this position.

Other Institutions for the Preparation of Teachers

In addition to the two-year training colleges, which may offer a third-year course for specialized training, and the university training departments, there are a number of institutions for the preparation of special teachers. Six colleges prepare teachers of infants and young children to take the examinations of the National Froebel Union, whose certificates are recognized by the Board. Teachers of handicrafts may be trained in the third-year course of a training college or in two technical institutions, Loughborough College and Shoreditch Technical Institute, which have organized two-year courses for the purpose. Teachers of domestic subjects may receive their training in special colleges which offer two-or three-year courses. Art teachers are prepared either in schools of art of in the third-year course of training colleges. Preparation of teachers of physical training is provided in the training colleges either in the regular two-year course or in the third-year course.[5]

Rural school teachers recieve their preparation either in secondary schools or in pupil-teachers centres. The former may become uncertificated teachers in rural schools after passing a First School Examination. Following a *Report of the Departmental Committee on the Training of Rural Teachers,* issued in 1929, it was decided to retain the pupil-teacher centres and to provide for them a course of study terminating in a special examination the conduct of which was placed in the hands of the Oxford Examination Delegacy and the Cambridge Examinations Syndicate. This examination differs from the First School Examination only in the fact that a foreign language is optional. The papers in English, history, geography, a foreign language, drawing, and needlework are identical with those set in the First School Examinations; those in elementary mathematics, natural science, music, gardening, hygiene with housecraft, and handicraft are based on special courses of study. Except for English, including an oral examination, and natural science, candidates are given permission to select from these subjects which are arranged in groups. Practical subjects are tested by inspection. The minimum age at which candidates take the examination is seventeen. Those who pass the examination may continue their further preparation in a training college.

The Departmental Committee reported that "the special needs of rural schools receive insufficient direct attention," and recommended that, in view of the reorganization of the school system into junior and senior schools, more important places be assigned to biological science, rural economics, professional subjects, and practical maintenance with rural school work, and that the content of courses in general should refer more directly to rural school teaching.

Certification of Teachers

The Board of Education recognizes for purposes of the grant three types of elementary school teachers: (1) The supplementary teachers whose only qualifications are age, physical fitness, and approval by the inspectors. The number of teachers of this type decreases every year; thus in 1931 there were 7270 supplementary teachers in regular employment as contrasted with 7497 in the previous year. It must again be made clear that such teachers are usually assigned to teach infants and younger children and never have charge of a school, as many happen with teachers with no better qualifications in the United States. (2) The uncertificated teachers whose qualifications at least guarantee a preparation equivalent to the requirements for admission to a training college. With the gradual disappearance of the pupil-teacher system and the student-teacher year, the new generation of uncertificated teachers will enter upon their work without any professional preparation. The abolition in 1929 of the acting teacher's certificate, granted on examination by the Board of Education to experienced but untrained teachers, the lower scale of salary paid to them, the refusal of the more progressive authorities to appoint them, and the absence of opportunities of promotion to principalships are already having their effect upon the number of uncertificated teachers. In 1931 there were regularly employed 30,632 uncertificated teachers, over seven hundred less than in 1930 (31,385). The larger authorities (London County and county borough) employed only about 18 per cent of the total number of uncertificated teachers. Their status will be further affected by the reorganization of the school system and the probability is that they will be limited to work in infants and junior schools. The opportunity is always open to those who wish, and can afford to do so, to enter a training college. (3) The third group consists of certificated teachers, who for the present include those who obtained their certificates by training and examination or by examination without training. The avenue to the second type of certificate (acting teachers' certificate) has now been closed. The improved scales of salaries and the adoption of a sound superannuation system, combined with the refusal of many authorities to employ any but certificated teachers, have increased their number; in 1931 there were in regular employment 126,245 certificated teachers as contrasted with 124,597 in 1930. Slightly more than fifty per cent of these teachers were in the service of the larger authorities.

The total number of teachers employed in public elementary schools in 1931 was 168,934, a number which included, in addition to the three types mentioned, teachers of special subjects and handicrafts who were not certificated. Of the total 43,775 teachers were sent and 125,159 were women. The general principle which is followed is that senior boys—that is, boys above the age of eleven—shall be taught by men.

Status of Teachers

The progressive improvement of the preparation of teachers has been accompanied by a marked improvement in their status. As contrasted with the practice which is common in other European countries, English teachers are not civil servants—that is, employees of the central Government, but of the local education authorities, or, in the case of non-provided schools, of the managers. Like all public employees, teachers hold their positions during the pleasure of the employing authority. Wherever positions are abolished owing to legally recognized re-organizations, teachers are entitled to compensation for loss of office. Local education authorities and managers of non-provided schools with the consent of such authorities may dismiss teachers on educational grounds or for misconduct; managers of non-provided schools have the further power to dismiss teachers on grounds connected with the giving of religious instruction. Teachers who are dismissed may of course resort to the courts. Their interests are protected by the powerful professional organization, the National Union of Teachers (N.U.T.), which places at their disposal, whenever necessary, the resources of its legal department. Dismissal of teachers are on the whole rare; this does not mean that all teachers are perfectly competent, but that it is extremely difficult to define in a court of law the meaning of teaching competence. Generally, measures are taken in cases of incompetence to give a teacher an opportunity in a different environment—

in another class or another school under a different headmaster. Nowhere, however, is the teachers so much at the mercy of the administrative officials or the local education authority as he is in the United States. The English system furnishes one of the best illustrations of indefinite tenure or "tenure during pleasure," which, on the one hand, because of tradition is free from the uncertainties which are found where there is no system of tenure, and, on the other hand, free from the abuses which are often found where teachers have secured the right to permanent tenure.

Salaries

Since teachers are not employees of the central authority, the Board of Education does not prescribe the scales of salary to be paid. The general principle is that salaries should be determined by those concerned in them, the teachers and their employers, the local education authorities; the interest of the Board of Education is involved because the central Government makes annual grants for educational purposes, including salaries. An improvement in the remuneration of teachers had long been overdue and, although increases were paid here and there to meet the higher cost of living following the War, they were uncertain and wholly dependent upon the he good-will of the local authorities. To correct this situation and to give reality of the new status of education which it had been the purpose of the Education Act of 1918 to promote, a number of Standing Joint Committees was set up in 1919 under the chairmanship of Lord Burnham to consider the drafting of scales of salary for elementary, secondary, and technical school teachers. The Committee on Salaries for elementary school teachers consisted of representatives of teachers through the National Union of Teachers and representatives of local education authorities through the County Councils Association, Municipal Corporations, and the Association of Education Committees. A provisional minimum scale was issued in 1920; a year later four scales of salary were drawn up, adjusted somewhat roughly to the cost of living in different parts of the country and subject to revision in 1925. The allocation of scales to the various areas was made by the Committee and accepted by all but 19 of the 318 local authorities; in these areas agreement was reached through the intervention of the Board. It must be noted that under the Education Act, 1918, the Board contributed grants on account of salaries equivalent to sixty per cent of the expenditure. Before the scales had been generally introduced, they were subjected in 1922 to a deduction of five per cent as a contribution toward pensions; in 1923 the teachers voluntarily submitted to another abatement of five per cent in view of the economic crisis at that time.

When the date for revision approached in 1925, there was evidence that the local authorities and the central Government were anxious to effect economies. Disagreement between the teachers and employing authorities on the amount of deduction to be adopted led to the reappointment of the Salary Committee, again with Lord Burnham as arbitrator. The result of the arbitration was the publication of new scales of salary which represented a compromise between the standards proposed by the teacher and those of the authorities. Under the new scheme a probationary year of service was introduced so that the first increment of salaries was not added until after two years of service. The amount of increment was reduced and the period between the minimum and maximum salaries was increased. The salaries of women were adjusted to approximately four fifths of those of men with similar qualifications. The Board of Education undertook to intervene by means of its grants in cases where the efficiency of the educational service was prejudiced or endangered by the unreasonable action of a local authority, an undertaking which was later incorporated in the Elementary School Code in the statement that "there shall be no saving to local rates by not paying the allotted scale if, in the opinion of the Board, the efficiency of the provision of elementary education is endangered." To permit flexibility in the award of special financial recognition for special work, the Board also expressed itself as ready to recognize such special arrangements for grant purposes.

The Burnham award was adopted for six years from March 31, 1925. When that period expired the existing arrangements were continued for another year, but a few months later the financial crisis developed, there was a change of government, and the demand for retrenchment, especially in public services, became urgent. An Economy Committee under the chairmanship of Sir George May had prior to this crisis recommended a cut of fifteen per cent in teachers' salaries, which was subsequently reduced to ten per cent. This reduction will continue until the end of the financial year when the whole question of salaries will again be reconsidered by the Burnham Committees. The local authorities and the Government desire to see a reduction in the scales corresponding to the reduction in the cost of living; the leading teachers' organization, the National Union of Teachers, claims that the salary scales were originally adopted in order to make teaching a profession which would attract ability, irrespective of any consideration of the cost of living; the women teachers have been opposed to the existing scales because of sex differentiation, while a section of the men teachers feel that the difference in the salaries of the two sexes is not great enough; a compromise between the two groups was a proposal to make additions to the normal scales in accordance with family obligations; head teachers or principals are discontented with the present method of calculating their salaries on the basis of the size of schools; and, finally, the reorganization of the school system into junior and senior schools and other schools on the secondary level may require more differentiation in the scales of salary than existed under the old system. The advance made since 1913 is indicated by a comparison of the average salary in that year (£119 for men and £74 for women, and £104 for all teachers) with the average salary in 1930 (£334 for men, £254 for women if certificated; £324 for all men, £217 for all women, and £245 for all teachers).

Pensions

The status of teachers was further improved by a radical revision of the pension system is 1922 and again in 1925. Elementary school teachers had, since 1898, enjoyed the benefits of a deferred annuity system which was inadequate in amount and which proved to be actuarially unsound. A Departmental Committee appointed in 1922 recommended the adoption of a contributory system to which teachers, employers, and the State would contribute. A superannuation scheme on this basis was established in 1922 and revised in 1925 (Teachers' Superannuation Act). The present system includes all elementary school teachers, administrative officers and inspectors, and teachers in grant-aided schools and institutions below those of university rank. The teachers and others eligible under the Act contribute five per cent of their salaries annually and the local education authorities an equal amount, which is reduced by grants from the Board of Education for this purpose to less than two and a half per cent of the cost of salaries. Teachers who have had thirty years of service may retire at the age of sixty, or, if the period of qualifying service[6] is less than thirty years, at the age of sixty-five, which is the age of compulsory retirement for all teachers. The superannuation allowance is one-eightieth of the average salary for the last five years of pensionable service for each year of service with a maximum of half of the average salary plus a lump-sum gratuity, paid at the time of retirement, of one thirtieth of average salary for each year of service with the same maximum. Disability allowances are paid after ten years of service, or, if disability occurs earlier, a short service gratuity of one twelfth of annual salary for each year of pensionable service is granted. To teachers who leave the profession or who fail to qualify for the benefits of the scheme or if the benefits are less than the accumulated contributions, the contributions, compounded at three per cent interest, are returned.

This scheme, while a considerable improvement on the deferred annuity system, has been subjected to a number of criticisms. The allowances are not calculated on the basis of accumulated contributions, but on length of service and average salary in the last five years of service at a time when salaries are subject to fluctuations. The cost of the system has only been vaguely estimated and the contributions are not funded but used to pay current annual obligations, most of which are on account of accrued liabilities, or allowances due to teachers who performed the major part of their service before the system was adopted. In other words, the future solvency of the plan depends on the pledge of the Government, which may at any time be overridden by national interests of greater importance. The progress of the system is to be watched and an actuarial survey is due in 1933; the probability is that it will then be too early to discover any trends of importance.

Conclusion

Despite the uncertainties of the pension scheme and the probable adjustment of salaries in the present year, there can be no doubt that there has been a considerable advance in the economic, professional, and social status of elementary school teachers since 1918. Increased or improved preparation, better remuneration and protection against disability and old age, greater freedom from administrative control and more sympathetic administration have completely changed the character of the elementary school teacher's career. To these may be added a rich and vigorous associational activity, which, as it becomes relieved of the burden of fighting for economic welfare, is directing increased attention to professional problems important to the schools and the public. This situation is reflected in the gradual but marked increase in "refresher" and other courses for general and professional improvement, conducted by universities, local authorities, professional groups, and the Board of Education. While training in service of this and other types is not as extensive as in the United States, it may also be said that it is not as much loaded in favour of professional courses as it is in this country. Finally, the absence of regimentation from above, whether by a bureaucracy or in the interests of "efficiency," leaves more to the teacher's freedom and initiative, but increases his sense of responsibility. The change in the status of English elementary school teachers can be illustrated in no better way than by referring to the high standard held before them, a standard which would have been inconceivable thirty years ago, by one who was during his whole career associated with them as teacher and inspector: "Every teacher should have his own theory of teaching and his own philosophy of education; but they can be built only upon long experience and mature reflection."[7]

2. FRANCE

History

The preparation of elementary school teachers in France is still based on the general lines on which the system was organized soon after the establishment of the Third Republic by Jules Ferry and Ferdinand Buisson. The idea of establishing normal schools for the preparation of teachers had already been adopted by the Convention acting on a report prepared by Lakanal in 1794 and was continued under Napoleon, but with little result until a normal school opened in Strasbourg in 1811 provided a model which was soon copied elsewhere. The regulations issued on December 14, 1832, under Guizot's influence required each department to establish a normal school offering a two-year course under state control. In 1842 the first normal school for girls was created, and three years later a regulation was issued requiring teachers in normal schools to have experience in elementary schools. The programmes of the normal schools were somewhat liberal in scope and for that reason aroused the suspicion that they tended to train teachers with a broader preparation than was regarded as necessary for teaching in elementary schools and thus to make them discontended with their work. This suspicion, which was also current in Germany at the same time, led in France to the reactionary *Loi Fallcux,* which reduced the programmes of the normal schools to the range of the elementary schools, but extended the period of preparation to three years. A more liberal spirit was introduced by Duruy in 1866; a year later, Duruy placed the preparation of girls on the same footing as that of boys.

The reorganization of the normal school system was effected by legislation introduced by Ferry and Buisson. In 1879 each department was required to maintain two normal schools, one for men and one for women; in 1880 a special examination was introduced for normal school professors of letters and science and was further defined in 1887; in the same year in institution (*école normale supérieure primaire*) to prepare candidates for these examinations was established at Fontenay-aux-Roses for women, followed two years later by the creation of a similar institution for men at Saint-Cloud; in 1882 an examination for candidates for directorships of normal school was introduced. In 1881 the normal school curriculum was liberalized by the inclusion of algebra, modern languages, and manual work. Except for a modification of the regulations in 1905, the character of the normal schools remained unchanged until 1920, when a new curriculum and courses of study were published.

THE PRESENT SYSTEM

Provision of Normal Schools

The preparation of elementary school teachers is entirely under the control of the State, which prepares the curriculum and courses of study, supervises the normal schools, selects the candidates, appoints the teachers, provides for the maintenance of the students, and bears the cost of teachers' salaries. Under the regulations each department is required to provide two normal schools, one for men and one for women, and to supply and maintain the buildings. Actually thee are only eighty-eight normal schools for each sex in France, and three for men and four for girls in Algeria and Tunis; in other words, two of the departments do not provide normal schools. Some of the institutions are very small, in some cases with less than thirty students, but local pride prevents the smaller departments from availing themselves of the legal provision to combine with their neighbours for the purpose of maintaining larger schools. All the normal schools are boarding institutions (*internals*), but provision is made for partial boarders and for day students.

Administration of Normal Schools

The normal schools are governed in general by state regulations, and are under the immediate supervision of the rector and inspectors of the academy in which they are situated. Each school has an administrative board consisting of an academy inspector, four members appointed by the rector, and two members delegated by the *conseil générale* of the department. The function of the board is to discuss problems of management, to prepare the budget, to visit the school with which it is associated once a month, and to submit an annual report through the prefect of the department to the rector on the material condition of the institution. Responsibility for the internal administration of a normal school is vested in the director, who is assisted by a bursar (*économe*), and the faculty which meets in conference once a month.

The Normal School Faculty

The faculty of a normal school consists of the director, the bursar, professors of letters and science, teachers of special subjects such as foreign languages, drawing, singing, music, gymnastics, and manual work, and the principal of the practice school. Each member of the faculty must possess the special qualifications prescribed for his position. For appointment as a professor of letters or science, candidates must hold the *certificat d'aptitude au professorat dans les écoles normales et des écoles primaires supérieures.* This certificate is awarded by the State under the following conditions: Candidates must pass two examinations separated by an interval of at least one year. For the first examination they must be at least nineteen years of age, be in good health, and hold the *brevet supérieur,* the *baccalauréat,* or the *diplôme de fin d'études secondaires.* For the second examination they must be at least twenty-one years of age, be in good health, and must have had at least two years of practical experience. The first examination is a qualifying examination, but is also required for admission to the higher primary normal school up to the number of vacancies at Fontenay-aux-Roses and Saint-Cloud, which are represented on the examining juries by their directors and professors. The second examination is competitive, only that number of candidates being selected which is necessary to fill available vacancies. Both examinations are based on syllabi issued each year by the Ministry of Public Instruction. The written test of the first part of the examination, from which holders of a *licence* in letters or sciences may under certain conditions be exempted, includes for the professorship in letters an essay on a question or text in French literature (five hours); an essay on a question or text in philosophy (four hours); an essay on a question in modern and contemporary history (four hours); and an essay on a question in geography (four hours). The oral examination includes an *explication* of a text in a foreign language (Latin or modern) after three quarters of an hour's preparation; questions in modern and contemporary history, and geography. For professors in science the written examination includes tests in arithmetic and algebra (three hours), geometry (three and a half hours), physics (four hours), chemistry (two hours), and natural science (five hours); the oral test covers the same subject with practical work, setting up experiments and reports on them in the sciences.

The second examination is organized in a similar way, but opportunity is provided for specialization; the professorship in letters may be in French language and literature, or history and geography, or in a modern foreign language (English, German, Italian, Spanish, and Arabic); that in science in the mathematical and physical, in the physical, chemical and natural, or in the applied sciences. In addition to the written and oral test there is a supplementary test in illustrative design and in handwork (wood or metal for men, dressmaking, knitting or embroidery for women).

The certificate of aptitude for a professorship (or a *licence* in letters or science) is the minimum requirement of candidates for the *certificat d'aptitude à l'inspection primaire et à la direction des écoles mamales*. They must be twenty-five years of age and must have had five years of practical teaching experience. Teachers who have had at least ten years of experience are exempt from the requirement of the certificate of aptitude for a professorship. The examination for the certificate of aptitude for a directorship (which is also valid for an elementary school inspectorship) is both written and oral. The written part, taken in the capital of an academy, consists of two essays (five hours being allowed for the preparation of each), one on education or educational psychology, and one on ethics or sociology based on the normal school course of study. Candidates who are successful in this part are summoned to Paris for the oral examination, which includes (1) the *explication* of a passage selected by lot from a list of authors issued every three years by the Ministry after one hour of preparation; (2) the discussion of an educational problem, after two hours of preparation; (3) the discussion of a problem of educational administration, after one hour of preparation; (4) report of a visit of inspection to a maternal, elementary, higher elementary, or normal school.

The principalship of a practice school connected with a normal school may be held by a professor who has had at least three years of experience in an elementary school or teachers who have their permanent certificate and have had at least ten years of experience in some institution of public education; an assistant in such a practice school must have had at least five years of experience.

Other members of the normal school staffs, including the bursar, must hold the certificates prescribed for their special fields of instruction or administration. In normal schools with more than seventy pupils, the number of professors is fixed at five; if the enrolment is between thirty-six and seventy, at four; if the number is less than thirty-six, at three. Each professor is expected to give twenty hours of instruction a week and to devote five hours a week to the supervision of study; directors are required to give six hours a week of instruction (always in ethics and education) in schools with more than thirty-six pupils and in addition ten hours of instruction in science or twelve in letters in smaller schools.

The scale of salaries of professors, men and women, is as follows:

Class	*Seine and Seine-et-Oise*	*Other Departments*
First	37,000 francs	30,000 frans
Second	34,000 "	27,000 "
Third	31,000 "	24,000 "
Fourth	28,000 "	21,000 "
Fifth	25,000 "	18,000 "
Sixth	22,000 "	15,000 "

Directors receive salaries on the same scale with residence and the addition of the following supplements:

Grade	*Seine and Seine-et-Oise*	*Other Departments*
1	7,000 francs	6,000 francs
2	6,000 "	5,000 "
3	5,000 "	4,000 "
4	4,000 "	3,000 "

Professors who also hold the position of bursar are entitled to residence and salary additions of 1000, 1500, or

2000 francs, according to grade. Those who are also principals of the practice school attached to the normal school receive the same additions to salary.

Admission of Students

Admission to normal schools is competitive. Each year the council of each department reports through the prefect and the rector to the Minister of Public Instruction the number of teachers which it is likely to need; on the basis of this export the number of students to be admitted to the normal schools is determined. Candidates for admission must be French, between the age of fifteen and nineteen, in good health and of good character; they are required to sign an undertaking that they will serve for ten years in a public school or refund to the State the cost of their maintenance in the normal schools, including the cost of board, laundry, books, and the value of scholarships for clothing, if they have held these. The selection of a normal school is a delicate matter, since every graduate must teach for a period of years in the department in which he has been trained unless he obtains permission to seek an appointment elsewhere.

The preliminary requirements for candidacy are followed by an commission, that for the *brevet elementaire* being used. This examination is based on the course of the general section of the higher elementary schools, in which most intending teachers receive their preparation. The examination is written and oral. The written tests, which are taken at local centres, include an easy in morals or literature (two and a half hours), a paper on history and geography (one and a half hours), a test in mathematics (arithmetic, algebra, and geometry, one and a half hours), and a paper on physical or moral sciences (one and a half hours); the first two papers are also marked for writing and spelling. The best candidates are permitted to proceed to a normal school for the oral test, which includes questions in mathematics, morals and civics, history and geography, physical and natural sciences, drawing, singing, gymnastics, and, for girls, needlework. The candidates who rank highest on the list are awarded scholarships of admission to the normal schools up to the limit prescribed by the Minister; those who obtain marks above the average but are not eligible for admonition are awarded the brevet *élémentaire*. The scholarships cover the cost of full or partial board and in some instances maintenance grants. The severity of the competition is indicated by the following table which gives the number of applicants and the number admitted:

	Men		*Women*	
	Applicants	*Admitted*	*Applicants*	*Admitted*
1927	4,700	1,787	6,659	1,911
1928	5,375	1,864	6,500	1,986
1929	6,101	1,967	7,198	2,104
1930	7,048	2,125	8,011	2,182
1931	6,327[8]	2,163	7,321[8]	2,176

Curriculum and Courses of Study

The latest regulations on the curriculum and courses of study in normal schools were issued on August 18, 1920. The new regulations aimed to give a more define character to the normal schools as institutions for professional preparation. It was felt that preceding the revision the normal schools suffered from a confusion of aims; on the one hand, they were too much like continuations of the higher elementary schools, and on the other they attempted to give the elements of a higher education. Under the regulations of 1905 the first two years had been devoted to general academic studies culminating in the examination for the *brevet supérieur* and the last year solely to professional studies. The regulations of 1920 seek to permeate all the work of the three years with the professional aim, while placing the general studies on a higher level; graduation from the higher elementary school is to furnish the starting-point leading up to the standard of the *classe de philosophie* in a secondary school or the work of the first year of a liberal arts faculty. The examination for the *brevet supérieur* has been postponed to the end of the course. The normal school is thus primarily a professional institution and not a university or a centre for educational research. Its work is differentiated from that of the higher elementary school, in the first place, by an avoidance of emphasis on the mere acquisition of information, and, secondly, by introducing the students to methods of research and the use of source materials. To this end the schools are encouraged to utilize activity methods and in the sciences to study the materials offered by the environment.

The curriculum includes the following subjects:

General and professional ethics
Elements of educational psychology and sociology; principles of science
Theory of education
French language and literature
One modern foreign language
History
Geography
Arithmetic and algebra
Surveying and levelling (for men)
Physical and natural sciences and their chief applications; hygiene, and,
for women, domestic economy and care of infants
Agriculture (for men), and horticulture
Drawing
Singing and music
Gymnastics
Manual work

The number of periods devoted to these subjects for week is given in the accompanying table:

Subjects	First Year		Second Year		Third Year		Total	
	M	W	M	W	M	W	M	W
Educational psychology and sociology. Education, Ethics, Philosophy of science	2	2	2	2	2	2	6	6
French language and literature	4	4	4	4	4	4	12	12
History and geography	3	3	3	3	2½	2½	8½	8½
Modern foreign language	2	2	2	2	2	2	6	6
Mathematics	3	3	3	3	2	1	8	7
Physical and natural sciences. Hygiene. Laboratory Domestic economy (for women)	4	4	4	4	4	5	12	13
Theory of agriculture	...	...	1	...	1	...	2	...
Drawing and modelling	2	2	2	2	2	2	6	6
Commercial drawing	1	1	1	1	1	1	3	3
Singing and music	2	2	2	2	2	2	6	6
Gymnastics	2	2	2	2	2	2	6	6
Manual work and agriculture	4	4	4	4	4	4	12	12
Total	29	29	30	29	28½	27½	87½	85½

An examination of the course of study (*Plan d'Eludes et Programmes des Ecoles Normales*), which for the first time leaves a certain latitude to the professors in the selection of topics and books for discussion and encourages adaptation to local differences, does not warrant the conclusion that the desire to permeate the work of the normal schools with the professional point of view has been carried out. General and professional studies are still kept distinct, and, although the professors are required to participate in the induction of the cadet-teachers (*élèves-maîtres* or *élèves-maîtresses*) into the practice of teaching, there is no indication in the courses of study that the subjects of general instruction are treated from the point of view of their use in elementary schools. Indeed, there appears to be a distinct separation between the two, since in the second year one hours a week is devoted, under the caption of *Pédagogie,* to the study of special methods in the elementary school subjects. The standards attained in general academic subjects have been raised, not only on the principle that every teacher must be an educated person, but to make possible the access of normal school graduates to the universities, which has been effected under certain conditions since the regulations appeared in 1920. Educational psychology still follows in the main the metaphysical approach, although opportunity is provided for general observation and measurement of school children and for the study of Binet-Simon tests. Educational theory includes the study of principles, general methods, and classroom management in the first year, special methods in the second, and the administration and organisation of education in the third. The course in educational sociology includes the discussion of the economic organization of society, the place of the family in society and its relation to the school and the child, civics, religion, art, and science studies from the sociological point of view. The study of general principles of science is a study in logic, methods of this various sciences, science of life, and science and reason. As in all French educational institutions the course in ethics (*morale*) is intended to take the place of religious instruction and deals in general with moral ideas and ideals, supplemented in another course by a study of professional ethics and the relations of the teacher to the pupils, their parents, the profession, and the authorities.

The preparation of the teachers on the professional side is extended by observation and practice. Each normal school has available for this purpose either a school directly associated with it (*école annexe*) or some other school in the locality designated for the purpose (*école d' application*). Normal schools for women must have access to a maternal and infant school either as a part of their own practice schools or assigned to them in the locality. The qualifications of the director of the *école annexe* have already been described; teachers in these schools must themselves be normal school graduates with at least five years of teaching experience. Directors and teachers in the *écoles d'application* are only required to be graduates of normal schools. The contact of students with the practice schools is continued throughout the three years of the course. All are required to spend at least fifty half-days a year in the schools; the first year is devoted to observation and reports; the second to observation and occasional teaching in the presence of the director, professors, or classroom teachers; in the last year opportunities are provided for more continued independent teaching in a number of subjects. The professors of general subjects as well as the normal school director participate in supervising the students' practice. In the last year of the course a weekly educational conference is held at which a demonstration lesson followed by discussion may be given, or a problem of method or discipline is discussed, or pupils' written work or school textbooks are criticized, or, finally, an extract from educational literature is critically analyzed (*expliquée*).[9] The members of the normal school faculty and the directors of the practice schools are present at these conferences.

The practical training of the cadet-teachers is not restricted to the schools associated with the normal schools. In order to extend the variety of their experiences they may be assigned for several weeks to selected teachers at a distance from the normal schools, or they may be required to participate in extra-school activities (*œuvres complementaires*) or to organize lectures or courses for adults. In general the tendency is to give the students as many opportunities as possible to become familiar with the possibilities of the profession of which they hope to become members.

Examinations

Students are examined at the end of each year and may be required to repeat the work of the year or be dismissed.

Each examination courts as a part of the examination for the *brevet supérieur,* which is also open to condidates not prepared in a normal school but who hold the *brevet élémentaire,* or the *brevet* of a higher elementary school, or have passed the first part of the *baccalauréat* or hold the *diplôme de fin d'éludes secondaires,* and who are at least seventeen years of age. The examinations, which are both written and oral, are based each year, in the case of normal school students, on the work of the year; other candidates may take all the tests at one time or in two separate sessions.

School Life

The normal schools, like other French schools, have not as yet developed an active corporate life. Not only is the programme of studies heavy, but the life and work of each day are carefully regulated. Slowly the schools are being affected by the general interest in athletics, but they do not yet constitute a recognized part of the school activities. The day of the normal school student is regulated as follows:

5.45 a.m.	Rise (dress and put room in order)
6.15 to 7.15	Study
7.15 to 7.30	Breakfast
7.30 to 7.55	Clean room
8.00 to 12.00	Classes (except on Thursdays)
12.00 to 12.30 p.m.	Lunch
12.30 to 1.30	Recreation
1.30 to 4.30	Classes; 1 Hour of study (except on Thursdays and Saturday afternoons)
4.30 to 5.00	Recreation and lunch
5.00 to 7.30	Study
7.30 to 8.00	Dinner
8.00 to 8.30	Recreation
8.30 to 9.30	Study
9.30	Retire

On Thursdays there are no classes, but two hours are devoted in normal schools for men to military instruction and three hours are left entirely free; on Sunday students are entirely free after 10 a.m.

Ten hours a day are thus normally devoted to classwork and study. Men students may leave the normal school premises only on Sundays and holidays; women are only permitted to go out at the request of their parents. Students are permitted to receive correspondence from persons listed by their parents. Such details may on the whole be unimportant and may have a different significance under different social regimes; they do, however, nerve to indicate that, while the new regulations seek to raise the intellectual level in the normal schools, the control and discipline of the pupils still follow the traditions of the nineteenth century. What the effect is on the professional initiative of the teachers it is impossible to estimate, since the same type of administrative discipline dominates the practices of the schools to which the normal school graduate proceeds. M. Lapie, who was in large measures responsible for the revision of the regulations for normal schools, advocated the introduction of self-government in these institutions in order to cultivate initiative and responsibility on the part of the students; his recommendations have not, however, been put into practice.[10]

Certification

The lowest qualification which is accepted for appointment as teachers is the *brevet élémentaire* already described, which at least guarantees three years of academic preparation beyond the regular elementary school; the minimum age for appointment is eighteen. It confers to claim to permanent appointment or assignment on the salary scale. The *brevet supérieur*, granted on the completion of the normal school course and the examination based on it, entitled the holder to appointment as an *instituteur* or *institutrice stagiaire*—that is, an elementary school teacher on temporary appointment made by an academy inspector. The temporary certificate may be converted, after at least two years of experience and passing the examination, for the *certificat d'aptitude pedagogique,* provided the candidates are twenty years of age. The examination is professional in character, and consists in teaching a class for three hours (the instruction must include singing and gymnastics) and questions on educational administration, school management, and practical problems in education; the exercise books of the candidate's class are examined. The certificate is not awarded to men until they have completed their period of military service. On obtaining the certificate the teachers become *titulaires* and are eligible to permanent appointment and advancement on the salary scale. The appointment as *titulaire* is made by the prefect of a department acting for the Minister of Public Instruction and on the advice of the academy inspector.

From this point on advancement depends upon the ability and ambition of the teacher. He may become the principal of a school; if he passes the necessary examinations he may advance to a position in a higher elementary or normal school on obtaining the *certificat d'aptitude au professorat des écoles normales et des écoles primaires supérieures,* which constitutes a stage to appointment as director of a normal school, or inspector of elementary schools on obtaining the *certificat d'aptitude a l'inspection primaire et à la direction des écoles normales.* The last two positions are the highest in the elementary branch of the educational system. A small number of passing the required examinations may transfer to the secondary branch; in general this procedure is unusual and promotion is sought within the elementary branch proper.

Training is Service

The continued training of teachers after their preliminary preparation is entrusted to academy and primary inspectors who organize conferences periodically for the teachers of one or more cantons. The conferences, which teachers must attend, are devoted wholly to the discussion of the theory and practice of education. Beyond this, the dependence of promotions on examinations services as a stimulus to continued study. Courses are available in universities and in normal schools, where they may be given by university professors. Scholarships are available for attendance at universities or for foreign travel in the case of teachers who plan to qualify as teachers of foreign languages. Each year the ablest teachers may compete for admission to the two higher primary normal schools at Saint-Cloud (for men) and Fontenay-aux-Roses (for women). These institutions prepare professors for higher elementary and normal schools as specialists in the two main branches of letters (French, foreign languages, history and geography) or sciences (physical and mathematical, chemical and natural, or applied) in a two-year course; a third year may be spent in preparation for the examination for normal school directorships or primary inspectorships. A few students from these institutions may take the examination for the *certificat d'aptitude à l' ensiegnement secondaire* and thence proceed through the *licence d'enseignment* to the *agrégation* and so enter service in the secondary schools. The members of the faculties of Saint-Cloud and Fontenay-aux-Roses are recruited from local secondary schools or from the Sorbonne. The students who succeed in obtaining admission received free tuition and board.

Status of Teachers

Since they are members of the civil service, the French teachers already enjoy a satisfactory status; in the smaller communes they may often be the best educated persons next to the priest; in the larger centres social graduations based on educational qualifications are still marked. Once appointed to office as *titulaires*, the teachers enjoy permanent tenure which can only be disturbed on account of serious misconduct or professional incompetence. They may be reprimanded, censured, suspended, or dismissed, but in all cases their interests are protected and no teacher may be dismissed without a hearing nor by any one superior official. The recommendation of dismissal may come from an academy inspector, but it is not carried out until the departmental council and the prefect have considered the case. All documents in the case are available to the teacher, who has the right to be represented by the professional organization of which he is a member and to appeal to the Minister and the Higher Council of Public Instruction.

On the material side the teachers enjoy salary scales fixed by the State for the country as a whole and allowances for disability and superannuation. Owing to the fluctuations in the cost of living and in the stability of the franc, salary scales have been revised several time since 1918. The present scale of salaries is as follows:

Stagiaires	10,500 francs
Sixth class	11,500 "
Fifth class	13,000 "
Fourth class	14,500 "
Third class	16,000 "
Second class	17,500 "
First class	19,000 "

The salary scales are basic for the whole country and are the same for men and women; in order to equalize them, the teachers are granted a number of supplements (*indemnites*) varying with the size of the locality in which they serve; in other words, they are adjusted to the cost of living in different parts of the country and to personal needs. Teachers are entitled to a residence or an allowance for rent which is paid by the communes according to their size and on a scale fixed by the prefect of the department; they range from 100 to 900 francs a year on the following scale:

Cities with less than 1,000 population	100 to 200 francs
Cities between 1,000 and 3,000	150 to 250 "
Cities between 3,001 and 9,000	180 to 400 "
Cities between 9,001 and 12,000	230 to 450 "
Cities between 12,001 and 18,000	260 to 500 "
Cities between 18,001 and 36,000	300 to 600 "
Cities between 36,001 and 60,000	340 to 650 "
Cities between 60,001 and 100,000	380 to 700 "
Cities over 100,000	450 to 900 "

A slight addition may be made to these sums in those cases, which are not infrequent, where both husband and wife are engaged in educational or other state service. Another allowance is paid varying with the locality in which the school is situated; this allowance ranges from 291.20 francs to 1747.20 francs, and is graded on the following scale:

Paris	1,747.20	francs
Suburbs of Paris	1,528.80	"
Cities of over 150,000 population	1,310.40	"
Cities between 100,001 and 150,000	1,092.00	"
Cities between 70,001 and 100,000	873.60	"
Cities between 40,001 and 70,000	728.00	"
Cities between 20,001 and 40,000	582.40	"
Cities between 10,001 and 20,000	436.80	"
Cities between 5,001 and 10,000	291.20	"

A further addition consists of family allowances depending upon the number of children in a teacher's family; the allowances are paid for each dependent child up to the age of sixteen, or, if the child is being educated, up to the age of twenty-one; the allowances increase progressively from 660 francs for the first child, 960 francs for the second, 1560 francs for the third, and 1920 francs for each child beyond the third.

Teachers who are transferred from one school to another are given a grant to defray the expenses of moving. In cases of ill-health, leave of absence on full pay is given up to three months; in the case of married women, leave of absence on full pay is granted for child-birth, one month before and one month after the confinement. Beyond this, teachers are given reductions on the railways for five trips a year, receive free tuition for their children who are day pupils in secondary schools, and for themselves if they study in a university for the *licence,* and may be given financial aid in serious cases of need. Additional allowances are paid to principals of schools, as follows:

Schools with 2 classes	800	francs
Schools with 3 to 4 classes	1,600	"
Schools with 5 to 9 classes	2,800	"
Schools with 10 or more classes	3,500	"

Protection against disability and old age is provided by a contributory system to which the teachers contribute six per cent of their salaries a year. They may retire at the age of fifty-five after twenty-five years of service on an allowance equal to one fiftieth of the average salary during the last three years of service multiplied by the number of years of completed service; these amounts may be increased if retirement is postponed; additions are also paid on the basis of the number of children raised up to the age of sixteen. Married women may retire after fifteen years of service, but do not become eligible to an allowance until they reach the age prescribed for it. A disability allowance is granted after fifteen years of service on the basis of one-fiftieth of average salary for each year of service; if disability occurs after less than fifteen years of service, life annuity based on the capitalized contributions is paid. The system makes provision for widows and orphans of deceased teachers.

Conclusion

Despite the apparently satisfactory conditions of service, there is considerable unrest among the elementary school teachers of France. The unrest on the whole is not primarily concerned with the material conditions of the teachers, but is due to discontent with their professional status and the class organization of the educational system as a whole. Professional organizations are recognized by law, but professional syndicalism, although prohibited, actually flourishes, and at present the *Syndicat des Instituteurs* is perhaps one of the strongest associations of the elementary school teachers, who may also be members of the *Fédération Générale de l'Enseignement*. The common bond of discontent brings together in the same groups teachers from different branches of education, and of different political, religious, and economic views. In general the associations would like to see a complete reorganization of the educational system on the basis of the common school, equal educational opportunities, and differentiation of post-primary education. So far as the normal school is concerned, their criticism is that it is still isolated, often located in small centres without adequate opportunities for intellectual growth and development. The preparation of teachers begins too early, and, although the latest regulations have attempted to raise the standard of general cultural education, the graduate of the normal school does not enjoy the same privileges as the *bachelier* of a secondary school. The situation is being remedied to some extent by the acceptance of the *brevet supérieur* for admission to some science faculties; the faculties of letters do not, however, recognize anything below the certificate for professors in normal and higher elementary schools. Postponement of the beginning of professional training, a sound general education in a secondary school, and preparation on a university level are among the proposals which are made. The universities, as at present constituted, are not equipped to prepare teachers, although here and there courses are offered in education and in educational and experimental psychology. Further, it is objected, although the admission of normal school graduates to the universities reduces the force of this objection, that they are not prepared for study at a university level, that they have too much of the *esprit primaire,* the primary mind which accepts all information and facts as of equal value without interest or ability to inquire into sources. The second objection the regulations of 1920 have attempted to meet.

The whole problem of teachers-preparation is closely associated with the character of the administrative system. Preparation on a higher level implies professional freedom and responsibility the intense centralization of the Frnech system assumes all responsibility by prescribing curricula and courses of study, methods to a large extent, and examinations, and restricts the freedom to a minimum even in the latest regulations of 1923, which permit some local adaptation. It is not, therefore, an accident that the same groups which are interested in the reorganization of the educational system and improvement in the preparation of teachers also advocate decentralization of the administrative system. Perhaps the best criticism of the professional preparation of teachers can be found in the educational journals[11] for elementary school teachers. Each of these contains in its weekly issue a section devoted to lesson plans based upon questions set in the examinations for the *certificat d'éludes primaires* or upon the prescribed courses of study; this, as nothing else could be, is evidence at least of the control exercised by the government regulations, if not entirely of the failure of the preparation given in the normal schools to provide the basis for professional freedom and growth.

3. GERMANY

History

In the preparation of teachers for elementary schools, Germany again bids fair to assume the leadership in the twentieth century as she did in the nineteenth. The political situation has changed and with it the status of the elementary schools, for although the organization of the school system as a whole has not been radically modified in the post-War period, the ideals governing the elementary schools have undergone a complete revision. In the nineteenth century, particularly in the second half of the century, the aim of elementary education had been the training of loyal, law-abiding subjects; the aim today is the development of free, intelligent, and active citizens. The change of aims has led to a profound change in the character of teacher-preparation. Under the old regime Germany had succeeded in developing a system for the preparation of teachers which was probably the most efficient that the worlk has seen with the exception of that of the Jesuits, if efficiency is defined as the best adaptation of means to secure clearly formulated ends. There was no break in gauge between the character of teacher-preparation and the work of the elementary schools. The responsibility of the elementary schools was to train submissive and unquestioning obedience to authority, and the duty of the teachers was to carry out the regulations prescribed by their official superiors in the same spirit. Curriculum, courses of study, and methods of instruction were prescribed by the Ministry of Education in each State, and the purpose of preparation was to train and discipline the teachers to carry these out without question. The teachers, in other words, were expected to be mouthpieces of the state governments, skilled craftsmen rather than independent practitioners of a profession guided by the demands of different environments for variety and adaptation. The regulations prescribed a certain amount of knowledge and information to be imparted to the pupils; the teachers were trained to impart this with the skill best adapted to secure the ends desired.

There were not, however, the principles upon which the system of teacher-preparation was established in the early part of the nineteenth century, when its great founders, Harnisch and Diesterweg, were influenced by the Pestalozzian movement. The aim at this time was to give teachers a general, intellectual training not limited to the subjects which they were to teach in the elementary schools. The future teachers must receive a liberal preparation and must be trained to think rather than be mere followers of routine and mechanical practices. Since the Prussian educational authorities did not define and prescribe the work of the normal schools, Harnisch at Weissenfels and Diesterweg and Mörs and later in Berlin were able, under the impulse of the liberal movement, to develop a system of preparation which went far to arouse a strong professional feeling among teachers not only in Prussia but throughout Germany. It was under the impulse of this professional consciousness that the teachers' associations were formed which were strong enough to formulate in 1848 the ideal bases for the further development of their profession. These demands were as follows: (1) Abolition of clerical control of schools. (2) The abolition of the isolated preparatory institutions and the preparation of candidates for entrance to normal schools in higher elementary schools. (3) A higher and more liberal curriculum in the normal schools. (4) The removal of the normal schools to university towns and their organization into professional institutions. (5) The recognition of teachers as civil servants and exemption from lower church duties. (6) Inspection of schools by professionally trained experts. (7) The representation of teachers on local school committees.

Only two of these demands, the fifth and seventh, were secured, it is interesting to note, before the Revolution of 1918. Indeed, the year 1848 marks the beginning of a reaction in the preparation and status of teachers. Placing the responsibility for the disorders of that year on the normal schools and the teachers that they had prepared, the Prussian Government in 1854 issued regulations which restricted the work of the normal schools to imparting those subjects which were taught in the elementary schools, controlled the reading of the students, limited the scope of the professional studies, and tightened more securely the political and clerical control over the teachers. The regulations of 1854 were modified in a more liberal direction in 1872, partly through the influence of Saxony, which in 1865 made access to the University of Leipzig possible for the best graduates of the normal schools, and partly through the active propaganda conducted in and out of Parliament by Diesterweg almost up to his death in 1866. Teachers were given the status of civil servants and the curriculum of the normal schools was expanded, particularly on the scientific side and by the introduction of French as an optional subject. Except for a slight modification in the curriculum in 1901, the general spirit of teacher-preparation remained unchanged until the recent reform.

The chief characteristics of teacher-preparation until this reform was introduced were as follows. Candidates were selected at the age of fourteen on completing the elementary school and began their preliminary training, in Prussia, in

Präparandenanstalten, where the elementary school course was continued for three years under teachers who were themselves elementary school teachers. At the end of the preparatory course candidates were admitted to the normal school (*Lehrerseminare*), maintained by the State and organized on a denominational basis. Here the three-year course was devoted, except for the study of physics and chemistry and French, to an intensive review of the subjects of the elementary school, professional subjects, and observation and participation in the work of the practice schools. The strength of the system lay in no sense in breadth of preparation, but in undeviating disciplining in the work which lay before the students. Every lesson had to be given in such a way that it could be reproduced in the elementary schools; every lesson was intensely practical, and, since the same instructor, himself trained in a normal school and with several years of teaching in elementary schools, was responsible for subject-matter, demonstration lessons, and supervision of the cadets in practice teaching, the whole of the work was closely integrated or professionalized, but at the level of the elementary schools. Discipline was strict; corporate activities were discouraged, the whole regime was almost military in character. Successful completion of the normal school course entitled the young teacher to probationary appointment which became permanent on passing a second examination and the completion, in the case of men, of the required military service. The only concession which was made to the recognition that normal schools were not merely exalted elementary schools was the grant to the graduates at about the age of twenty of the one-year military service privilege, obtained by secondary school pupils at about the age of fifteen.

Despite this somewhat limited but efficient preparation, which turned out skilled craftsmen, there was an intense professional activity among the teachers directed wholly by their own organizations. Discontent with a system, which isolated the normal schools from all other institutions at a higher level and refused to admit into the lives and minds of the future teachers the breath of anything but the elementary spirit, had its political effects; teachers, although they could not be members, because since 1872 they had been given the status of civil servants, sympathized in large numbers with the programmes of the Social Democratic Party. On the educational side there were widespread discussions of plans for reorganization of the system, demands for the preparation of teachers on a higher level, and proposals for the improvement of curriculum and methods. It was no accident that after the War the first Prussian Minister of Education, Karl Haenisch, was a former elementary school teacher, and that a large number of elementary school teachers won places in the state and federal Parliaments.

The Revolution of 1918 made possible the realization of the demands of the elementary school teaching profession for preparation on a higher level, a preparation which would substitute for the traditional apprenticeship type of training a new system based on principles governing the preparation for other professions. The recognition that a new responsibility and a new status were to be assigned to the elementary schools, that a change in the political character of the State inevitably implied a change in the character of education, was widespread. But the demands of the teachers had social and economic implications as well; improved training on a professional rather than a craftsmanship basis would, it was expected, mean an improvement in their status which had been depressed, it was felt, because of the character of their preparation.

The fundamental principle upon which the reform was to be based was defined in the federal constitution of 1919. According to Article 143, 2, "The preparation of all teachers shall be uniformly regulated for the *Reich* according to principles which apply generally to higher education." This provision spelt the abolition of the traditional preparatory and normal schools, the preliminary education of future teachers in schools leading up to the universities, and their professional preparation at the university level. A discussion of the problem at the *Reichsschulkonferenz* (the Federal Educational Conference), which was held in 1920 and offered to representatives of the branches of education and others concerned in its provision and maintenance an opportunity of considering the basic principles of reform, resulted in the acceptance of a number of theses bearing on the preparation of teachers. Since all teachers are members of the same profession, they should have a common preliminary preparation followed by a period of study, varied according to the needs of the various types of schools, in a university. Elementary school teachers should be required to follow a three-year course in pedagogical institutes as constituent parts of universities in which the members of the different faculties would give instruction. Separate teachers colleges, whether in the universities or not, were rejected. The courses for teachers should include both professional and academic studies with opportunities for intensive study of one subject elected by the student according to his own interests.

For some time it was expected that the Federal Government would issue regulations and suggestions to serve as a common basis for the organization of institutions for preparing teachers. This expectation was bound up with the hope that the Federal Government would also participate in the new system with financial aid. After it was announced in the Third Federal Tax Ordinance, issued in 1924, that the Government had neither the resources nor the intention of aiding any part of the education system, it was understood that the States were free to proceed alone with the organization of education without waiting for a lead from the Federal Government.[12] Steps were immediately taken, if not already begun, to abolish preparatory and normal schools; in Prussia the last of these were closed in 1926; in most of the other States, except Bavaria, in 1928. Owing to the great excess in the supply of teachers, quick action was not needed to recognize the system of preparation.

THE PRESENT SYSTEM

The Constitution had set up only the common basis of providing for the preliminary education of all intending teachers in institutions leading to the universities—that is, in secondary schools; beyond this, each State by the inaction of the Federals Government was left free to devise its own system of preparing teachers. The problem of selecting the type of secondary school course best adapted to the future needs of elementary school teachers was not difficult; it was decided that such a course should be modern in character—that is to say, the *Gymnasium* and *Realgymnasium* were practically ruled out; for the modern courses a choice remained between the *oberrealschule* and the *Deutsche Obserschule.*[13] Since the latter emphasized German cultural subjects, it was generally regarded as preferable to the *Oberrealschule.* There was, however, another problem to be solved; in the past a large number of teachers had been recruited from the rural districts and small towns which in general were not provided with secondary schools or else only with those of the classical type. The abolition of the normal school which was generally located in these areas left a number of buildings available for other purposes. These were converted into a new type of secondary school, the *Aufbauschule,* open to boys and girls entering from elementary schools at the age of thirteen. The *Aufbauschule* offers a six-year course, following the curriculum of either the *Oberrealschule* or the *Deutsche Oberschule,* and leading up to the *Abiturientenprufüng,* which carries with it the privilege of university entrance. The regulations do not discourage preliminary education in any of the secondary schools, but ordinarily the *Deutsche Oberschule* type, whether in the nine-year school or in the *Aufbauschule,* is preferred.

More serious and difficult was the question of the type of institution to be created for professional preparation. The Constitution provided that it must be at the university level, but did not specify that it must be a part of, or affiliated with, the universities. The teachers in general desired the preparation to be given in the existing universities. Against this course it was argued that the universities are primarily institutions for academic study and research; that they are not equipped to provide professional preparation, only one part of which—philosophy and education—could be offered; that new arrangements would have to be introduced to provide training in practice and in the skill subjects required in the elementary schools; and that, in Prussia at any rate, secondary school teachers are not prepared professionally in the universities. In these arguments there was, of course, a great deal of truth, but political considerations entered. The universities would have been overwhelmed with a great increase of students for whom special provision would have to be made; the temptation would always be present to devote a little more time to university studies and transfer to the secondary school branch; and, finally, preparation in the universities might make the teachers dissatisfied with the prospect of entering upon the humble but important work of the rural school. The solutions reached in the different States followed somewhat the political lines. Thus Prussia and Bavaria with learning towards the Right favoured the two-year independent *Pädagogische Akademie* (teachers college); Saxony, taking a middle position, compromised by splitting the preparation between the universities and pedagogical institutes; Socialist Hamburg incorporated the preparation in the local university. The story of the development of the system in Thuringia to some extent illustrates the shift from one point of view to another as influenced by the political changes in that State. Thuringia from 1918 until 1924 had been overwhelmingly Socialist; during that period it was proposed to prepare teachers at the University of Jena. In 1924 political control was transferred from the Left toward the Right and the immediate consequence was a modification of the plan in favour of that adopted by Saxony—academic preparation in the University and professional in a pedagogical institute. The smaller States follow one or other of the three systems indicated, or delegate the preparation of their teachers to other States.

Prussia decided to adopt the two-year teachers colleges; the general principles on which they were to be established were defined in a Memorandum on the Preparation of Elementary School Teachers (*Neugestaltung der Volksschullehrerbildung*) issued on July 20, 1925. The aim of these colleges was not to be merely the training of classroom teachers, but educators and teachers of the people, living in contact with them and with the realities of life, able to develop their cultural needs and to cultivate the intellectual, moral, and aesthetic values ever present in their environment. The teacher must be equipped with knowledge of this subjects, but he must during his period of preparation acquire ability, not necessarily in academic research, but insight into the cultural possibilities of the environment in which he may be placed. Through professional studies he must acquire a professional ideal which will inspite every aspect of his work and give him a realization of the significance of education for the development of local and national culture and for the promotion of social welfare. In the work of the teachers colleges the emphasis must be on the development of personality rather than of skilled craftsmanship.

It was planned to establish ultimately thirty-five teachers colleges (*Pädagogische Akademien*). Three were opened at Easter, 1926, two Protestant institutions at Kiel and Elbing, and one Catholic at Bonn, the first two for men and women, the last at the first for men alone. In 1927 an interdenominational college was opened at Frankfurt-am-Main; in 1929 four more were added at Breslau, Erfurt, Hannover, and Dortmund (all Protestant and co-educational), and in the following year further additions were made at Frankfurt-a-d-Oder, Stettin, Halle, Altona, Cassel (Protestant) and Beuthen (Catholic). By 1931 fifteen colleges had been established. It is to be observed that the colleges were organized, with the exception of that at Frankfurt-am-Main, as sectarian institutions and that they were practically all co-educational.[14] The original intention of admitting three hundred students to each college was not carried out owing to the oversupply of teachers already available.

Students who seek admission to the colleges must present a biography, a certificate a graduation from a secondary school, and a certificate of health. Successful applicants must pass a further test in music (singing and the playing of the violin, piano, or organ); women candidates must demonstrate their ability is sewing. The students do not pay tuition fees, but provide for their own maintenance, state assistance being granted in necessitous cases. Dormitories are not provided in the colleges, but day homes or unions and reading-rooms are made available for the students who live in lodgings. It is estimated that the annual cost of living for each student is 1000 Mark. An important innovation is the encouragement of student self-government, particularly in the care and organization of the homes or unions which are placed at their disposal. The social relations between students and faculty are more intimate and genial than they used to be in the traditional normal schools.

The Faculty

The teachers colleges are under the general supervision of the Ministry of Education, one member of which is delegated to cooperate with the faculties. All appointments are made by the Minister of Education. The faculties consist of a director, professors, docents, and instructors. Responsibility for administration is vested in the director with the cooperation of his colleagues. Some difficulty was experienced in the initial stages of the new venture in securing the type of personnel best adapted to the work. Fundamentally the character of teacher preparation is determined by the needs of the elementary school and of public education. On the one hand, the future teacher must be given a thorough mastery of subject-matter directed to use in the elementary school; on the other, he must receive the necessary preparation in professional studies, methods, practice, and the skill subjects (music, art, handwork); the teachers colleges, however, are on the university level. The problem was how to find professors and instructors who had had a university training and experience in elementary schools. During the period of transition a solution could not be found immediately and a compromise had inevitably to be accepted; the faculties were made up of members, some of whom had had elementary school experience without academic training, while others were university trained, but had no experience in elementary schools. It is hoped that in time it will be possible to establish requirements for appointment which will combine both types of preparation. To emphasize the recognition of teachers colleges as institutions of university rank, the members of the faculties, with the exception of the teachers of the skill subjects, have been given the title of "Professor." The salary scales in the teachers colleges were as follows according to the regulations of 1927: Director and about one fourth of the professors, 9000 Mark, rising to 14,000 Mark (in exceptional cases to 15,000 Mark); one half of the professors, 7500 mark, rising to 11,600 Mark (13,600 Mark in exceptional cases); and the remaining fourth of the professors, 5700 Mark, rising to 9000 Mark (11,600 Mark in exceptional cases); to the salaries are added indemnities for rent.

Curriculum, and Courses of Study

The Ministry of Education, recognizing the experimental character of the teachers college, refrainted from issuing uniform curricula and courses of study, but in 1927 issued suggestions on the basis of which the faculty of each college was expected to formulate its own-course of study. The curriculum is distributed into four main divisions: (1) professional subjects; (2) materials and methods of instruction in elementary school subjects; (3) training in skill subjects, combined with observation and practice teaching; (4) elective studies. The distribution of subjects by hours is indicated in the following table:[15]

	Hours	
Education		
Theory	4	
History	8	
School hygiene	2	
School management—economy	2	
Materials—methods of elementary school subjects	17(18)	
Sociology	3	
Practice teaching	19	(55)(56)
Allied Sciences:		
Philosophy	4	
Psychology	9	
Religion	2	
Geography (local)	2	
Ethnology (local)	1	
Animal and plant biology (local)	1	
Physiology and Anatomy	1	
Political and Social economy	2	21
Fine and Practical Art Training:		
Music	20(16)	
Speech	1	
Manual training or sewing	3(6)	
Physical training	12	
Drawing	2	38(37)
		114 Sem. hrs.

The organization of the curriculum may be illustrated by the organization of the curriculum at the Bonn Teachers College.

In addition, students are required to attend a number of lectures and practical offered in a variety of fields: education; religion; German; hisstory and civics; Geography, local and folk study; mathematics; natural science; music, drawing; manual training; and physical training.

The programme of each student requires about thirty hours of required studies each week; beyond this, he is expected to attend the special lectures which he may elect. The two years of the course hardly suffice to carry out the aims set before the teachers colleges. The chief difficulty is that of reconciling the claims of study of academic subjects at the higher level and the needs of the teachers in their future work. Although the students enter the colleges with a rich background of liberal education obtained in the secondary schools, it must be reorganized for purposes of the elementary schools. Great stress is placed, however, not so much upon lecturing about the various subjects of the elementary school curriculum, but upon training the cadet-teachers in independent development of the materials of instruction by studying and analyzing the opportunities provided in different environments; in other words, just as *Bodenständigkeit* and *Ileimatkunde,* leading to *Lebernskunde,* constitute the basis of the elementary school work, so it becomes the aim of the colleges to impart a profound understanding of the meaning of these terms for the development of a curriculum. Class instruction and lectures are supplemented by special study rooms, laboratories, and excursions for shorter or longer periods, which create opportunities for the development of free activity groups (*freie Arbeitsgemeinschaften*) of students who have a common interest. While these methods aim at cultivating initiative and independence on the part of the student and to open his intellectual vision to a world that is not bound up in books, it is not the intention of the teachers colleges to train research workers; the aim is rather to enable the students to see how knowledge and information have been developed rather than to extend their limit by new discoveries. Essentially the difference between the methods of the old and new type of teacher-preparation lies in the attempt to develop activity and curiosity rather than to fill the minds of the students.

The function of a teachers college is not, however, wholly academic and intellectual, but ultimately practical. Here the colleges are confronted by another difficulty created by the decision of the Ministry to abandon the practice school attached to the training institutions. Administrative and financial difficulties were too great to provide a separate school directly under the control of each college. Accordingly, it is expected that public elementary school in the locality of a college will be employed for purposes of observation, participation, and practice by the students. Such schools, while provided and administered by the local authorities, are placed under the supervision of the directors or some professors of the local teachers college, thus giving them a certain latitude in determining the character of the schools and in the selection of some of the teachers. Students are inducted into the practical aspects of teaching through observation which begins in the first semester and is continued throughout the course in such a way that opportunity is provided for them to become familiar with the content, method, and practice in nearly all the subjects of the elementary school curriculum. Practice teaching begins in the third semester; generally, students in small groups of four or five are assigned to a class for several subjects, each one being expected to be ready to give the lesson, if called upon, while the others observe; at the end of four weeks the groups are rotated and sent to other classes. Lesson plans are prepared and supervised by the subject-matter specialists of the college and the conduct of the lesson is discussed with the group by them and the teacher in charge of the practice class. Generally, each student is expected to have some practice in teaching religion, German, and arithmetic. The chief criticism of the arrangements made for practice teaching is that the teaching is not consecutive, but broken up into a number of isolated lessons. To obviate this criticism, students are encouraged to become assistants in rural and other schools during the college vacations, when they might obtain complete charge of a class under the supervision of the regular teachers.

In order to extend the range of their observation and a knowledge of the scope of the school organization, students are expected to visit, not only a number of elementary schools, but schools for defectives, schools in elementary institutions, garden schools, open-air schools, experimental schools, kindergartens, nursery schools, recreation centres, and other educational agencies. The same puirpose underlies the more extended tours, not only to educational institutions, but to museums, social welfare institutions, conferences, and so on.

First teacher's examination (*Erste Lehrerprüfung*). The two-year course in the teachers colleges culminates in a final examination which is also the first teachers' examination, regulated by a decree issued on April 10, 1938. Candidates must submitted a biography, a maturity certificate from a secondary school, and a certificate of regular attendance at a teachers college and participation in elective courses and practice. Attached to the application for examination are the reports of the professors and instructors of the candidate's record. Candidates may be refused admission to the examination if for any reason the records of the applicants are unsatisfactory. The examination committee, which consists of the teachers college faculty and an educational official of the country (*Regierung*) in which the college is situated, is presided over by a chairman appointed by the Ministry; a representative of the Protestant or Catholic denomination, as the case may be, is also invited to attend the examination.

The written part of the examination consists of an essay on a problem in education or in an allied field selected by the candidates from lists drawn up by the instructors of the field chosen; eight weeks are allowed for the preparation of the essay, which is marked by a member of the examining committee appointed by the chairman. All the essays must be available to all the examiners at least three days before the oral examination. The subjects of the oral examination fall into two main groups:

(1) *Professional*—theory of education, history of education, psychology, philosophy, school management, school hygiene, and educational sociology. All candidates are examined in theory of education and psychology, and any two of the other subjects.

(2) *Subject-matter and methods*—(a) religion, German, and arithmetic or geometry; (b) history, civics,

> geography, and nature study (c) music, drawing, manual work (or sewing); (d) physical training. All candidates are examined in the subjects under (a) and one subject in the other groups at their choice. The examination in religion may be dispensed with by candidates who refuse to take it on conscientious grounds. In the subject-matter and methods examination, candidates must show familiarity with the *Suggestions for the Curricula of Elementary Schools* and a knowledge of the most important methods of instruction in five subjects as well as ability to determine the educative value of curriculum materials and to discuss them in relation to the ages and maturity of pupils at various levels and to the needs of a locality or the nation as a whole. The test, in other words, is not so much verbal mastery of content, but professional judgement and standards of application.

The results of an examination are determined by a candidate's performance—not only in the subjects in which he is examined and in the essay, but also on his record in other subjects as reported by his instructors. Success or failure is decided by vote of the whole committee; the grades are "excellent," "good," "satisfactory," "failed." Those who pass the examination receive a certificate which entitles them to appointment as probationary teachers.

Second Teachers's Examination

Permanent appointment is dependent upon the successful passing of the second teachers' examination (*Zweite Lehrerprüfung*), the regulations for which were issued on June 25, 1928, to become effective on April 1, 1929. The requirements for permanent appointment in existence before the new regulations were issued were continued until March 21, 1930 under these requirements teachers could obtain permanent appointment by successful participation in a study course (*Arbeitsgemeinschaft*) for two years. The new regulations require teachers to present themselves for the second examination after from two to four years of active employment. Each applicant must submit the certificate of the first teachers' examination and a full account of his professional career and further study; to the application is added a report from the inspector (*Schulrat*) of his district. The county school board decides on the admission of a candidate to the examination, which is conducted by a committee consisting of a county educational official (*Regierungsrat*) or inspector as chairman, the inspector of the candidate's school, a member of the teachers college faculty appointed by the Minister of Education, and an elementary school teacher or principal selected from a list prepared with the advice of the district teachers' council (*Bezirkslehrerrat*); the principal of the candidate's school may be present at the examination. If the examination includes religious instruction, the examiner must be of the same denomination as the candidate; if the candidate is a woman, the examining committee must include a woman.

The examination, which takes place in the candidate's school, is wholly professional and practical. The committee observes the instruction of the teacher in his own class in at least two subjects which must be selected from religion, German, arithmetic or geometry, history, civics, geography, and natural science. The instruction observed is followed by a discussion in which the teacher is expected to show a scientific grasp of principles of teaching and education and the administrative regulations for schools. The results of the examination are marked "excellent," "good," "satisfactory," or "failed." Teachers who fall twice in the examination or who do not present themselves for the examination within five years after passing the first teachers' examination are dismissed from the service.

Training in Service

The period of probation required before appointment is made permanent services as a stimulus to further study. But beyond this, German elementary school teachers have always been active in continuing their education, both academic and professional, largely through their own organizations. Study groups (*arbeitsgemeinschaften*) have increased in number as a result of the greater professional freedom which has been given to teachers, particularly in the development of curricula and courses of study and in the advancement and encouragement of experimental schools. The teachers colleges have also assumed a certain responsibility for the further training of teachers who return to their own institutions for conferences and lecture courses. Similar provision is made by local authorities and by the *Zentralinstitut für Erziehung und Unterricht* in Berlin which has become an active agency in this work; it arranges exhibits, demonstrations, conferences and courses, and conducts study tours in Germany and abroad. Finally, the increased participation of teachers in the administration of their own schools and of education in general through their school, district, and regional council has been an effective measure in developing both their status and their professional consciousness.

Status of Teachers

Teachers are civil servants even though they may not be appointed directly by the State. Their position as civil servants does not, however, diminish in any way their rights and duties as citizens. They may belong to any organizations, political or otherwise, that they please, may participate activity in party politics, and may hold political office. A large number of them are today found as members of local councils and as representatives in the state and federal Parliaments. Their status from this point of view is likely to continue to improve as more teachers enter the service after a period of preparation in the teachers colleges.

Salaries

As public employees teachers receives salaries which are determined by a federal salary law for the whole country, even though the salaries are not paid by the Federal Government. The amount of basal salary paid depends upon the salary group or category to which they are assigned; there are altogether twelve groups for all public employees. The remuneration of elementary school teachers includes the basal salary, rent indemnity, and allowance for children, and provisions for disability and retirement. The basal salary rises in Prussia from 2800 Mark to 5000 Mark in twenty years from the date of permanent appointment, with four increments of 250 Mark each and six of 200 Mark each. Head teachers and principals receive an additional annual grant ranging from 200 Mark to 1400 Mark, varying with the size of school and number of teachers employed. The rent indemnity, where a house is not provided, varies with the teacher's position and salary and the location of the school, and ranges from 258 Mark to 1152 Mark. The allowance for children is 20 Mark a month for the first two, 25 Mark a month for the next two, and 30 Mark a month for each child beyond the fourth; the allowances are paid for children up to the age of sixteen and may be continued up to twenty-one if the child is engaged in study.

The retiring and disability allowances have been included as part of the remuneration, for, since the system is not contributory, the allowances are technically provided for by deferred payments; that is to say, salaries are reduced by the amount which must be reserved to meet the obligations created by these allowances ultimately. Teachers become eligible to disability allowances after ten years of service and may retire voluntarily at sixty-five. The allowance after ten years of service consists of thirty-five per cent of salary, rising by two per cent annually for each year of service up to twenty-five and thereafter by one per cent of salary up to forty years of service, with a maximum of eighty per cent of final salary. For pension purposes only basal salary and rent indemnity are taken into account. Windows of teachers receive allowances of sixty per cent of the pension which the teachers received if retired or to which he would have been entitled. Children of deceased teachers receive one fifth of the widow's allowance, if she is alive, or one third, if not.

Preparation of Teachers in other States

A number of German States have adopted systems of preparing teachers similar to that of Prussia—that is, in teachers colleges or training institutions; among these are Baden, Mecklenburg-Schwerin, Oldenburg, Waldeck, and Bavaria. Other States have not reorganised their systems or have teachers trained in a neighbouring State or have adopted a three-year course in affiliation with or as part of the universities. Those which have adopted the affiliated plan are Saxony, Thuringia, Hesse (two-year course), and Brunswick; Anhalt and Lippe use the facilities provided by Thuringia in Jena. Hamburg prepares teachers wholly in the university of that city.

In Saxony the preparation of teachers, following a regulation passed on April 3, 1923, was organized on a three-year basis in part at the University of Leipzig and the Technical University (*Technische Hochschule*) in Dresden and pedagogical institutes (*Pädagogische Institute*) in the two cities. In general, the responsibility of the universities is to provide the courses in general and academic subjects, and of the pedagogical institutes to give the training in the theory and practice of education. Thus, every student in Dresden is expected to take the following courses at the *Technische Hochschule:* history and principles of education, psychology of childhood and adolescence, anthropology and hygiene, German language and literature, government, and one elective subject; eighty of the total of one hundred and eighty semester hours of the three-year course are devoted to these subjects. The arrangements of subjects is somewhat similar at the University of Leipzig, but the amount of time devoted to them is less. The pedagogical institutes in both cases assume the responsibility for the professional preparation in special and general methods, introduction to practical instruction, and training in the skill subjects (art, music, and physical training). As compared with the two-year course in Prussian teachers colleges, the system adopted in Saxony has the obvious advantage of an additional year which furnishes opportunities for the more intensive study of the materials and methods of instruction in the elementary schools, especially in the practical. Observation, demonstration, experiments, research, and some practice teaching take place in the schools belonging to the institutes. Each of the members of the faculty of the institutes is responsible for instruction in the practice schools. In Dresden observation is continued during the first three semesters; actual participation in teaching is provided for usually in local public schools, when the institutes are closed for the summer vacation.

The examination at the close of the course in Saxony includes the preparation of two essays, one on a problem of practical education; two months are allowed for their preparation. The oral examination includes questions on the following major subjects: education, school management, school organization and law, and special methods on two elementary school subjects, philosophy, history of education, and psychology; the minor subjects are anthropology and hygiene and one elective subject. Saxony does not require a second examination for final appointment.

Elementary school teachers in Hamburg receive their preparation wholly in the School of Education of the University under a law issued on December 20, 1926. The length of the course is three years and it includes the following main divisions of study: education, philosophy, and psychology; elective academic or skill subject, art, remedial education, and observation and practice. Observation, participation, and practice are provided for in the demonstration school of the School of Education. Upon the observation and demonstrations in this school are based the study of methods of instruction in the subjects of the elementary school curriculum. More intensive practice teaching is arranged for in the public schools of the city under the supervision of its teachers; it is continued for six weeks between the third and fourth semesters and is followed by a second period between the fifth and sixth semesters of four weeks' participation in social welfare work and educational activities for children and adolescents. The first examination at the end of the course for eligibility to appointment as a probationary teacher includes: (1) the preparation of two essays, one in education and one in an elective subject; (2) written examinations on education, philosophy, and psychology, and one other subject selected from the elementary school curriculum or any other academic subject; (3) an oral examination on the same subjects as in the written test; and (4) a practical examination at the choice of the examiners in teaching, physical training, fine arts, or natural science. Permanent appointment is based on a second examination taken after at least three years of school experience; this examination is practical in character and is similar to the second examination in Prussia, with the additional requirement that candidates must demonstrate their ability in the teaching of physical training, drawing, music, manual training (for men), and sewing and household arts (for women). Opportunities for further study are provided in a special institute for the training of teachers in service.

Conclusion

There forces have been influential in determining the present reform in the preparation of teachers in Germany. Discontent with their status, economic and political, under the Imperial regime contributed very largely to the demand for a type of professional preparation which would improve it in both aspects. Undoubtedly the narrow, even though effective, character of the training given in the old normal schools justified this discontent. The Revolution and the realization that its success and the development of a new national spirit which would give real expression to the best in German culture led to the recognition that the schools must be given a new orientation the responsibility for whose success would devolve upon the teachers. Inevitably the traditional form of training was inadequate for the assumption of such a responsibility. From another point of view the development of education as an independent science or field of knowledge, with its own content and methods, inspired the plea for autonomy in education (*Eigengesetzlichkeit der Erziehung*), a movement for professional freedom and self-determination, which could only be realized by a new system of professional preparation more nearly akin to the spirit underlying the preparation for other liberal professions. Those who feared that the increased demands, both in the length and cost of the preparation which has been adopted, would diminish the number of suitable candidates failed to take into account the inspiration of the youth movement (*Jugendbewegung*) and the missionary spirit which influenced German youth immediately after the War.[16] Actually far more candidates present themselves for admission to the teachers colleges of various types than can be accepted. To some extent, but not wholly, this may be attributed to the intense economic struggle which confronts youth everywhere, but more particularly in Central Europe.

Whatever the causes, Germany has taken the lead in adopting for the preparation of teachers for elementary schools the highest standards to be found anywhere in the world. The nature of there standards may bring about a change in the social group from which teachers have in the past been recruited—the rural and artisan classes; but opportunities are already being provided to retain these by means of scholarships and other financial aid. The problem is whether teachers, trained in the new system, will be willing to serve, even during the probationary period, in the small rural school. The German answer has always been that physicians and the clergy have always been ready to settle in rural areas; the advanced training will probably not prove a deterrent, but rather a stimulus to the young teacher to contribute to the rebuilding of his country. The serious crisis through which Germany is now passing and which has already compelled the authorities to close a number of teachers colleges postpones for many years the opportunity of estimating the results of the reform, which is of supreme interest for all interested in education. The experiment means more than an improvement in the professional preparation of elementary school teachers; it means with the gradual approximation of the time spent on preparation to that of secondary school teachers, the ultimate development of a single teaching profession, prepared according to the various functions which it is called upon to perform.

4. ITALY

History

The reform of education following the Fascist Revolution inevitably affected the status and the preparation of elementary school teachers. A reorganization in this field had long been overdue, for it had been the subject of a special investigation in 1918. The preparation of teachers for elementary schools had been provided for under the Casati Law of 1859 in separate normal schools for boys at the age of sixteen and girls at the age of fifteen. The training was mainly a continuation of the work of the elementary school with an emphasis on practice teaching in the second and third years of the three-year course. In 1896 the course of study was modified by the Gianturco Law which required the organisation of practice and infant schools in connection with the normal schools and introduced a final examination for a teacher's certificate, which was a condition of eligibility for the competitions for appointment to vacancies. In 1911 a two-year course of training for elementary school teachers was instituted in *ginnasi* with four-year courses. In 1912 the *Unione Magistrale Nazionale* (National Teachers Union) at its Congress in Bologna recommended a complete reorganization of the system and the establishment of institutions with a seven-year course, five to be devoted to general education and two to professional preparation. Beyond this, the Union advocated the creation of facilities for further training of teachers in service. In the following year the Ministry of Public Instruction appointed a committee to consider a number of problems in the preparation of teachers: how to meet the demands of general and professional training; the length of the course as a whole and the distribution of time between the two parts; and curricula and courses of study. The recommendations of the committee were identical with those of the Union. A reform along these lines was proposed in a bill introduced by Minister Credaro in 1914: the whole course was to be seven years in length following elementary education; the first five years were to be devoted to general culture and the last two to a review of general education with special reference to the elementary schools, and to the study of education and social ethics with practice teaching; in the last year the study of agriculture, hygiene, and physical training were to be included. Nothing came of this plan, which was again modified in 1918 in a proposal to organize a seven-year course, separate for men and women, the first six years to be devoted to general education and the last year to professional preparation.

During the same period there had been established two higher normal schools, in Rome and Florence, to provide opportunities for women teachers who wished to prepare for positions as principals of schools; similar opportunities had also been created in schools of education for men in the universities and in special courses elsewhere for advanced study (*corsi di perfezionamento*). The characteristics of both stages of training were the same; the institutions were virtually isolated from the main currents of education and devoted closely to preparation for the elementary schools; in both the greatest difficulty was the problem of adjusting the claims of general culture studies and of professional preparation.

The problem, on the whole was not difficult when considered from this point of view or in the light of the character of elementary education. Italy had long been under the influence of positivist philosophy and in education this meant an emphasis on the acquisition of an organized body of knowledge. In practice this emphasis resulted in memorization, formalism, and bookishness. On the professional side the task was to prepare teachers with a thorough command of methods and techniques. The same consequences followed also from the introduction of the Herbartian principles.

THE PRESENT SYSTEMS

The New Orientation

The Gentile reform, which emphasized humanism and the awakening of the spirit, the cult of personality through activity and sympathetic insight on the part of the teacher into the meaning of the Italian tradition and of humanism, on the one hand, and into the inner urge of the pupils for spiritual expression and activity, on the other, was not compatible with a mythology which stressed mechanisms and artificial devices as something extrinsic both to subject-matter and to the personality of the pupils. In other words, the Gentle reform was in essence opposed to the traditional practices in preparing teachers. The leading exponent of the new approach was Professor Ernesto Codignola, Director of the *R. Istituto Superiore di Magistero* in Florence, who had for many years been a critic of the normal schools and the principles upon which their work was based. Education, according to Codignola, is a spiritual process and anything which stands between the teacher and the pupil disturbs this process. Methods tend to dominate and to mechanize the spirit and to reduce instruction to mere routine. Hence the best preparation of the teacher lies, not in the study of principles of education and of methods of teaching, but in the thorough penetration of the humanistic spirit. On the professional side the best preparation of the teacher is provided by the study of philosophy, of which education is a part, and whose function it is to illustrate the nature of the spirit and the process of its development. Methods are only meaningful, not as external devices, but as the expression of a spiritual form, constantly active and constantly changing as conditions, pupils, or environment change. Not mastery of methods nor even an encyclopedic command of knowledge alone makes the good teacher, but an active mind, a firm will, an exquisite feeling for art, and consciousness of the harmonious and universal in man. Applied to the problem of preparing teachers, this means a different approach; the problem is not what knowledge or methods are necessary for the teacher, but what is best adapted to giving him that consciousness of his own and the pupils' humanity. Not didactic formulas, but how to reach the inner souls of the pupils and how to respect the human spirit in them, is the lesson that the future teacher must learn. This lesson can, in Codignola's opinion, be acquired only by thorough study of the humanities and of philosophy which seeks to interpret them in the light of universals.[17]

The reorganization of the preparation of elementary school teachers followed the principles advocated by Codignola. All existing institutions—the normal schools and courses in *ginnasi,* the *corsi di perfezionamento,* and the schools of education in universities—were abolished, and were replaced by new institutions (*istituti magistrali*) as a part of the secondary school systems. Institutions of this type may only be established by government decree. Pupils, boys and girls, are admitted on completing five years of the elementary school at the minimum age of ten and on passing an entrance examination. The length of the course in the *istituti magistrali* is seven years, divided into two periods of four and three years each. Transfer from the lower to the upper section of the course is based on an entrance examination.

The curriculum of the *istituti magistrail* is wholly academic. The subjects and the weekly time-distribution are given in the accompanying tables.

Time Schedule *Instituto Magistrale*

Subjects	Lower Course			
	I Year (hours)	II Year (hours)	III Year (hours)	IV Year (hours)
Indian language	8	4	4	4
Latin language	...	6	6	6
History and geography	4	2	2	2
Mathematics	3	2	2	3
Foreign language	...	4	4	4
Drawing	3	2	2	2
Music and singing	2	2	2	2
Musical instrument*	(2)	(2)	(2)	(2)
Total	20	22	22	23

*Optional

The *istituto magistrale* does not differ in content or methods of instruction or in organization and administration from other schools at the secondary level.[18] The only connection between this institution and the obvious purpose for which it is created is to be found in the discussion of educational theory in the philosophy course. Every institute is required to have associated with it a kindergarten, or *casa dei bambini,* primarily for purposes of observation and not for practice teaching.

Time Schedule *Istitutio Magistrale*

Subjects	Upper Course		
	I Year (hours)	II Year (hours)	III Year (hours)
Indian language and literature	4	5	4
Latin language and literature	5	4	4
Philosophy and education	4	5	6
History	3	4	4
Mathematics and Physics	3	4	4
Natural science, geography and hygiene	3	2	3
Drawing	2	1	1
Music and singing	2	1	1
Musical instrument*	(2)	(2)	(2)
Total	26	26	27

*Optional

At the end of the whole course candidates must pass an examination in all the subjects of the upper section. The oral examination in philosophy and education which are characteristic of the normal institute covers the following programs:

Knowledge and evaluation of children's literature.

Selections from the history of schools and of educational theory.

The aesthetic problem and teaching of art. The candidate must show a knowledge of at least one of the following works: Plato, *Republic,* X; Aristotle, *Poetics* (extracts): Vico, *Sciensa nuova* (extracts referring to the problem of art); Kant, *Critique of Judgment* and *Æsthetic Judgment;* Croce, *Breviario di Estetica.*

The problem of religion and the teaching of religion. The candidate must show a knowledge of at least one of the following works: Plato, *Euthyphro;* Aristotle, *Metaphysics,* XII; Cicero, *De Natura Deorum* (Part I or II); Saint Paul's *Epistles;* Vico, *Sciensa nuova* (Providence); Mazzini, *Idee religiose* (extracts); Gioberti, *Riforma Cattolica* (extracts); Royce, *The Problem of Christianity.*

The problem of consciousness and the teaching of science, based on a knowledge of at least one of the following works: Aristotle, *Organon;* Descartes, *Meditations* (extracts); Locke, *On the Understanding* (extracts); Leibniz, *Nouveaux Essais;* Kant, *Critique of Pure Reason* (extracts) and *Prolegomena;* Galluppi, *Saggio* (extracts); Rosmini, *Esposizione del suo Sistema;* Spaventa, *Logica e Metaphysica* (Part I).

The moral problem and moral instruction, based on a knowledge of at least one of the following works: Aristotle, *Nichomochean Ethics* (extracts); *New Testament;* Spinoza, *Ethics* (Part III); Kant, *Critique of Practical Reason* and *Metaphysics of Morals;* Rosmini, *Principi di Scienza morale* and *Storia dei Sistemi.*

Discussion of an educational classic selected from the following: Comenius, *Great Didactic; Ratio Studiorum;* Locke,

Thoughts on Education; Basedow, *Appeal to the Friends of Humanity;* Vico, *De Ncstri Temporis Studiorum Ratione* (extracts); Rousseau, *Emile;* Kant, *On Pedagogy;* Cuoco, *Pagine scelte;* Pestalozzi (selected writings); Froebel, *Education of Man* and selected writings; Fichte, *The Vocation of Man* and *Addresses to the German Nation;* Schelling, *Lectures on the Method of Academic Studies;* Necker de Saussure, *L'Education Progressive;* Richter, *Levana;* Rosmini, *Del Principio supremo.*

Discussion of a modern or contemporary educational work: Capponi, Lambruschini, Gioberti, Mazzini, De Sanctis, Gabelli, Ardigo, James, E. Caird, Arnold, Laberthonnière, Boutroux, etc.

According to the regulations in aim of the oral examination is not so much to test the knowledge acquired by the candidates as their ability to discuss questions and problems from the philosophical point of view. When it is recalled that pupils begin the study of philosophy and education at the age of fourteen or fifteen, that they are examined at the age of seventeen or eighteen, and that the duration of the oral examination is but thirty minutes, some doubt may be expressed of the virtue of such a course. The pupils acquire a certain glibness in discussing theories and principles, wide in range, but, although the use of textbooks and compendia is forbidden, the feeling cannot be resisted that the glibness is the result of instruction by the teacher rather than "inner penetration of the spirit" of the sources read.

Appointment

Candidates who pass the final examination in the *istituti magistrali* are given the *abilitazione all' insegnamemto elementare* or *abilitazione magistrale,* a certificate of aptitude as elementary teachers, which is the minimum qualification required, not for appointment, but for the competition for appointment, in an elementary school. Vacancies are advertised each year by the *proveditore aglistudi* or regional superintendent of public education or by the councils of autonomous communities.

Candidates must submit with their applications the certificate, a statement of physical fitness, proof of citizenship, and testimonials of character; if men, they must be over eighteen years of age, and, if women, over seventeen years of age. They are then submitted to a public competitive examination (*concorso public*) conducted by commissions appointed either by the superintendent or the autonomous community which may delegate the conduct of the examination to the superintendent. The examination consists of a written essay on an education problem and an oral test based largely on the programmes of the *istituto magistrale*. On the basis of the result the candidates are arranged in order of merit and the best are assigned to the available vacancies in boys', girls', or mixed schools; the highest on the list have, of course, a certain preference in the choice of a position.

After obtaining their firm appointments, teachers must serve a probationary period of three years as *maestri straordinari*, corresponding to the French *institutors stagiaires;* at the end of this period they are appointed on the favourable report of the inspectors as *maestri ordinari*, the French *instituteurs titulaires*. No teacher may transfer from one school to another unless he has spent two years in the same post; exceptions are made only for reasons of health or for family considerations.

The line of advancement of elementary school teachers in within the field of elementary education itself. The *maestro elementare* may become a *direttore didattico* or supervisor and then an *ispettore scolastico*. Promotion is secured by further study in the *Istituti Superiori di Magistero*, three maintained by the State in Rome, Florence, and Messina, and three private in Milan, Turin, and Naples. The Royal Higher Teachers Colleges offer two-year courses preparing for positions as *direttori didattici*, and four-year courses preparing teachers of literature in secondary schools, of philosophy and education in normal institutes, and inspectors. Admission is secured by competitive examination which is the same for all courses. The examination is written and oral; the written test includes an essay in philosophy and education, or history or Italian literature and a translation from Latin; the oral test is on philosophy and education, Italian and Latin language and literature, and history and geography. The annual fees are 350 lire for tuition and 140 lire for the examinations in the four-year course; additional fees are charged for the entrance examination, matriculation, contribution to the school fund, the examination for the diploma, and the diploma (445 lire for the four-year course and 210 lire for the two-year course). The Government each year selects by competition forty teachers who are assigned to the two-year course and retain their salaries and positions during their period of study; one fourth of these teachers are selected from the new provinces. In addition, fees are remitted wholly or partially to candidates who rank highest in the competitive examination and can prove the need of financial assistance. Finally, the Minister of Public Instruction awards a number of scholarships annually to students recommended by the administrative council of each institute.

The curriculum for the two-year course leading to the *diploma di direzione didattica* includes the following subjects: Italian and Latin language and literature, education, German language and literature (two-year courses in each), and history, geography, philosophy, elements of public law and educational legislation, school hygiene, and foreign literature (one-year course in each). The diploma awarded by examination at the end of the course is a certificate of eligibility for the competitive examination by which the *direttori didattici* are selected each year up to the number of available vacancies. The minimum age for appointment is thirty; candidates must have had at least three years of teaching experience. The function of the *directori didattici* is in the main supervisory; they assign teachers to their classes, issue time-schedules and programmes of work, arrange for examinations, and in general supervise instruction and progress in the schools, reporting each year to the inspectors of their districts; in the larger areas they may be assisted by sub-directors.

The four-year courses for teachers of philosophy and education and for inspectors includes in the first two years the following subjects: Italian and Latin language and literature, philosophy, education, and German language and literature (two-year courses in each) and English language and literature, history, geography, elements of public law and educational legislation, and school hygiene (one-year course in each). The subjects of the last two years are Latin language and literature (two-year course) and philosophy and education (one-year course in each) and at least two other courses selected from the subjects of the first two years and pursued for one year. The final examination leads to the award of the *diploma di pedagogia filosofia* or the *abilitazione all'ispettorato scolastico,* both of which are only certificates of eligibility for the competitive examinations for appointment. Candidates for inspectorships must be *directori didattici* with two years of experience or teachers with fifteen years of experience; appointments are divided equally between the two groups; one fifth of the inspectorships are reserved for women.

Status of Teachers

Before appointment teachers, like all public officials, must take the following oath:

I swear loyalty to the King and his successors, to observe the Constitution and other laws of the State faithfully, to fulfill and the duties of my office diligently and with zeal for the public good and the interests of the Administration, scrupulously guarding the secret of office and conducting myself, in public and private, in accordance with the dignity of my position. I swear that I do not nor will belong to associations or parties whose activity cannot be reconciled with the duties of my office. I wear to carry out all my duties to the sole end of the inseparable good of the King and my country.

As recently as 1928 teachers were not required to be declared Fascists, but a strong hint had already been given by Mussolini in one of his addresses (*Discorso All'Augosteo*) to the effect that teachers were expected to support the Fascist regime. After a number of dismissals for political reasons, the question whether teachers were or were not Fascists ceased to be of importance. Many of the teachers are members of the Party and many are officers of the *Balilla* organization.

After appointment as *ardinari,* teachers enjoy permanent tenure, but are subject to dismissal for incompetence or misconduct, with the right of appeal to the disciplinary council of the regional superintendent (*provveditore agli studi*) and beyond it to the Higher Council of Public Instruction. The organisation is thus hierarchical with responsibility fixed by law at each stage. The importance of this organization, which is the result of the Gentile reform, can only be understood in the light of the conditions which prevailed in the profession in the period preceding it. Insubordination, lack of discipline, frequent and readily condoned absences, and professional incompetence, as indicated by the examination of pupils and in the competitions for advancement, had produced a state of chaos; efforts at improvement led to strikes among the teachers. The situation was immediately improved by the removal of the incompetent and superannuated, by a reform in the system of preparation, by the introduction of a hierarchical system, and above all by an amelioration of the salary conditions, which were probably more responsible for the unrest and discontent than any other cause.

Under the Gentile reform the salaries of elementary school teachers were almost immediately doubled; from a minimum of 3000 lire a year and a maximum of 5600 lire they were raised to a minimum of 5600 lire and a maximum of 9500 lire. Since 1923 salaries have been further increased to a minimum of 5900 lire, rising in twenty-eight years to a maximum of 10,000 lire, with a supplement for active service ranging from 1300 to 1800 lire a year and an addition of 800 lire a year for service in schools with double sessions. No provision is made for teachers' homes or for rent or other indemnities as in France. Local communes, particularly in rural areas, may provide homes, but teachers are not entitled to such a benefit as of right.

A pension fund (*monte-pensioni*) for elementary school teachers was established in 1878; after periodical revision the regulations governing the system were codified by Royal Decree of March 23, 1931 (*Regio Decreto,* 23 Marzo, 1931, No. 707). The system has been placed under the supervision of the Administrative Council of the Loan and Trust Fund and the State Insurance Associations. The cost of administration of the pension fund is provided for annually by appropriations granted on the recommendation of the Minister of Finance. The fund is mode up of contributions paid by the teachers in elementary schools and their employers (the State, communes, or other recognized educational corporations) and gifts and bequests. The decree regulates the nature of the investments and provides for quinquennial valuations. Teachers are required to pay into the fund eight per cent of their salaries annually, which is duplicated by their employers. Disability and retirement allowances are paid out of the fund accumulated at compound interest. Teachers may be retired on account of ill-health with an allowance after ten years of service or on reaching the age of sixty after the same period of service; a retiring allowance may be obtained on reaching the age of sixty after twenty years of service or after forty years of service without any age requirement. Disability allowances consist of three- fourths of the allowance to which a teacher would be entitled if eligible for retirement; the retiring allowances consist of the annuities purchasable with the accumulated contributions standing to a teahcer's account, but limited to a maximum equal to the average of the salary received in the last three years of service and raised to certain prescribed minimal based on the length of service. Provision is made under the same scheme for the protection of widows and orphan of teachers who die in service or after retirement. A somewhat different system exists for the retirement of administrative officials (inspectors and supervisors), who may be retired at the age of sixty after twenty years of service or after forty years of service without any conditions as to age. The retiring allowance in such cases consists of one-fortieth of the first 4000 lire of the average salary received in the last three years of service and an addition of one-sixtieth of the balance of the average salary over 4000 lire for each year of service, with a maximum allowance of four-fifths of the average salary.

Conclusion

The new Italian system of preparing teachers for the elementary school, determined as it is by the idealistic philosophy underlying the whole reform of education, is frankly a challenge to the traditional and current practice. Sound in insisting on a broad cultural and general background for every teacher, the complete negation of the value of professional training raises many doubts of the ultimate success of the system. That there is much truth in the view that overemphasis on methodology tends to lead to sterility and mechanization cannot be denied, but it is questionable whether the difficulty can be solved by talking about education and avoiding the practical induction of the young teacher into its conduct. The result in practice will be that Italian teachers will secure their initiation into practice at the expense of the pupils entrusted to them during their three years of probation with such guidance as they may receive from *direttori didattici* and *ispettori scolastici*—a reactionary step which has in it the inherent danger that the teacher may become more mechanical and formal than without any professional preparation. This is particularly serious at a time when the essence of the elementary school reform is to impose greater responsibility upon the teacher in framing courses of study adapted to the local environment and in conducting instruction on activity principles. In other words, in seeking to make the teacher free, as the new system of preparation does, it fails on the practical side to give him that professional training which alone can make him free.

The reform has, however, achieved one notable accomplishment—a change in the status of elementary school teachers and of elementary education by incorporating both as essential parts of the great national Revolution. Incorporation of the normal institutes into the secondary school system, improved salaries, opportunities for advancement, better discipline, and more freedom have already exercised their influence. Beyond this, a new sphere of activity has been opened for elementary school teachers in the service of educating adolescents and adults outside of regular school hours and in participating in the national movement as officers in the *Balilla* organisation. The new spirit is perhaps more marked in smaller and remote corners of Italy where the rural school teachers seem to be inspired with missionary zeal; in the cities the opportunity provided for experimentation produces the same result. In both cases, however, it is doubtful whether the new spirit can yet be attributed to the new system of teacher-preparation; the new spirit was in fact already present under the influence of the cultural wakening which had begun in Italy many years before the Revolution.

5. RUSSIA

The preparation of teachers in the Soviet Union is dominated by two main objectives. The first is to secure teachers who are loyal to the existing political ideology; the second is to reorganize the character of the preparation in such a way as to promote the close relationship between education and the economic goals which are to be attained. In the pre-Revolutionary system elementary school teachers had been trained in normal schools of the traditional type and in girls' *gymnasia*. Through the organisation in 1905 of the All Russian Teachers' Union, in which membership was open to teachers in all grades of schools and universities, a strong professional spirit had begun to be developed, even though there was no great improvement in the material conditions of teachers in elementary schools. The part which education was to play in the social reconstruction of the Revolution was immediately recognized, and it was with this in mind that Lenin declared that "We must raise our teacher to a height such as he had not attained and never will be able to attain in a bourgeois society." Despite this declaration the conditions of the teaching profession, socially and materially, continued to be unimproved until the past year.

The preparation of teachers was not reorganized until 1924, when, instead of being assigned to separate institutions, it was provided in the technicums or in the last two years of the nine-year secondary schools. In these institutions are prepared teachers for pre-schools, first grade schools, and for lower schools for political enlightenment. The character of the preparation is thus determined by the predominantly vocational bias of the institutions in which it is given. Admission to the pedagogical technicum is based on the completion of the seven-year school, which usually takes place at about the age of fifteen. The length of the course is four years. Each pedagogical technicum has an industrial or agricultural bias, determined by the predominant local conditions. As contrasted with the academic and professional emphases found elsewhere and with the movement for autonomy in education, the preparation of teachers in the Soviet Union is subordinated to the aims of the unified labour school and of participation in socially useful labour. There is, in other words, no break in gauge between the preparation of the teacher and the aims of education, which are determined by the needs of the workers. This synthesis is emphasized all the more because the teacher is expected to be a leader in the cultural work of his locality. Labour thus becomes the centre in the scheme of teacher training as it is in education. Accordingly, the future teacher is expected to acquire a certain amount of skill whether in a trade or in agriculture, for it is from variety of practical experience that his influence will be determined. Beyond this, the studies must include the scientific studies which are fundamental to an understanding of the nature of the child and of the educative process (anatomy, physiology, biology, pedology, and psychology), and the social sciences, with an emphasis on Marxian philosophy and dialectic materialism.

The first two years of the four-year course in the pedagogical technicum are devoted to general and professional studies, visits to all types of educational institutions, and a study of the educational systems in the Soviet Republics. The last two years are more intensively professional in character and are devoted to the study of social science, methods, and practice, with participation in the work of the locality (industrial or agricultural), and to training in conducting campaigns against illiteracy, work with homeless children, children's clubs and libraries, and participation in youth movements. At a recent meeting of the Central Committee of the Communist Party (reported in *Izvestia*, September, 1931) it was resolved that all teachers be required to learn the fundamentals of production in factories, Soviet farms, machine tractor stations, and collective farms, and the methods of the work of polytechnization. Increasingly the statement is repeated that the teacher is not only the chief agent in the educative process, but the organizer and leader of his community.

The curriculum and time-distribution for the various subjects of the four-year course in a pedagogical technicum with an agricultural bias in the Russian Republic are shown in the accompanying table.

The courses in the pedagogical sections of the nine-year secondary schools, which are given in the eighth and ninth years, are similar in general to those in the first two years of the pedagogical technicum, the major part of the time being devoted to professional studies and practice.

Status of Teachers

The All-Russian Teachers' union was dissolved early in the history of the Revolution and recognized, but without restoring the confidence of the authorities in the teachers. That many of the older teachers (and the majority had inevitably been trained under the old regime) did not sympathize actively

Curriculum and Time-Distribution in the Pedagogical Technicum

Subjects	Number of Hours per week	
	I year	*II year*
Mathematics	4	4
Physics	3	3
Chemistry / Natural science (bracketed together)	6	6
Agriculture	2	2
Vernacular	5	5
Foreign language	2	2
History of the class struggle	2	2
Economic geography	3	..
Political economy	..	3
Activity instruction*	3	3
Drawing	2	2
Music and singing	2	2
Physical education	2	2
Introduction to pedology	2	3
Educational system of R.S.F.S.R.	2	2
Total	40	40

Subjects	Number of hours per week	
	III year	*IV year*
Theory of evolution	3	..
History of the class struggle	3	..
Economic policy	2	..
Constitution	1	..
Historical materialism	..	3
Environmental study	1	..
Foreign language	2	2
Pedology	4	..
Problems of the organization of instruction by complexes	1	2
Methods of the vernacular	2	2
Methods in arithmetic	2	2
Methods in nature study	2	2
Methods in social sciences	1	2
Methods in activity instruction*	2	1
Methods in drawing	2	1
Methods in singing	2	1
Methods in phyical education	1	1
Pedagogical practice	6	13
Pedological practice	..	2
Political enlightenment	..	2
Total	37†	36†

* It is not clear, from the use of the term *Arbeitsunterricht* employd in the report from which this table is taken (see note following), whether it refers to manual instruction or the activity principle.

† The totals given in the last two columns are 41 and 40 respectively in the publication of the People's Commissariat for Education in the R.S.F.S.R., *Die Volksbildung in der Russisches Socialistischen Föderativen Sowjetrepublik*, p. 34 (Moscow, 1920).

with the Revolution is certain. About 1924 the Union was reorganized as the Educational Workers' Union, including all workers in public education, students, school medical officers, clerks and janitors, and was made a constituent part of the General Workers' Union. In 1925 the Educational Workers' Union declared its loyalty to the Communist Party and decided to throw in its lot with the workers in the construction of the new life and the new order. That suspicion is not altogether allayed was indicated at the conference of the Central Committee of the Communist Party (referred to above) which urged all members to take an interest in the schools and to supervise the teachers, especially those of the social and political disciplines the Central Committee of Komsomols was at the same time encouraged to select candidates for the teaching profession from trust-worthy Pioneers.

Materially the conditions of teachers continued without improvement until 1931, when it was decided by the Council of People's Commissars in Russia to raise the existing salaries by twenty-five to thirty per cent and to extend to teachers the privilege of purchasing provisions and merchandise at the same rates as workers. Salaries, the same for men and women, are established in five zones and vary with the cost of living, and the grade of school. In 1927-28 elementary teachers in rural areas received about 46 roubles and in cities 54 roubles a month; in 1932 salaries were raised to 90 roubles a month, a rouble being worth about 50 cents. Teachers in the first grade schools are required to teach twenty-four hours a week; in the second grade schools eighteen hours a week, with additional compensation for additional work. Lodgings are provided for teachers in villages; unemployment benefits and medical care are provided for all; married women may retain their positions and two months' leave of absence are granted for childbirth. Teachers, like workers, enjoy special concessions for the education of their children, may retire on a non-contributory pension after twenty-five years of service, and are entitled, like workers, to the privilege of purchasing supplies and of using clubs and rest-houses.

The Educational Workers' Union, to which all engaged in public education must belong, is supported by contributions from the members of two per cent of salary, and has a membership of 800,000. All education bills and plans for curricula and courses of study, which are drawn up by the Education Department (*Narkompros*), are presented to the Union for suggestion and final approval; its advice is sought in the appointment of principals, and the People's Commissar for Education makes an annual report at the Conference of the Union. The extent of this participation implies, as does the character of the preparation given, that the teacher is expected above all to be a partisan, and not a member of a free profession, which in Soviet ideology would for education be a contradiction in terms. Up to the present the teacher in the Soviet Republics is still far from having attained, from the point of view of professional preparation or of status, the exalted position which Lenin assigned to him.

6. UNITED STATES

History

The great variety of practices and standards which prevail in the educational systems of the United States is nowhere so well illustrated as in the preparation of teachers. Here are reflected the wide divergences which prevail in the economic conditions, the popular attitude to education, the weakness of local control, and the status of teachers. All levels of teacher-preparation are found from high school training classes, country normal schools, and state normal schools to teachers colleges and education departments in colleges and universities. While the educational system was gradually developed during the nineteenth and rapidly expanded during the twentieth century on the principle of equality of opportunity and adaptation to changing social demands, the institutions for the training of teachers, which began to be provided in the third decade of the nineteenth century, continued to maintain an existence almost isolated from the influences which governed the growth of the rest of the system. This was due in the main to two causes: first, the control and administration of education were to a large degree decentralized, and, second, the normal schools, until an adequate supply of secondary education was available, had to perform a dual function in providing both the preliminary academic education and the professional training. To these a third cause, closely associated with the first, might be adduced in the reluctance of the state authorities to enforce basic standards for the certification of teachers, with the result that in some localities teachers were appointed on the basis of simple examinations conducted by the local school committee or on the basis of a variety of certificates granted by several overlapping authorities and valid for terms of different duration from one year to life. Only within the last two decades has there been a concentrated effort to secure some order out of the confused and complicated situation, and to define certain minimum requirements for the preparation of teachers; but, although progress has been made in this direction, the reorganization of the systems of certification has barely been initiated.

The desirability of giving teachers some preparation for the work which they were to undertake began to be advocated in the second decade of the last century, when the establishment of teacher-training institutions began to be urged by James L. Kingsley, William Russell, Samuel R. Hall, Thomas Gallaudet, and James G. Carter. The movement gained momentum in the thirties as a consequence of reports on the Prussian system of teacher-training which were disseminated widely by Charles Brooks, Calvin E. Stowe, and Alexander D. Bache, and particularly by the translation of Cousin's *Report on Public Instruction in Prussia*. To James G. Carter, who was assisted in his efforts by Horace Mann, is due the credit for the establishment of the first state normal school in the country at Lexington, Massachusetts, in 1839. The institution severed as a model for other States and in time superseded the practice adopted in New York state in 1827 of training teachers in academies or secondary schools which received special grants for this purpose. Cnnecticut through the efforts of Henry Barnard established the first state normal school at New Britain in 1850; Michigan followed in 1853 with the opening of the state normal school at Ypsilanti; and even New York State was influenced by the practice of creating independent institutions for the training of teachers in the establishment of the New York State Normal School at Albany in 1843, while remaining for some time the academy system. From these early beginnings the normal school system spread throughout the country. Unfortunately, certification requirements were not made dependent on training, so that the majority of teachers, until within the last twenty years, although certificated, were untrained professionally.

While the normal schools helped to keep alive and to foster the idea of professional preparation for teachers, they were confronted with serious difficulties. The length of the course was unstandardized and even where it was defined many students failed to complete it; the entrance requirements were low, often not more than an elementary education, with the result that the course of training had to include both academic and professional preparation; frequently the academic work consisted of little more than a review of the subjects of the "common school" branches, while the so-called professional courses—principles of education, methods, and practice—consumed a major part of the time. Two traditions were built up during this formative period, which contained almost up to 1910; one was the restriction of academic studies to the subjects of the elementary school; the second was an overemphasis on the professional subjects or techniques.

With the gradual expansion in the supply of high schools after 1905, it became increasingly possible to raise the entrance requirements to normal schools and to demand graduation from high school for admission, a practice which had already been introduced in the New York State Normal College at Albany in 1890 and in Massachusetts in 1894.

Beginning in 1908, a definite movement was launched to set up as the minimum period of preparation a two-year course in a normal school following graduation from high school. This standard was urged again in 1920 as the result of an extensive inquiry into the *Professional Preparation of Teachers for American Public Schools* conducted by the Carnegie Foundation for the Advancement of Teachers. Scarcely had this standard begun to be adopted, when, as a result of the improved economic status of teachers, the prosperity of the country, and the expanding programme of the elementary school, a new movement was initiated to extend the period of preparation to four years and to convert the normal schools into teachers colleges.

This, the latest movement in the organization and advancement of teacher-preparation, was not new. As long ago as 1879 a paper had been read before the Normal Department of the National Education Association on *Professional Degrees for Teachers,* which were already being granted in several States. The nomenclature of these degree it is not necessary to discuss here; it was not until after 1900 that some institutions began to expand this courses to four years and to award not only the degree of Bachelor, but that of Master of Arts. A number of institutions had already adopted the title of college; the Michigan State Normal School at Ypsilanti because the Michigan State Normal College in 1897; Illinois had gone even further when it established its training institution in 1857 as the Illinois State Normal University. The introduction of degree did not, however, mean the discontinuance of shorter courses in the same institutions. The real significance of the movement was that the teacher-training institutions were entering into competition with the liberal arts colleges and were undertaking the preparation of teachers for high schools as well as for elementary schools. By 1930 a number of States had raised the period of preparation for elementary school certificates awarded on the basics of training from two to three years; a smaller number, including California and New

York, required four years of preparation. The direction of the movement for raising normal schools to the status of teachers colleges was defined by the American Association of Teachers Colleges, which was organized in 1917.

The result of all these tendencies is a bewildering variety of practices ranging from high school training to preparation requiring four years of study at the collegiate level. Cutting across the array of practices between these extremes are the certification requirements which have in many States not been adjusted to the systems of training. The situation can, of course, be explained in part by the existence of a large number of small single-teacher schools in which teachers receive low salaries and are under annual contracts of employment only, and in part by the fact that the centralization of educational control in the hands of the state authorities is in its initial stages in many States. There is thus a range of schools from the small single-teacher rural school, with a term of about one hundred and twenty days, to the urban school, elaborately equipped, providing a varied curriculum, employing specialized teachers, and having a term of about two hundred days. The various types and degrees of preparation of teachers are thus determined by economic and social status, by the grade of work, and by the public interest in education.

THE PRESENT SYSTEM

Since there is such a variation in the practices of preparing teachers in the United States, ranging from the high school to the universities, it is impossible to do more than present a general picture.

The outstanding tendency at present, due to the increase in teachers' salaries during the past decade, is the gradual elimination of the lowest types of preparation. The preparation in high schools consists of a few simple courses in education in addition to academic subjects; in the country training classes the major part of the work of the year following, as a rule, graduation from high school is devoted to the study of professional subjects. Teachers prepared in this way secure employment in rural schools of which they are in sole charge, responsible for the work of all the grades.

Since 1920 there has been a marked tendency to set up as the minimum desirable requirement two years of preparation following graduation from the high school. This preparation is given in state, county, and city normal schools, in private normal schools, and in teachers colleges. In 1930 the number of these institutions was as follows: state normal schools, 66; city normal schools, 26; county normal schools, 47; private normal schools, 58; teachers colleges, 134; and private teachers colleges, 6. The current trend is in the direction of a decrease of normal schools of different types and their conversion into teachers colleges, which offer a variety of courses ranging from one to four years. The majority of the teacher training institutions, except where indicated in their description, are maintained by the state authorities, which meet the greater part of the annual cost of operation by appropriations. Until recently most of the normal schools and teachers colleges were administered by their own governing bodies, a practice still found in twelve States; the objection to this practice is that it encourages excessive rivalry and competition for appropriations. The defects of this situation have been overcome in many States by placing the institutions concerned directly under the state department of education, as in Alabama, California, Connecticut, Louisiana, Maryland, Massachusetts, New Hampshire, Oklahoma, Tennessee, Vermont, and Virginia; in other States special boards have been created to supervise the preparation of teachers, as in Colorado, Indiana, Maine, Michigan, Minnesota, Nebraska, Texas, and Wisconsin; in thirteen States one board has been established for all state institutions of higher education, including universities, liberal arts colleges, teachers colleges, and normal schools. While these systems of coordinating the preparation of teachers in each State represent a great advance, there is still left the difficulty of adjusting the relations between the teachers colleges and normal schools and the state institutions for higher education, particularly as these are also concerned with the preparation of teachers.

Standardization

Although there have for a long time existed organizations for the consideration of problems affecting institutions for the preparation of teachers, it has only been within the last few years that a concerted effort has been made to definite minimum standards for their organization. This task was undertaken and has been promoted by the American Association of Teachers Colleges, which performs the same function as the associations for standardizing secondary schools and colleges. The Association defines as a teachers college a state, municipal, or incorporated private institution which admits students who have completed a high school course, offers at atleast one four-year unified curriculum devoted to the preparation of teachers, and has the legal right to confer degrees; a normal school is a similar institution offering curricula of two or more years in length, but not leading to a degree. The members of the faculty of such institutions must hold the master's degree or its equivalent. The standards further define the desirable maximum of the number of teaching periods per week, and require the maintenance of a practice school, the provision of adequate library facilities, the appropriate organization of curricula, and the prescription of organized requirements for the award of degrees.

The standards prescribed by the Association represent the direction in which it is desired to move. During the present period of transition many teachers colleges still offer one-, two-, and three-year courses in addition to the four-year course, while many normal schools offer three- as well as two-year courses. This confusion is attributable, however, not merely to the transition stage, but to the fact that certification laws have not yet adjusted their requirements to the new trends, and many institutions undertake to prepare teachers for high schools as well as for elementary. While there is a tendency to define the function of teachers colleges and normal schools, the criticism is still current that they are undertaking more than lies within their province and are thereby in danger of missing the primary objective for which they exist. A few teachers colleges, besides providing courses which lead to the bachelor's degree, are beginning to offer graduate work and to award higher degrees.

The creation of teachers colleges offering four-year courses, the increase in salaries, and an oversupply of teachers have rendered it possible to raise the minimum requirement for the certification of elementary school teachers to two years of preparation, as is done in Colorado, Connecticut, Idaho, Indiana, Louisiana, New Jersey, Oregon, Pennsylvania, Utah, and Vermont; three States have raised the requirement to three years—Arizona, Massachusetts, New York, and Washington (to become effective in 1933); California and the District of Columbia (to become effective in 1934) and a few cities, such as New York, require four years of preparation.

Admission Requirements

The minimum requirement for admission to normal schools and teachers colleges is graduation from high school. The oversupply of teachers has had the effect of introducing selective methods of admission. These include the requirement that candidates for admission must have had a high record of scholarship in their high schools, or the use of intelligence or standard achievements tests. One State admits candidates by examinations. Others require a personal interview. A health and physical examination, and recommendations and statements of character from high school principals, are required generally. Only nine States demand a declaration of intention to teach. Experiments have been undertaken to devise personality and diagnostic tests of fitness for the teaching profession, but up to the present without any great degree of success. In general, from the scholastic point of view it is claimed that the students entering normal schools and teachers colleges are slightly inferior to those who proceed to liberal arts colleges. From the social point of view the few investigations which have been made indicate that intending teachers are drawn from the homes of skilled and unskilled labour in industrial areas and from farm homes in agricultural areas. Tuition fees are not charged in public institutions for the preparation of teachers; generally matriculation and incidental fees must be paid. The students are themselves responsible for the payment of the cost of board and lodging; they may receive aid for this purpose from loan funds or defray their expenses by "working their way through" the period of preparation.

Curricula

Serious consideration has been given to the problem of curricula in the institutions for the preparation of teachers. While it has always been a subject of discussion, attention was directed to the problem as a result of the publication by the Carnegie Foundation for the Advancement of Teaching of its *Curricula Designed for the Professional Preparation of Teachers,* in 1927, and of its report on the *Professional Preparation of Teachers for American Public Schools,* in 1920. The problem is more complicated than in most other countries, not only because most institutions have until recently enjoyed a great deal of independence from any state control, but also because of the practice, which is common; of providing preparation in the same institution for different branches of the educational service. Hence, while the European institutions tend on the whole to provide one type of preparation for elementary school teachers leaving to special institutions the preparation of teachers of young children, the American normal schools and teachers colleges attempt to prepare teachers for the kindergarten, the kindergarten-primary grades, the primary, intermediate, and upper grades, rural school, junior high school, and senior high school.

The problem became somewhat more complicated with the introduction of three- and four-year courses, for which no precedents existed except in the liberal arts college. The tendency in the four-year courses was to prolong general, liberal education for the first two years and to concentrate on professional preparation in the last two years, a practice which brought the teachers colleges into direct competition with the junior colleges, which have spread rapidly in the last decade. The normal school courses of two years had themselves not developed a sound policy. The development of high schools had by 1920 made it unnecessary for them to stress general or academic preparation; the practice of concentrating on reviews of elementary school subjects had already begun to disappear. Fundamentally the crucial problem, it began to be recognized, particularly after the publication of the reports of the Carnegie Foundation, was not one of choosing between a liberal or general education, and professional preparation for the future teacher, or of superimposing professional or liberal courses, but of devising curricula in which the professional needs of the teacher would serve as the integrating nucleus. The preparation of teachers in the United States has suffered, and perhaps still suffers, from an overemphasis on professional subjects divorced from content. Since, however, the teacher's tools are subjects to be used for the attainment of particular ends, it was realized that appropriate professional preparation consists in the professionalization of subject-matter, a principle of which Professor W.C. Bagley has been the outstanding advocate. on the one hand, it is not enough for the teacher to be a master of the subjects which he professes, and on the other to study methods divorced from content is inadequate. The teacher must see the subjects in the light of their place in the development of culture and civilization and from the point of view of the growing child. Professionalization serves to integrate mastery of subject-matter with methods and with practice and gives a functional unity to the preparation of the teacher. It does not, as is sometimes objected, mean a restriction of the academic subjects to the standards needed in the elementary schools, but demands, indeed, a breadth of knowledge and perspective which are not present when academic subjects are taught in separate compartments devoid of any application. The principle of professionlization of subject-matter does more than orient the organization of subjects; it incorprorates more directly than ever the utilization of the practice or training school as an essential adjust in the preparation of teachers for purposes of observation, participation, demonstration, and practice teaching. The simplicity of this principle, which *mutatis mutandis,* applies equally to preparation for other professions, does not reduce the administrative difficulties involved in the provision of practice schools adequate in size to meet the new place assigned to it. Properly organized, the practice school serves as a point of concentration for the work of normal schools and teachers colleges and provides the best opportunity of eliminating the traditional dualism between academic and professional subjects by directing attention to the main objective of these institutions—the education of the child. The objective may be sometimes forgotten in faculties composed of specialists in academic subjects with little preparation in education and specialists in professional subjects who are apt to overestimate the importance of the technical studies.

This dualism, which has been traditional not only in the United States but also in other countries, is being gradually attacked, although some recent studies, such as that of W.W. Charters and D. Waples in the *Commonwealth Teacher-Training Study* (Chicago, 1929), influenced by the job analysis technique employed in industry, indicate that the solution has not yet been reached. Such studies seek to analyze the duties and traits of teachers, to draft an itemized and detailed list of the activities of teachers, and to rate these in order of importance as a basis for making curricula for teacher-training institutions. Such studies would result in perpetuating the apprenticeship principle of preparing teachers rather than in promoting the professional character of the work.

As at present organized, the curricula of teacher-training institutions include three main divisions, the extent to which they are coordinated depending upon whether the whole task is looked upon from a unitary point of view. These divisions are: (1) academic and cultural subjects (generally English, history, and social sciences, economics, science, and physical training); (2) professional subjects (generally principles of education or teaching, special methods, educational psychology, history of education, and educational methods); and (3) observation, participation, and independent practice. As a rule room is left in most curricula for the election of some subjects by the students. Within this general framework provision is made for functional specialization for various branches of educational service—kindergarten, kindergarten-primary, primary, intermediate or upper grades, and junior or senior high school.

Curricula and courses of study are either prescribed by state authorities or prepared in each institution. In both cases their preparation is entrusted to numerous committees assisted by experts in the preparation of teachers. The principles which serve to guide such committees vary. In some cases they are based on the method of job-analysis—the needs of the area to be supplied, the duties of the teacher, and the traits of teaching success; in others they are more directly adapted to the prevailing curricula and courses of study in schools for which teachers are being prepared; in others again, but less frequently, the whole framework of the curricular organization is inspired by a definite philosophy of education which starts with the needs of the growing child. In the first type there is inherent the danger of emphasizing the "tricks of the trade"; in the second, it is objected that curricular may be adapted too much to the *status quo;* in the third, the aim is to permeate the whole of the curriculum with a philosophy which is to guide the future work of the teacher and give him a certain degree of flexibility and independence. While it is obvious that the third type is the ideals and emphasizes the professional rather than the craftsmanship ideal of teaching, it encounters the difficulty that under the prevailing practices of administration and organization the teacher in the United States is still too much controlled from above—by prescribed curricula and courses of study, supervision, tests of various kinds, and textbooks, all of which involve the danger of creating a gap between the system of preparing teachers and school conditions as they exists.

Whatever the principle upon which the curricula are based, they include academic and professional subjects. The selection of the academic subjects is determined partly by the type of teaching in which the intending teacher plans to specialize and partly by the need of extending his general cultural education. The professional subjects tend to be more closely adapted to the work of the teacher. History of education, which at one time held a commanding position, is gradually being subordinated to other subjects and the emphasis placed more upon recent developments with greater stress on the growth of practice than on theory or philosophy. Philosophy of education is generally postponed to the last year of a four-year course or to the period of post-graduate study. Educational sociology, whose scope is as yet not clearly defined, is as a rule not a required subject. The emphasis is placed upon educational psychology (the growth of the child, individual differences, laws of learning, psychology of various subjects), principles of teaching or general methods, special methods, and classroom management. Generally, a foundation for these studies is laid in a course which is usually called "introduction to teaching" or "introduction to education." In all the subjects more stress is placed upon the practical than the theoretical aspects of education, but on the whole the nature of the content as well as the selection of subjects is determined by the availability of textbooks. Closely linked up with both academic and professional studies and observation and practice in the training or practice schools.

The majority of teacher-training institutions have their own practice schools; others use the local public schools. The practice schools are organized under a director of training and have their own staffs of critic teachers, who serve as demonstrators and advisers of the young teachers in practice. Critic teachers are teachers who have been selected or in many cases have had special training for their positions, which are somewhat better paid than those in the ordinary public schools. The practice schools serve as centres for observation, participation or occasional teaching practice and assistance to the critic teacher, and independent practice. To an increasing extent members of the normal school and teachers college faculties are closely associated both with the work of the practice school and the supervision of the students in the own subjects. The chief difficulty which is always encountered is the problem of securing schools of adequate size for the large number of students usually enrolled. As a consequence a large number of students leave the teacher-training institutions without any practice at all. The amount of practice teaching also varies considerably in different institutions. In 1929-30 the median number of hours of practice was 190 in state normal schools, 270 in city normal schools, 26 in county normal schools, 225 in private normal schools, and 150 in teachers-colleges. One result of these variations in the practice of placing young and inexperienced teachers under special supervision during a probationary period; in some cases the supervision is conducted by supervisors in the school system to which the teacher is appointed, in others by members of the faculty in which he was appointed. A few institutions have adopted the practice of conducting special conferences for recent graduates who return for a week to discuss the problems and difficulties which they have encountered during their first year of teaching; their places during the conference are taken by senior students in the institutions where the conference is held.

In the following pages are presented a few samples of curricula in two-, three-, and four-year teacher-training institutions.

Two-Year Curriculum for Primary Teachers, State Teachers College, Fredericksburg, Virgina[19]

Fall Quarter	*Winter Quarter*	*Spring Quarter**
	First Year	
General art	Art in the elementary grades	Reading and language
Educational psychology	Educational psychology	English fundamentals
English fundamentals	English fundamentals	Gymnasium
Music	Music	History of the United States
Gymnasium	Gymnasium	
Geography of the United States	History of the United States	
One of the following:		
History of education	History of education	History of education
Children's literature	Children's literature	Children's literature
Arithmetic	Arithmetic	Arthmetic
	Second Year	
Art appreciation	Children's literature	Nature Study
Educational sociology	Oral reading	Citizenship
Tests and measurements	Music appreciation	Geography of Eurasia or Geography of Southern Lands
Supervised teaching	Gymnasium	
Principles of teaching		

* In addition to the subjects listed students may elect courses in Art appreciation, Public school music, or Music appreciation.

In the second year students may elect courses in music or other subjects by permission. The students are divided into three groups, each of which is assigned to teaching practice for one of the three quarters. The only course taken during the period of supervised teaching is that in principles of teaching.

Three-Year Curricula for Kindergarten-Primary, Intermediate and Grammar Grade Teachers State Normal School, Cortland, New York[20]

Semester I	*Semester II*	*Semester III*
Introduction to teaching and observation Library methods Science History of civilization Geography Written expression Art Penmanship	Educational psychology Literature Health education Oral expression Arithmetic Music Educational biology	Kindergarten theory Methods of teaching history Literature Methods of teaching geography Methods of teaching reading Health education Art Special kindergarten-primary methods
Semester IV	*Semester V*	*Semester VI*
Principles of education Educational methods Methods of teaching arithmetic Children's literature Practice teaching Elective	Specialized psychology Sociology Music Technique of teaching Art Practice teaching Modern European history	History of education Economics Electives Practice teaching Methods of teaching penmanship

The institution has a practice or training school with seven hundred pupils; students are required to spend more than one hundred hours in observation and ten weeks in actual teaching with charge of a class for stated periods each day. The curricula for each of the three groups—kindergarten-primary, intermediate, and grammar grade teachers—are selected from the above list of subjects according to its needs.

Four-Year Course, State Teachers College, Greeley, Colorado

The curricula are built upon four principles: (1) the inclusion of a common group of general, cultural, and background courses; (2) the inclusion of a common group of professional courses; (3) the inclusion of a group of courses in each curriculum to give adequate instruction and preparation for a specific teaching job; (4) leaving ample room for individual choices by students so that their education may be suited to their own likes and preferences while preparing them for a definite place in the teaching profession.

The Core Required Subjects

First Year	*Second Year*	*Third Year*	*Fourth Year*
Fall			
Introduction to the social world Introduction to education Hygiene Introduction to science Physical education	Student teaching Psychology of learning Physical education		Student teaching
Winter			
Art appreciation Outline of literature Outline of music Introduction to science Physical education	Contributions of the ancient and medieval world to modern civilization Physical education	General sociology	
Spring			
Outline of literature Pre-teaching observation Introduction to educational psychology Physical education	Expansion of European civilization in modern times Physical education		Philosophy of education

Requirements for Majors

Kindergarten Primary Major *First Year*	*Rural Major* *First Year*
Winter	*Winter*
Language arts in primary grades	Agriculture for teachers
Spring	*Spring*
Pre-teaching observation	Pre-teaching observation
Social arts in primary grades	Language arts in intermediate grades
Teaching of history and civics	Teaching of history and civics
Second Year	*Second Year*
Fall	*Fall*
Student teaching	Student teaching
Winter	*Winter*
Music, rudiments and method	Rural school management
Fine art methods	Principles of education
Kindergarten-primary methods	Electives
Child development	
Spring	*Spring*
Biological elementary science	Biological elementary science
Principles of education	Methods and materials in geography for intermediate grades
Rural school problems	Methods and materials in arithmetic
Home geography	Fine art methods in intermediate grades
	Electives
Third Year	*Third Year*
Fall	*Fall*
Instruction in spelling and reading	Instruction in spelling and reading
Making the school curriculum	Recent developments in rural life
Electives	Social and industrial history of the United States
Winter	*Winter*
Instruction in content subjects	Methods and materials in

Contd . . .

Third Year	*Third Year*
History of education in the United States	geography for intermediate grades
Industrial arts methods	Electives
Electives	
Spring	*Spring*
Instruction in handwriting, composition, and arithmetic	Instruction in handwriting, composition, and arithmetic
Teachers' classroom tests	Teachers' classroom tests
Elective	Expansion of European civilization in modern times
Fourth Year	***Fourth Year***
Fall	*Fall*
Creative education	Making the school curriculum
Electives	Electives
Winter	*Winter*
Genetics and eugenics	Instruction in content subjects
Electives	Electives
Spring	*Spring*
Personality and social behaviour	Personality and social behaviour
Electives	Electives

Courses are similarly organized for teachers who plan to teach in intermediate, upper grades, and junior high schools, and as specialist teachers in high schools; the last group is expected to take courses organized into majors and minors. The State Teachers College grants both undergraduate and graduate degrees.

Student Life

Very few normal schools or teachers colleges have their own dormitories; students live in boarding-houses, clubs, fraternity or sorority houses, which are under the general supervision of the authorities. Student life is organized very much like that in liberal arts colleges. While sports and physical activities are everywhere encouraged, the preponderance of women prevents that emphasis on athleticism so common in the colleges. The social life of the students is promoted by the clubs, sororities, and fraternities, and a variety of societies organized for cultural or recreational purposes. The responsibility for government and the control of student affairs in entrusted to student representative councils or to the whole student body.

Certification of Teachers

The chief obstacle in the way of the progressive development of teacher-preparation lies in the vagueness and diversity of the practices of granting teachers' certificates. Traditionally certificates were awarded by local authorities on the basis of examinations often with little or no specific requirement as to preparation, whether academic or professional. The present tendency is in the direction of more rigid control by the state authorities, the implication of practices, the elimination of examinations, and the award of certificates on the basis of diplomas earned in recognized institutions. Although the movement is in this direction, the goal is still far from being reached; there still exist low-grade, emergency, temporary, provisional, and life certificates awarded on the basis of examinations and renewable, except in the last type, periodically. The following examples of certificates may be cited:

In California the state board of education issues a life diploma in all schools of the State upon recommendation of a county board of education, which in turn is authorized upon presentation of credentials issued by the state board to grant a great variety of certificates, valid for two or five years and renewable for the same terms, for school administration, general, special, or departmental supervision, kindergarten-primary or general elementary schools, junior high school or general secondary, special subjects, educational research and guidance, vocational arts and trade and industrial occupations, and health and development certificates.

In Kansas the State Teachers College issued life diplomas valid in any school, life certificates valid in elementary, junior, and two-year high schools, and special subject life certificates, as well as three-year certificates. The state board of education grants in addition life certificates on college graduation, three-year certificates renewable for life, permanent certificates, three-year certificates renewable for three-year periods on the basis of further study or examination, and special certificates for special subjects or departments. Still another type of certificates, the first grade certificate valid for three years and the second grade certificate valid for two years, are granted by county boards of examinations.

In Massachusetts certificates may be issued by the state or by local committees. There are, however, two marked tendencies: the first is to centralize the power of certification in the hands of the state authority, and, second, to abolish certification by examination in favour of the acceptance of credentials based on a specified period of study in recognized institutions. Both tendencies will make the improved organization of teacher-preparation possible.

Appointment of Teachers

The minimum requirements for appointment have been indicated in the discussion of the methods of preparation and certification; as may be expected, they show a wide range of variation from less than high school graduation for teachers in rural schools to four years of preparation in the more progressive cities. In 1930-31 in cities with population of 2500 and over, 74.7 per cent of the teachers were required to have two years of preparation, 16.1 per cent three years, and 6.1 per cent four years beyond the high school. In addition to preparation, many cities require candidates for appointment to have some experience; 18 per cent require one year, 22.4 per cent two years, and 1.1 per cent more than two years. The majority of the cities will not appoint married women teachers, but the practice varies when a single woman teacher already in service marries—in three fifths of the cities they are required to resign at once or at the end of the school year, and in the remainder they may continue to teach. Leave of absence without pay is provided for maternity in a number of cities. Despite serious objections to the practice, more than half of the cities prefer to appoint local residents, a practice which is still more common in rural areas. The selection of candidates for appointment is a function of the superintendents of education, who in most cases interview candidates personally and in addition use other methods, such as application blanks, recommendations, written and physical examinations, and observation of instruction. The sources from which suitable candidates are available are: (1) commercial agencies; (2) appointments bureaus in normal schools, colleges, and universities; and (3) appointment bureaus maintained by state departments of education or state teachers association. Appointments are held from the boards of education.

Tenure

The most common practice throughout the country is the appointment of teachers on annual contracts which may be renewed or discontinued, often without notice. While this practice of "hire and fire" is most usual in rural areas, the annual contract is still the most commonly found even in cities, of which 60.1 per cent elect teachers annually or enter into contracts for one year only; 27.5 per cent grant permanent appointments after a probationary period, usually of three years; 12.1 per cent appoint teachers to indefinite tenure subject to termination at the end of any year. Teachers are protected by state-wide tenure laws in Indiana, Maryland, Montana, New Jersey, and New York, and in California in districts with eight teachers or more; the larger cities have their own tenure laws. The argument for annual appointments is that incompetent teachers can be more easily dismissed; the argument for permanent tenure is that it is the only method by which teachers can be protected against wrongful dismissal for political or other reasons not always connected with teaching ability; the obstacle to the introduction of indefinite tenure, which is generally recognized as the soundest practice, is the difficulty of defining teaching ability and competence in such a way that the courts would accept reasons for dismissal on such grounds. Efforts to establish merit or efficiency scales have up to the present proved to be unsatisfactory.

Salaries

Teachers' salaries have followed a decidedly upward trend in the past ten years. The median salaries paid to teachers in city kindergartens and elementary schools in 1930-31 are shown in the accompanying table on page 619.[21]

The median salaries paid to elementary school principals in the United States were as follows in 1931:

Cities	*Teaching Principals*	*Supervising Principals*
Over 100,000	$2,436	$3,519
Between 30,000 and 100,000	2,011	2,646
Between 10,000 and 30,000	1,572	1,925
Between 5,000 and 10,000	1,583	2,239
Between 2,500 and 5,000	1,409	2,175

Salary scales have been adopted in more than three-fourths of the cities with populations over 2500, but are more frequently found in the larger than in the smaller cities. The scales are based on the number of years of service, amount of professional training, ratings on efficiency scales, position held, and sex. The periods within which the maximal on the scales adopted range from five to fifteen years, although longer scales are found. About three-fourths of the school systems require continued professional or other study in summer schools or extension courses as requirements for salary increases. Although efficiency ratings are regarded as desirable bases for the award of salary increases, rating scales have not yet been devised which give complete satisfaction or command the confidence of teachers; the mistrust of such devices is indicated by the fact that less than eleven per cent of the cities employ them. In theory an adequate array of arguments may be produced in favour of a single salary scale for all teachers, irrespective of the type of school in which they teach; in practice its adoption is beset by many administrative difficulties and particularly by the problem of supply and demand for certain positions. At present the single salary scale has been adopted by an insignificant number of school systems. The question of sex differentiation in salary scales is relatively unimportant in elementary schools, since the percentage of men teachers is so very small; in the junior high schools 42 per cent and in the senior high schools 54.8 per cent of the cities pay higher salaries to men than to women. Supermaximum salaries are paid in 44.1 per cent of the cities to teachers who have exceptional qualifications as indicated by successful classroom instruction and continued professional study.[22] The two tables on page 306 indicate the methods of organizing salary schedules.

Pensions

The improvement of salaries for teachers has been accompanied by the development during the past few years of sound retirement systems. Teachers' retirement systems have been in existence since the close of the last century, but it was not until the Carnegie Foundation for the Advancement of Teaching began to study the problem of the principles underlying sound system that a revision of them began to be made. The older systems either were based on inadequate contributions or elsewere of the free or non-contributory type. The sound systems which have been established recently are based on contributions of teachers and employers accumulated at compound interest and provide protection against old age and disability. To protect the funds measures are taken to meet the accrued liabilities—that is, the payment of allowances to teachers already in service when the systems are launched. The return of contributions, optional form of allowances, periodical actuarial evaluations, the keeping of individual accounts and establishment of a reserve basis, and optional and compulsory limits for retirement are some of the features of the sounder systems.

There are at the present time state retirement systems in the District of Columbia and twenty-two States (Arizona, California, Connecticut, Illinois, Indiana, Maine, Maryland, Massachusetts, Michigan, Minnesota, Montana, Nevada, New Jersey, New York, North Dakota, Ohio, Pennsylvania, Rhode Island, Vermont, Virginia, Washington, Wisconsin). In addition, a large number of cities, both within these States and in others, have their own systems. Normally, membership in retirement funds is optional with teachers already in service, but compulsory for new entrants into the service. Of the state systems, nineteen require both the employer and the teacher to pay contributions. Practice varies as to the contributions of teachers; some systems require a flat annual payment, others a percentage of salary. Provision is made in most systems for the return of contributions in whole or in part in cases of death or on leaving the service prior to retirement. The conditions of retirement are governed by length of service, which varies in range from ten to forty years—thirty years being the most usual—and age, usually sixty as the minimum requirement and seventy as the compulsory limit. The amount of the retiring allowance is either a flat rate or in the sounder systems an annuity purchased by the contributions accumulated at compound interest; disability allowances are determined in the same way.[23]

Improvement of Teachers in Service

The in-service training of teachers is probably more widespread in the United States than in other countries. Arising at a time when the initial preparation was inadequate, the practice has been retained and extended, not only to meet the rapid advance of the science of education, but as a method for the continuous improvement of teachers. The methods of inservice training are many and varied. Reference has already been made to the follow-up systems used by normal schools and teachers colleges to keep in touch and assist their graduates in the first year or two of their experience. This is supplemented in all systems by supervisors, general and special, who not only visit teachers in their classrooms, but

Elementary School Teachers' Salary Schedules

1. Springfield, Massachusetts

Schedules	*Years of Training*	*Minimum*	*Yearly Increments*	*Maximum*
I.	Successful completion of a two-year course in normal school or equivalent	$1200	8 × $100	$2000
II.	Successful completion of a three-year course in normal school or equivalent	1300	9 × $100	2200
III.	Successful completion of four years of college work with a standard bachelor's degree or equivalent	1400	9 × $100	2300

2. Bronxville, New York

Training	*Years of Experience*												
	0	1	2	3	4	5	6	7	8	9	10	11	12
Two years' normal	$1500	$1800	$2034	$2209	$2341	$2441	$2516	$2576	$2626	$2676	$2726	$2756	$2786
Three years' normal or third college year	1563	1926	2223	2398	2530	2630	2705	2765	2815	2865	2915	2945	2975
A.B., B.S., Ph.B	1563	1926	2244	2587	2719	2819	2894	2954	3004	3054	3104	3134	3164
A.M.	1563	1926	2244	2587	2908	3008	3083	3143	3193	3243	3293	3323	3353

conduct conferences on special problems. Teachers' institutes and conferences are organized very generally, in some localities by the educational authorities, in others by the teachers' associations. Rating scales of efficiency, of which the use of achievement tests constitutes a part, are employed by nearly half of the city school systems as a method of improving teachers; it will be noticed that rating scales are more frequently used for this purpose than for promotion on salary schedules. Generally such scales are the results of the cooperative action of the administrators, supervisors, and teachers. Although used fairly extensively, there is still no widespread confidence in such scales. By far the most general system employed for the improvement of teachers in service is attendance at summer sessions, which are now conducted by colleges and universities, normal schools and teachers colleges; it is estimated that about one teacher in four spends the summer vacation in attendance on courses in summer schools. About five per cent of the cities either grant bonuses for such attendance or take it into consideration for salary increases. Another practice which is also distinctively American is the granting of extended leave of absence for professional improvement either by formal study or by travel. In 1930-31, 616 cities reported that they granted leave of absence for professional improvement, 290 for travel, and 352 for rest. In practically all but 10 per cent of the cities such leave of absence is granted without salary; 31 cities, mostly the largest, grant leave of absence with half salary, and a few with full salary less the pay of a substitute.

Status of Teachers

Considerable contribution to the improvement of the professional status of teachers has been made by their professional organizations, especially the National Education Association and the state associations, which conduct conferences, publish journals, and maintain bureaus of research and information. The full growth and development of these organizations have been recent, so that it is difficult to estimate their contribution to educational politics. The local organizations in the larger cities have in the main been concerned with the promotion of the interests of their own members, sometimes in opposition to the policies of the authorities. The larger associations have limited themselves too narrowly to education and instruction, and, as contrasted with the activities of similar associations in England, France, and Germany, their work has been mainly that of assembling, disseminating, and interpreting information on current tendencies rather than of leadership. Whether due to the fact that the overwhelming majority of teachers are women, or whatever the cause, the teachers of the country, despite their numbers, have not taken concerted steps to promote and protect their professional, as contrasted with their material, interests. The result is that the principle upon which education in the United States is based, that it is a public concern, is still interpreted to mean that the public has the right to interfere in matters which are properly not its concern—teacher tenure, curriculum prescription, acceptance or rejection of textbooks for reasons which are not educational. Undoubtedly much of this situation can be attributed to the fact that teaching in general has only recently begun to evolve out of what has been described as a procession into a real profession. The rising standards of preliminary preparation, improved salaries and retirement systems, and better conditions of tenure are tending to produce more stable conditions and longer professional service. One defect still remains: the fact that the rewards of the profession do not lie in its separate branches, with the result that teachers not only tend to move from one place to another, but also from one branch to another—from elementary schools to junior or senior high schools or to the administrative branches or to higher institutions. While from one point of view mobility of teachers from place to place or from one branch of education to another is salutary, it tends to develop a restlessness from which in the long run the smooth progress of education, particularly in the smaller areas, is likely to suffer.

REFERENCES

1. These grants were reduced by Amendments to the *Regulations* issued in 1931 and 1932.
2. Both ordinary and advanced standards unless otherwise indicated.
3. Sense boards include voice training, reading and recitation, drawing and handwork among these subjects.
4. These sums were reduced in 1931.
5. In 1930-31 the total number of students in training was 19,484 (6,737 men and 12,727 women), distributed as follows: university training departments, 6,492 (3,393 men and 3,069 women); post-graduate training colleges, 70 (7 men and 63 women); two-year training college 11,941 (3,354 men and 8,587 women); training colleges for domestic subjects, 988 women; 23 graduate students (3 men and 20 women) were in training in secondary schools under a scheme somewhat like the Prussian.
6. Various types of services may be calculated for this purpose—recognized service before April 1, 1926, contributory service subsequent to that date, and approved external service in other than grant-earning Schools, Universities, Scotland, the civil service, or such may be approved by the Treasury.
7. Ward, H. (formerly Chief Inspector for the Training of Teachers in the Board of Education), "The Training of Teachers," in Wilson, J. Dover, *The Schools of England,* p. 370 (London, 1928).
8. The reduction in the number of applicants for admission in 1931 is explained partly by the abolition of fees in secondary schools and partly by the fact that the fall in the birth out during the War is beginning to show itself at this stage.
9. The terms *expliquer* and *explication de texts* have a definite connotation in French educational literature. Originally developed by the Jesuits and carried over very generally in classical instruction for nearly three centuries, it has in France been applied to a variety of subjects. The method involves the detailed, critical analysis of any written text with a thorough and minute discussion and implication of almost every word. In the United States the method has been introduced by M. de Sauzé in the teaching of modern language in Cleveland, and by Professor A. Cru in Teachers College, Columbia University.
10. See Lapie, P., *Pédagogies francaise* (Paris, 1926).
11. For example: *L'Ecole et la Vie, Manucl d'Enseignement, L'Ecole Libératrice.*

12. On the relation of the Federal Government to education see Chapter V.
13. On the secondary schools, see Chapter VIII.
14. The oversupply of teachers and the serious financial crisis which imposed severe measures of economy on the Government compelled into in November, 1931, to decide on the closing of five teachers colleges at Easter, 1932 and to distribute their students among the remaining colleges, which were not to admit any new students at that time.
15. Alexander, T. *The Training of Elementary Teachers in Germany,* p. 73 (New York, 1929).
16. For the change which has taken place and the intensely narrow spirit of nationalism which is now sweeping Germany the intransigent attitude of some foreign powers, which have produced the present situation, rather than the domestic situation itself, must bear the responsibility.
17. See *La Riforma della cultura magistrale* (1917): *Il Problema dell' Educasione nazionale in Italia* (1925).
18. See Chapter VIII.
19. This institution offers in addition to the curriculum here given, curricula for the grades (two years) elementary teachers, principals, and supervisors, high school teachers, principals and supervisors, commercial education, physical education, music, and home economics (all four-year courses).
20. The institution also offers three-year courses in physical education, nutrition, and open air classes.
21. Based on the Research Bulletin of the National Education Association, Vol. IX, No. 3, May, 1931, *Salaries in City School Systems,* 1930-31 (Washington, D.C. 1931).
22. On teachers' salaries see Elsbree, W.S. *Teacher's Salaries* (New York 1931), and Research Bulletin of the National Education Association, *Salaries in City School Systems, 1930-31,* Vol. IX, No. 3, May, 1931.
23. On the subject of pensions see the reports and bulletins of the Carnegie Foundation, and the Research Bulletins of the National Education Association, especially *Current Issues is Teacher Retirement,* Vol. VIII, No. 5, November, 1920, which contains a bibliography.

Index

U

❑❑❑